The
Amphibians and Reptiles of Missouri

The Amphibians and Reptiles of Missouri

by Tom R. Johnson

Photographs and drawings by Tom R. Johnson

Edited by Kathy Love

Missouri Department of Conservation

**Missouri Department of Conservation
P.O. Box 180
Jefferson City, MO 65102-0180**

Front cover: a three-toed box turtle; watercolor by the author

To the children of Missouri, whose natural curiosity and lack of fear of these interesting and often misunderstood creatures should be an example for us all.

CONTENTS

Acknowledgments

During the eight years that have passed since work began on this volume in November, 1978, I had the assistance and support of many people. I have particularly appreciated the patience and understanding of my supervisor, Jim Henry Wilson and our Natural History Officer, John E. Wylie. I have also appreciated the support of my colleagues in the Natural History Section throughout our years together. They have provided an atmosphere of professionalism that inspired me to continue to strive for accuracy and give my best.

The entire book was typeset by Mitzi Crump, who skillfully prepared the final text for publishing. This book was edited by Kathy Love. Her dedication and expert handling of all aspects of producing this book are greatly appreciated.

During the early typing of the reptile accounts I had the valuable assistance of Verita C. Ponder and Jeannette M. Gunther. Barbara Singleton typed the bibliography. Several copies of the entire manuscript were typed by Freida E. Fisher. Without her special help this work would have taken much longer and had many misspellings. Donna Pasley was immeasurably helpful in the final proofreading stages.

Part I, Amphibians, is a revision of my book, *The Amphibians of Missouri* (1977), published by the Museum of Natural History, University of Kansas, Lawrence. I wish to thank Natural History Museum Publications Editor Joseph T. Collins for permission to use much of the original sections, photographs and drawings in this book.

I am grateful to Ronald A. Brandon, Joseph T. Collins, Michael A. Morris and William J. Resetarits, Jr. for critically reading the amphibian and reptile family and species accounts. Their comments, corrections and additions enhanced those sections.

For sharing valuable tips on rendering tadpole drawings I wish to thank Linda Trueb. The photograph of Julius Hurter was kindly supplied by James A. Houser, director of the St. Louis Museum of Science and Natural History. The photograph of the late Paul Anderson was graciously supplied by his son Roy Anderson. I wish to thank Bert W. Landfried for giving me permission to use his photograph of Paul Anderson in this book. I am also grateful to Lauren E. Brown and Richard S. Funk for kindly supplying the gray treefrog sonograph.

I am deeply grateful to my friend Roger Conant for writing the Preface. Roger Conant is the author of *A Field Guide to Reptiles and Amphibians of Eastern and Central North America* which was my "bible" while growing up in central Wisconsin and learning about amphibians and reptiles. He is Director Emeritus of the Philadelphia Zoological Garden and is currently Adjunct Professor in the Department of Biology at the University of New Mexico.

My good friend Joseph T. Collins has been a constant source of inspiration during the course of this book. His belief in my work and his encouragement helped me overcome various problem areas that always appear in projects of this type.

Many of the dots representing county records on the various distribution maps are the result of new county records generously supplied by Robert Powell of Avila College. His contributions were the result of many field trips and I am very thankful.

So many people have helped me with various aspects of the herpetology of Missouri over the years that it is inevitable I have forgotten some of them. This by no means diminishes my gratitude, but simply indicates a weakness of the human mind. I offer my thanks to the following persons who helped me in a variety of capacities—from specimens to county records, from reprints to field assistance, and many other kindnesses: Rebecca N. Anderson, Robert N. Bader, Barbara K. Bassett, Dale and Sharon Becker, Tom Bell, Jeffrey H. Black, Randy Bloyd, Ronald A. Brandon, Lauren E. Brown, John Bursewicz, Mike J. Christensen, Robert F. Clarke, Joseph T. Collins, Charles J. Cole, Roger Conant, Hollis D. Crawford, Mike Crocker, Ronald Crombie, Ann Day, Wayne J. Drda, David A. Easterla, Gerald Elick, Carl H. Ernst, Dennis E. Figg, Terry R. Finger, George W. Foley, Richard S. Funk, James E. Gardner, Carl Gerhardt, J. Whitfield Gibbons, John A. Goddard, Ron Goellner, Berlin Heck, Mike P. Hemkens, John Hess, Richard Highton, Charles H. Hoessle, Diel Howard, Diane M. Johnson, Mike Johnson, Michael Jones, Donald A. Kangas, John A. Karel, Ed Katzenberger, Stephen A. Kemp, Arnold Kluge, Christopher P. Kofron, Robert L. Krager, Randy Krohmer, Douglas Ladd, Jeffery W. Lang, Richard L. Lardie, Bob and Linda Leis, Jim Lowery, Hymen Marx, Louise Mathis, Dean E. Metter, Sam Mitchell, Loren D. Moehn, Don Moll, Richard R. Montanucci, David Moore, Michael A. Morris, Robert W. Murphy, Clarence J. McCoy, Joseph E. McCray, Roy W. McDiarmid, Tom Nagel, Paul Nelson, Max A. Nickerson, Gary D. Novinger, Larry Page, Donna S. Pasley, William L. Pflieger, Gary D. Pogue, Robert Powell, Dennis B. Ralin, Michael F. Rapp, William J. Resetarits, Jr., Meril Rogers, Tom R. Saladin, Bruce Schuette, Bud Schuller, Richard A. Seigel, Owen J. Sexton, Donald D. Smith, Dorothy M. Smith, Philip W. Smith, Elaine M. Stewart, Molly Striker, Richard H. Thom, Thomas E. Toney, Stanley E. Trauth, David L. Tylka, Virginia K. Wallace, James R. Whitley, Robert Wilkinson, Steven J. Young, George R. Zug, Nancy L. Zuschlag and Richard G. Zweifel.

Finally, I wish to express my sincere thanks to the Missouri Department of Conservation for publishing this book.

Tom R. Johnson
January 1987
Jefferson City, Missouri

Preface

More than three score years and ten—the biblical span of life—have passed since the first comprehensive *Herpetology of Missouri* was published. In 1911, Julius Hurter, Sr., gave us a scholarly review of the information then known about the subject. He wrote for only a handful of scientists and serious-minded naturalists at a time when, to the common man, all snakes were vermin, small frogs and salamanders were good only for fish bait, and basking turtles were prime targets for a rifle or shotgun. Most contemporary Missourians had little appreciation for the state's amphibians and reptiles, save for the gustatory value of frogs' legs and the meat of certain turtles.

Now we have a splendid new book on the subject, beautifully illustrated and authoritatively written for the layman.

What great changes have occurred during the seventy-odd years that have passed between the publication of the two volumes. An enormous amount of new information has accumulated on the herpetofauna, and the attitude of the general public has shown a commendable improvement. Intelligent people are now well informed about the value of these cold-blooded vertebrates as members of the food chain and their usefulness in helping to control rodent and insect pests. An awareness of the value of all wildlife has prompted enlightened Missourians to give financial support, through the ballot box, to their state's widely known and highly respected Department of Conservation.

Not all changes have been for the good, however. The destruction of habitats, which began when the early settlers started clearing the forests and plowing the prairies, has continued at an accelerating pace and has been compounded by such problems as pollution, the silting of streams and the indiscriminate use of pesticides. All of these have taken their toll. One of the chief functions of the Missouri Department of Conservation, through its Natural History Section, is to accumulate detailed information on species of wildlife and plants that are under stress and to designate ways of protecting them and their habitats. Another is to disseminate information about the various groups, and that has been done to perfection for amphibians and reptiles by this excellent book.

The value of state and regional handbooks cannot be overstated. They provide the public with concise, accurate and usable facts, but they also serve as important tools for scientists whose objectives are to study individual species or groups of animals or plants and to plot their general ranges on distribution maps.

Tom Johnson is eminently qualified to compile and illustrate this book. He is a talented, self-taught artist and photographer and a thoroughly competent herpetologist who has conducted field work in all parts of Missouri, seeking information about its amphibians and reptiles, which unfortunately are still relatively little known and misunderstood by many people. The volume, prepared with great care and thoughtfulness, will go a long way toward dispelling the superstitions and absurd folklore that still linger in many parts of Missouri as well as America as a whole.

Roger Conant
Department of Biology
University of New Mexico
Albuquerque, NM 87131

INTRODUCTION

This book is about the amphibians and reptiles native to Missouri. As a group, the salamanders, toads, frogs, turtles, lizards and snakes are the least known and understood of all the vertebrate animals in this region. One reason is that few Missourians come in direct contact with the majority of these animals: amphibians and reptiles have secretive habits and are inactive during the winter. Fear and myth still surround many amphibians and reptiles, due largely to a lack of knowledge. It is my hope that the availability and use of this book will reduce negative attitudes and replace them with understanding, tolerance and an appreciation of amphibians and reptiles as a natural part of outdoor Missouri. An informed public is vital to a successful wildlife conservation program. A variety of individuals from the casual amateur naturalist to the serious student and professional biologist should benefit from this book.

Scientists currently recognize 3,266 species of amphibians and 5,954 reptile species living on earth (Duellman, 1979). Approximately 460 species of amphibians and reptiles are known to occur within the continental United States. At present, a total of 107 species of amphibians and reptiles are native to Missouri. Of this total, only five species (venomous snakes) are considered dangerous to humans. The majority of Missouri's amphibians and reptiles are benign creatures of little direct economic consequence to people, but add immeasurably to the complexity, diversity and esthetics of our region.

A Brief History of Missouri Herpetology

The first major contributions to the knowledge of Missouri's amphibians and reptiles were made by a Swiss-born engineer named **Julius Hurter, Sr.** (1842-1916). Around the turn of the century, Hurter published several papers and one book about Missouri amphibians and reptiles (see bibliography).

Julius Hurter was born in Schaffhausen, a city located along the Rhine River in extreme northern Switzerland. Upon graduation from high school in 1858, he became a millwright apprentice and later a draftsman in Kriens, a small city in central Switzerland. He spent two years as a mechanical engineer in Paris, then emigrated to the United States (1865). He lived briefly in Minnesota and Chicago, and finally settled in St. Louis in 1866. He became a mechanical engineer and chief draftsman at a foundry and remained there until 1906.

Although his vocation was mechanical engineering, Hurter had a strong avocation for the study of natural history. He spent many days observing and collecting Missouri birds (the study skins he gathered are still housed at the St. Louis Museum of Science and Natural History).

Hurter's fieldwork eventually led him to observe and gather amphibians and reptiles in many areas of Missouri. A number of his specimens are in the permanent collection at the U.S. National Museum of Natural History in Washington, D.C. Hurter's book, *Herpetology of Missouri*

Julius Hurter, Sr., *(1842–1916). Photo*
courtesy of the St. Louis Museum of
Science and Natural History.

(1911), was the only major reference available on Missouri amphibians
and reptiles for decades. The Hurter's spadefoot, *Scaphiopus holbrookii*
hurterii, was named in honor of Missouri's early herpetologist (Conant,
1975). Julius Hurter, Sr., died in St. Louis on December 6, 1916, at the
age of 74.

Paul Anderson (1914–1962) was another contributor to the knowledge of Missouri's amphibians and reptiles and he also lacked a formal
education in herpetology. A resident of Independence (Jackson County),
Anderson had a life-long interest in reptiles; he was self-taught and
became recognized as an authority on Missouri herpetofauna by many
professional herpetologists. He worked at a petroleum refinery for 28
years but spent his free time collecting, preserving and cataloging thousands of Missouri amphibians and reptiles.

Anderson wrote 19 technical papers, many of them published by
the Chicago Academy of Science, and corresponded with a number of
professional herpetologists and several budding zoologists. While in his
20s, he became interested in writing a book on the herpetology of Missouri; most of the specimens he collected and observed in captivity were
for the book.

Anderson was assisted by the late Philip Evans and Howard K.
Gloyd; his late wife, Zelma, typed the manuscript.

Anderson's untimely death in 1962 at the age of 48 came when the
reptile section was nearly ready to go to press. The University of

Paul Anderson, *(1914–1962). Photo by Bert W. Landfried.*

Missouri–Columbia published it as *The Reptiles of Missouri* in 1965. Anderson's storehouse of information on Missouri amphibians, however, remained in his field notes. A major part of Anderson's preserved amphibian and reptile collection was donated to the Natural History Museum of the University of Kansas after his death. The Chicago Academy of Science gained many specimens over the years through Anderson's close association with that institution.

The final major contribution to the reference work on Missouri's amphibians and reptiles was the publication of *The Amphibians of Missouri* in 1977. This book, which I authored, was published by the Museum of Natural History of the University of Kansas. The project began less than a year after I moved to St. Louis in 1973; the book took nearly four years to complete. During this period, I worked as a reptile keeper at the St. Louis Zoo, and wrote the book in my spare time.

Natural Divisions of Missouri

This information is furnished to familiarize the reader with the physical characteristics of the state. These physical features have a strong influence on the kinds of plants and animals occurring in various parts of Missouri (Thom and Wilson, 1980).

Rolling hills are characteristic of the glaciated plains of north Missouri.

Glaciated Plains: The physical features of this region reflect the southern-most movement and eventual retreat of the Kansan period of glaciation, which took place about 400,000 years ago. The rolling hills and broad, flat valleys were caused by the leveling effect of the glaciers. Soils developed from the glacial till and loess deposits. Marshes, native prairie and upland deciduous forests were dominant plant communities during presettlement time. Most of the region has been altered by agricultural activities. The eastern edge of Missouri, along the Mississippi River, has limestone bluffs and steep hills of till or loess soils (Lincoln Hills) which likely escaped glaciation. Average annual precipitation is 91 cm (36 inches). Some of the amphibians associated with this area are the eastern tiger salamander (*Ambystoma tigrinum tigrinum*), plains spadefoot toad (*Scaphiopus bombifrons*), northern crawfish frog (*Rana areolata circulosa*) and plains leopard frog (*Rana blairi*). Reptiles occurring in this province include the Illinois mud turtle (*Kinosternon flavescens spooneri*), western painted turtle (*Chrysemys picta bellii*), western fox snake (*Elaphe vulpina vulpina*), western plains garter snake (*Thamnophis radix haydeni*) and massasauga rattlesnake (*Sistrurus catenatus*).

4

An area of rugged hills and bluffs, the Ozark border region occurs along the lower Missouri River and the western edge of the Mississippi.

Ozark Border: This region includes a narrow band along the lower Missouri River and the eastern edge of the state along the Mississippi River. This area has rugged river hills and bluffs with deep, rich soils, deciduous forests and wide river valleys. The Ozark Border has the appearance of the Ozarks, but its steep-sided sandstone canyons have generally more productive soils, and plant species occur here which are not commonly found in the Ozarks. Amphibian species found in this region include the smallmouth salamander (*Ambystoma texanum*) in the river valleys, and the ringed salamander (*Ambystoma annulatum*) and wood frog (*Rana sylvatica*) in the forested hills. Reptiles of the area include the broadhead skink (*Eumeces laticeps*) and redbelly snake (*Storeria occipitomaculata*).

Ozark Plateau: This region is characterized by rough terrain, thin soils, limestone bluffs, springs, caves, clear streams and rocky glades. The Ozarks make up nearly 40 percent of the state. Most of the forest cover is oak and hickory with some maple. Shortleaf pine is a common tree species in the southeastern section of the province. The eastern section of the Missouri Ozarks has Precambrian (igneous) bedrock and steep hills which are known as the St. Francois Mountains. This area has the highest elevation point in the state—Taum Sauk Mountain, 1,772 feet above sea level. The forest products industry has been important here and several large areas are under the management of the U.S. Forest Service. However, major sections of the Ozark forest have been cleared and seeded in cool-season grasses for pasture. The average annual precipitation is 102 cm (40 inches). Amphibian and reptile species indicative of this region include: Ozark hellbender (*Cryptobranchus*

Nearly 40 percent of the state is made up of the rugged, scenic terrain of the Ozark plateau.

Upland glades characterized by thin, rocky soils and rocky outcroppings are also prominent features of the Ozark plateau.

alleganiensis bishopi), graybelly salamander (*Eurycea multiplicata griseogaster*), grotto salamander (*Typhlotriton spelaeus*), pickerel frog (*Rana palustris*), three-toed box turtle (*Terrapene carolina triunguis*), eastern collared lizard (*Crotaphytus collaris collaris*), southern coal skink (*Eumeces anthracinus pluvialis*), rough green snake (*Opheodrys aestivus*) and western pygmy rattlesnake (*Sistrurus miliarius streckeri*).

Most of the state's last native tallgrass prairies are located in the Osage prairie region of west central Missouri.

Osage Plains: This unglaciated region in the west central section of Missouri is characterized by rolling hills, prairie streams and tallgrass prairie plants. The majority of Missouri's last native tallgrass prairies are located in this area. Amphibians typifying this province include the Great Plains narrowmouth toad (*Gastrophryne olivacea*) and northern crawfish frog (*Rana areolata circulosa*). Reptiles associated with the Osage Plains: ornate box turtle (*Terrapene ornata ornata*), Great Plains skink (*Eumeces obsoletus*), bullsnake (*Pituophis melanoleucus sayi*), blotched water snake (*Nerodia erythrogaster transversa*) and Osage copperhead (*Agkistrodon contortrix phaeogaster*).

Mississippi Lowlands: The southeastern corner or "Bootheel" of Missouri is mostly a broad, flat alluvial plain. The area has an average elevation of 325 feet above sea level; the lowest point in the state (located in Dunklin County) is 230 feet above sea level. A ridge of low hills of sand, gravel and bedrock runs diagonally across the lowlands from northern Dunklin County to northern Scott County; this elevated area is known as Crowley's Ridge. Most of the area was bald cypress, tupelo swamp and bottomland hardwood forest during presettlement time. Extensive lumbering and drainage programs during this century have converted most of the area to agriculture. Average annual precipitation is 116.6 cm (46 inches). Some amphibians and reptiles typical of the southern United States range into Missouri in this province: mole sala-

7

Don Kurz

The native swamplands of southeast Missouri provide unmatched habitat for many species of amphibians and reptiles, but the natural features of the area are threatened by drainage and destructive agricultural practices.

mander (*Ambystoma talpoideum*), three-toed amphiuma (*Amphiuma tridactylum*), green treefrog (*Hyla cinerea*), Mississippi mud turtle (*Kinosternon subrubrum hippocrepis*), western mud snake (*Farancia abacura reinwardtii*) and broad-banded water snake (*Nerodia fasciata confluens*).

Natural Divisions of Missouri

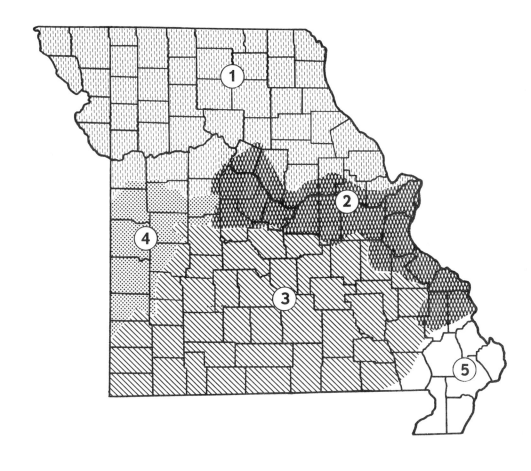

① **Glaciated Plains**
② **Ozark Border**
③ **Ozark Plateau**
④ **Osage Plains**
⑤ **Mississippi Lowlands**

Explanation of Family and Species Accounts

Accounts: The 22 families of amphibians and reptiles native to Missouri are presented in the sequence used by Smith (1961) and Collins (1982). These accounts are furnished to acquaint the reader with the general characteristics common to each family. Some species which occur outside of Missouri are discussed in order to give the reader an idea of the relationships and distributions of amphibians and reptiles on a broader scale. A typical example of each family is illustrated at the beginning of each family account.

Common and Scientific Names: The common and scientific names used throughout this book are those currently accepted by most authorities. These names follow the recommended usage by Collins, *et al.* (1982) in *Standard Common and Current Scientific Names of North American Amphibians and Reptiles*. If there has been a recent change in any name, a comment to that effect will be found in the Remarks section of the species account. To help standardize reptile and amphibian nomenclature, usage of the names contained in this book is recommended.

The genera found in each family are placed in alphabetical order and the species are placed in alphabetical order within each genus. For an understanding of the scientific naming of animals, it is helpful to refer to a biology or general zoology textbook.

Description: The description of species outlines characteristics to help identify each species; it includes general shape, a brief description of color and pattern and, when appropriate, a discussion of external characteristics that help separate the sexes.

The size of each species is given in both metric and English units. Total length is given for salamanders, lizards and snakes (i.e., length from snout to end of tail). Sizes of toads and frogs are given in snout-vent length (i.e., from the tip of the nose to the vent or anus). Turtle sizes are of the carapace or upper shell length. Record sizes of Missouri specimens are those reported by Powell *et al.* (1982) and are not necessarily the maximum lengths that these animals are capable of reaching.

Habits and Habitat: Aspects of the natural history of each species are discussed. These include habitat preferences, daily and seasonal activity, food and specific behavioral traits.

Breeding: The reproductive biology of Missouri's amphibians and reptiles is discussed in this section: courtship, mating, egg-laying, descriptions of eggs or newborn young, births or hatching. Also included are the duration of the breeding season and, in the case of toads and frogs, a description of their breeding calls. Much of this information has been gleaned from published papers in technical journals or from the works of Bishop (1943), Wright and Wright (1949), Smith (1961), Ernst and Barbour (1972), Conant (1975) and Collins (1982).

10

Subspecies: This section is offered only in those species accounts where more than one subspecies or geographic race occurs in Missouri. Descriptions used to distinguish the races are presented.

Remarks: The Remarks section provides special information such as taxonomic changes or problems, rare or endangered species status, hybridization or comments on unusual behavior.

Distribution and Maps: At the end of each species account is a brief description of the species range in Missouri. A map of Missouri showing county lines illustrates the presumed range of each species and/or subspecies (shading) and the known county records (black dots). Sections of the state where subspecies are thought to intergrade are shown by overlapping shading. An open circle in a county indicates a field observation with no available museum voucher specimen.

Preserved amphibian and reptile specimens were examined and/or county records were gathered from the following institutions:

American Museum of Natural History, New York, NY
Carnegie Museum of Natural History, Pittsburgh, PA
Chicago Academy of Science, Chicago, IL
Culver-Stockton College, Canton, MO
Field Museum of Natural History, Chicago, IL
Illinois Natural History Survey, Urbana, IL
Milwaukee Public Museum, Milwaukee, WI
Museum of Natural History, University of Kansas, Lawrence, KS
National Museum of Natural History, Smithsonian Institution, Washington, D.C.
Northeast Missouri State University, Kirksville, MO
Northwest Missouri State University, Maryville, MO
Southern Illinois University, Carbondale, IL
Southern Missouri College, Joplin, MO
Southwest Missouri State University, Springfield, MO
St. Louis Museum of Science and Natural History, Clayton, MO
University of Michigan, Museum of Zoology, Ann Arbor, MI

Missouri specimens collected as county records for this book have been deposited at the Museum of Natural History, University of Kansas in Lawrence.

For those readers who wish to learn about the distribution of amphibians and reptiles outside the confines of Missouri, I suggest referring to *A Field Guide to Reptiles and Amphibians of Eastern and Central North America*, by Roger Conant (1975).

Photographs: Photographs have been selected to show each animal in a natural setting while clearly illustrating individual characteristics. Each species account has one photograph to assist in identification, plus one or more photographs to illustrate a subspecies, show a calling male toad or frog, eggs or larvae, hatchlings, etc. Unless otherwise indicated, all photographs were taken by the author.

CHECKLIST OF MISSOURI AMPHIBIANS AND REPTILES

Class Amphibia

Order Caudata—Salamanders

Family Cryptobranchidae—Giant Salamanders
Eastern Hellbender . . . . . *Cryptobranchus alleganiensis alleganiensis* (Daudin)
Ozark Hellbender . . . . *Cryptobranchus alleganiensis bishopi* Grobman
Family Sirenidae—Sirens
Western Lesser Siren . . . . *Siren intermedia nettingi* Goin
Family Ambystomatidae—Mole Salamanders
Ringed Salamander . . . . *Ambystoma annulatum* Cope
Spotted Salamander . . . . *Ambystoma maculatum* (Shaw)
Marbled Salamander . . . . *Ambystoma opacum* (Gravenhorst)
Mole Salamander . . . . *Ambystoma talpoideum* (Holbrook)
Smallmouth Salamander . . . . *Ambystoma texanum* (Matthes)
Eastern Tiger Salamander . . . . *Ambystoma tigrinum tigrinum* (Green)
Family Salamandridae—Newts
Central Newt . . . . *Notophthalmus viridescens louisianensis* (Wolterstorff)
Family Amphiumidae—Amphiumas
Three-toed Amphiuma . . . . *Amphiuma tridactylum* Cuvier
Family Plethodontidae—Lungless Salamanders
Longtail Salamander . . . . *Eurycea longicauda longicauda* (Green)
Dark-sided Salamander . . . . *Eurycea longicauda melanopleura* (Cope)
Cave Salamander . . . . *Eurycea lucifuga* Rafinesque
Graybelly Salamander . . *Eurycea multiplicata griseogaster* Moore and Hughes
Oklahoma Salamander . . . . *Eurycea tynerensis* Moore and Hughes
Four-toed Salamander . . . . *Hemidactylium scutatum* (Schlegel)
Ozark Zigzag Salamander . . . . *Plethodon dorsalis angusticlavius* Grobman
Slimy Salamander . . . . *Plethodon glutinosus glutinosus* (Green)
Southern Redback Salamander . . . . *Plethodon serratus* Grobman
Grotto Salamander . . . . *Typhlotriton spelaeus* Stejneger
Family Proteidae—Mudpuppies and Waterdogs
Red River Mudpuppy . . . . *Necturus maculosus louisianensis* Viosca
Mudpuppy . . . . *Necturus maculosus maculosus* (Rafinesque)

Order Salientia—Toads and Frogs

Family Pelobatidae—Spadefoot
Plains Spadefoot . . . . *Scaphiopus bombifrons* (Cope)
Eastern Spadefoot . . . . *Scaphiopus holbrookii holbrookii* (Harlan)
Family Bufonidae—True Toads
Eastern American Toad . . . . *Bufo americanus americanus* Holbrook
Dwarf American Toad . . . . *Bufo americanus charlesmithi* Bragg
Great Plains Toad . . . . *Bufo cognatus* Say
Fowler's Toad . . . . *Bufo woodhousei fowleri* Hinckley
Woodhouse's Toad . . . . *Bufo woodhousei woodhousei* Girard
Family Hylidae—Cricket, Chorus and Treefrogs
Blanchard's Cricket Frog . . . . *Acris crepitans blanchardi* Harper
Cope's Gray Treefrog . . . . *Hyla chrysoscelis* Cope
Green Treefrog . . . . *Hyla cinerea* (Schneider)

12

Northern Spring Peeper .... *Hyla crucifer crucifer* Wied
Eastern Gray Treefrog .... *Hyla versicolor* Le Conte
Illinois Chorus Frog .... *Pseudacris streckeri illinoensis* Smith
Upland Chorus Frog............... *Pseudacris triseriata feriarum* (Baird)
Western Chorus Frog .... *Pseudacris triseriata triseriata* (Wied)
Family Microhylidae—Narrowmouth Toads
Eastern Narrowmouth Toad .... *Gastrophryne carolinensis* (Holbrook)
Great Plains Narrowmouth Toad .... *Gastrophryne olivacea* (Hallowell)
Family Ranidae—True Frogs
Northern Crawfish Frog .... *Rana areolata circulosa* Rice and Davis
Plains Leopard Frog... *Rana blairi* Mecham, Littlejohn, Oldham, Brown and Brown
Bullfrog .... *Rana catesbeiana* Shaw
Bronze Frog .... *Rana clamitans clamitans* Latreille
Green Frog .... *Rana clamitans melanota* (Rafinesque)
Pickerel Frog .... *Rana palustris* Le Conte
Northern Leopard Frog .... *Rana pipiens* Schreber
Southern Leopard Frog .... *Rana sphenocephala* Cope
Wood Frog................................. *Rana sylvatica* Le Conte

Class Reptilia

Subclass Anapsida

Order Testudines—Turtles and Tortoises

Family Chelydridae—Snapping Turtles
Common Snapping Turtle .... *Chelydra serpentina serpentina* (Linnaeus)
Alligator Snapping Turtle............. *Macroclemys temminckii* (Troost)
Family Kinosternidae—Mud and Musk Turtles
Yellow Mud Turtle .... *Kinosternon flavescens flavescens* (Agassiz)
Illinois Mud Turtle .... *Kinosternon flavescens spooneri* Smith
Mississippi Mud Turtle.......... *Kinosternon subrubrum hippocrepis* Gray
Stinkpot .... *Sternotherus odoratus* (Latreille)
Family Emydidae—Box and Water Turtles
Western Painted Turtle.................... *Chrysemys picta bellii* (Gray)
Southern Painted Turtle .... *Chrysemys picta dorsalis* Agassiz
Western Chicken Turtle .... *Deirochelys reticularia miaria* Schwartz
Blanding's Turtle .... *Emydoidea blandingii* (Holbrook)
Map Turtle .... *Graptemys geographica* (Le Sueur)
Mississippi Map Turtle...................... *Graptemys kohnii* (Baur)
Ouachita Map Turtle ..... *Graptemys pseudogeographica ouachitensis* Cagle
False Map Turtle .. *Graptemys pseudogeographica pseudogeographica* (Gray)
Missouri River Cooter .... *Pseudemys concinna metteri* Ward
Three-toed Box Turtle .... *Terrapene carolina triunguis* (Agassiz)
Ornate Box Turtle .... *Terrapene ornata ornata* (Agassiz)
Red-eared Slider .... *Trachemys scripta elegans* (Wied)
Family Trionychidae—Softshell Turtles
Midland Smooth Softshell .... *Trionyx muticus muticus* Le Sueur
Western Spiny Softshell ...... *Trionyx spiniferus hartwegi* Conant and Goin
Eastern Spiny Softshell............... *Trionyx spinifer spinifer* Le Sueur

13

Order Squamata—Lizards and Snakes

Suborder Sauria—Lizards

Family Iguanidae—Iguanid Lizards
Eastern Collared Lizard .... *Crotaphytus collaris collaris* (Say)
Texas Horned Lizard .... *Phrynosoma cornutum* (Harlan)
Northern Fence Lizard .... *Sceloporus undulatus hyacinthinus* (Green)
Family Scincidae—Skinks
Southern Coal Skink .... *Eumeces anthracinus pluvialis* Cope
Five-lined Skink .... *Eumeces fasciatus* (Linnaeus)
Broadhead Skink .... *Eumeces laticeps* (Schneider)
Great Plains Skink .... *Eumeces obsoletus* (Baird and Girard)
Ground Skink .... *Scincella lateralis* (Say)
Family Teiidae—Racerunners
Six-lined Racerunner .... *Cnemidophorus sexlineatus sexlineatus* (Linnaeus)
Prairie-lined Racerunner.......... *Cnemidophorus sexlineatus viridis* Lowe
Family Anguidae—Glass Lizards
Western Slender Glass Lizard .... *Ophisaurus attenuatus attenuatus* Cope

Suborder Serpentes—Snakes

Family Colubridae—Garter Snakes, Rat Snakes, Kingsnakes, etc. (non-venomous)
Western Worm Snake............ *Carphophis amoenus vermis* (Kennicott)
Northern Scarlet Snake .... *Cemophora coccinea copei* Jan
Eastern Yellowbelly Racer .... *Coluber constrictor flaviventris* Say
Southern Black Racer........ *Coluber constrictor priapus* Dunn and Wood
Prairie Ringneck Snake .... *Diadophis punctatus arnyi* Kennicott
Mississippi Ringneck Snake .... *Diadophis punctatus stictogenys* Cope
Great Plains Rat Snake .... *Elaphe guttata emoryi* (Baird and Girard)
Black Rat Snake....................... *Elaphe obsoleta obsoleta* (Say)
Gray Rat Snake ... *Elaphe obsoleta spiloides* (Dumeril, Bibron and Dumeril)
Western Fox Snake .... *Elaphe vulpina vulpina* (Baird and Girard)
Western Mud Snake.............. *Farancia abacura reinwardtii* Schlegel
Dusty Hognose Snake .... *Heterodon nasicus gloydi* Edgren
Plains Hognose Snake .... *Heterodon nasicus nasicus* Baird and Girard
Eastern Hognose Snake .... *Heterodon platyrhinos* Latreille
Prairie Kingsnake .... *Lampropeltis calligaster calligaster* (Harlan)
Speckled Kingsnake .... *Lampropeltis getulus holbrooki* Stejneger
Red Milk Snake .... *Lampropeltis triangulum syspila* (Cope)
Eastern Coachwhip.............. *Masticophis flagellum flagellum* (Shaw)
Green Water Snake........ *Nerodia cyclopion cyclopion* (Dumeril, Bibron
and Dumeril)
Yellowbelly Water Snake .... *Nerodia erythrogaster flavigaster* (Conant)
Blotched Water Snake .... *Nerodia erythrogaster transversa* (Hallowell)
Broad-banded Water Snake .... *Nerodia fasciata confluens* (Blanchard)
Diamondback Water Snake ...... *Nerodia rhombifer rhombifer* (Hallowell)
Midland Water Snake................. *Nerodia sipedon pleuralis* (Cope)
Northern Water Snake .... *Nerodia sipedon sipedon* (Linnaeus)
Rough Green Snake .... *Opheodrys aestivus* (Linnaeus)
Western Smooth Green Snake ..... *Opheodrys vernalis blanchardi* Grobman
Bullsnake .... *Pituophis melanoleucus sayi* (Schlegel)
Graham's Crayfish Snake .... *Regina grahamii* Baird and Girard

Ground Snake .... *Sonora semiannulata* Baird and Girard
Texas Brown Snake .... *Storeria dekayi texana* Trapido
Midland Brown Snake .... *Storeria dekayi wrightorum* Trapido
Northern Redbelly Snake .... *Storeria occipitomaculata occipitomaculata*
(Storer)
Flathead Snake .... *Tantilla gracilis* Baird and Girard
Western Ribbon Snake .... *Thamnophis proximus proximus* (Say)
Western Plains Garter Snake .... *Thamnophis radix haydenii* (Kennicott)
Eastern Plains Garter Snake .... *Thamnophis radix radix* (Baird and Girard)
Red-sided Garter Snake .... *Thamnophis sirtalis parietalis* (Say)
Eastern Garter Snake .... *Thamnophis sirtalis sirtalis* (Linnaeus)
Central Lined Snake .... *Tropidoclonion lineatum annectens* Ramsey
Northern Lined Snake .... *Tropidoclonion lineatum lineatum* (Hallowell)
Rough Earth Snake .... *Virginia striatula* (Linnaeus)
Western Earth Snake .... *Virginia valeriae elegans* Kennicott
Family Viperidae—Copperheads, Cottonmouths, Rattlesnakes (Venomous)
Southern Copperhead .... *Agkistrodon contortrix contortrix* (Linnaeus)
Osage Copperhead .... *Agkistrodon contortrix phaeogaster* Gloyd
Western Cottonmouth .... *Agkistrodon piscivorus leucostoma* (Troost)
Timber Rattlesnake .... *Crotalus horridus* Linnaeus
Eastern Massasauga .... *Sistrurus catenatus catenatus* (Rafinesque)
Western Massasauga .... *Sistrurus catenatus tergeminus* (Say)
Western Pygmy Rattlesnake .... *Sistrurus miliarius streckeri* Gloyd

Keys to the Amphibians and Reptiles of Missouri

How to Use the Keys

The illustrated keys which follow are furnished to help the reader identify *adult* amphibians and reptiles known to occur in Missouri. These keys have been designed to identify living animals, not preserved specimens. Tadpoles, salamander larvae, and some young adults of many Missouri species cannot be identified using these keys.

Keys used to identify plants or animals are organized into a series of numbered couplets which furnish a choice of characteristics (*a* and *b*) in each couplet. By choosing the description which best fits the animal being identified, and by continuing to refer to the next couplet numbered at the end of the appropriate characteristics, the reader is eventually directed to a couplet which ends in the name of the animal. Illustrations of important characteristics are furnished and labeled. The page numbers, in parentheses at the end of the species name, refer to the page where each species account begins.

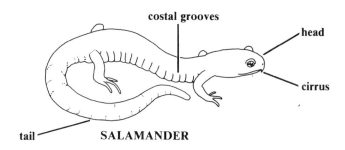

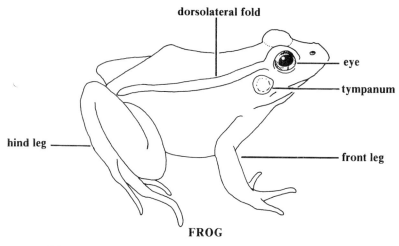

Fig. 1. Generalized drawing of a typical salamander and frog.

Key to the Salamanders of Missouri

1a Body eel-like; with or without gills; legs reduced or hind legs absent 2
1b Body not eel-like; with or without gills; legs well developed 3
2a Only front legs present; with gills; tail compressed vertically; color dull brown; no opening present on either side of the rear of the head .... Western Lesser Siren, *Siren intermedia nettingi* (Fig. 2A; p. 43).
2b Front and hind legs present, tiny with three toes on each leg; no gills; tail not compressed; color dark gray-brown to black; opening present on either side of the rear of head .... Three-toed Amphiuma, *Amphiuma tridactylum* (Fig. 2C; p. 64).
3a Both front and hind legs with four toes 4
3b Front legs with four toes; hind legs with five toes 5
4a Large feathery gills; tail compressed; color tan to dull gray-brown; numerous dusky or dark spots over dorsum and tail ..... Mudpuppy and Red River Mudpuppy, *Necturus maculosus* (Fig. 2B; p. 86).
4b No gills; tail rounded and constricted at base; white belly with black spots .... Four-toed Salamander, *Hemidactylium scutatum* (p. 75).
5a Costal grooves absent......................................6
5b Costal grooves present 7
6a Size 70–100 mm (2 7/8 to 4 inches); head small, body rounded; color: olive-brown dorsum with two rows of tiny red spots, belly yellow with numerous black spots; found in ponds and swamps ..... Central Newt, *Notophthalmus viridescens louisianensis* (p. 60).
6b Size 290–510 mm (11 1/2 to 20 inches); head wide and flattened, body with longitudinal wrinkles; color: gray to reddish-brown dorsum, belly grayish brown; found in Ozark rivers .... Hellbender, *Cryptobranchus alleganiensis* (Fig. 2D; p. 39).

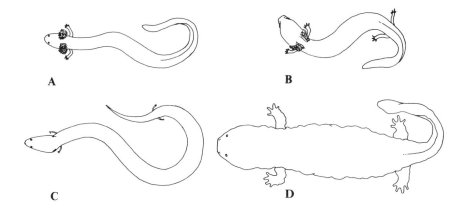

Fig. 2. *Outline drawing of aquatic salamanders:*
(A) siren   (B) mudpuppy   (C) three-toed amphiuma   (D) hellbender.

7a   Tail thick, same length as body or shorter; no naso-labial grooves 8
7b   Tail slender, as long or longer than body; naso-labial groove present 13
8a   Tail as long as head and body length; dorsum with grayish flecks or crossbands; costal grooves 14–15 9
8b   Tail as long as or shorter than head and body length; dorsum with flecks, round spots, cross bars or large blotches; costal grooves 10–15 10
9a   Body and tail plain or with numerous gray flecks; no rings ....Smallmouth Salamander, *Ambystoma texanum* (p. 55).
9b   Body and tail with narrow, transverse white or yellowish rings .... Ringed Salamander, *Ambystoma annulatum* (p. 46).
10a Transverse gray or silvery bars; costal grooves 11–12 ...... Marbled Salamander, *Ambystoma opacum* (p. 51).
10b No transverse bars; uniform dark color or with spots or blotches; costal grooves 10–15 11
11a No yellow spots or blotches; with or without faded lichenlike gray flecks; costal grooves 10–11 .... Mole Salamander, *Ambystoma talpoideum* (p. 53).
11b Yellow spots or large yellowish blotches over body and tail; no lichenlike gray flecks; costal grooves 11–15 12
12a Dorsum with two rows of round, yellow spots; white flecks on sides of body; costal grooves 11–12 .... Spotted Salamander, *Ambystoma maculatum* (p. 48).
12b Dorsum with olive-brown, yellow or occasionally white irregular blotches; no white flecks on sides of body; costal grooves 12–15.... Eastern Tiger Salamander, *Ambystoma tigrinum tigrinum* (p. 57).
13a Tail long and slender; with dorsal and ventral fins; with or without gills; costal grooves 19–21 14
13b Tail rounded or slightly compressed, without fins; no gills; costal grooves 14–20 15
14a Tail fins present; gills present (neotenic); two rows of white spots along sides of body; belly pale and without markings; no rows of chevrons along midline of dorsum; costal grooves 20–21 ......Oklahoma Salamander, *Eurycea tynerensis* (p. 73).
14b Tail fins present or absent; gills present or absent (sometimes neotenic); one row of white spots along sides of body; belly gray, may have some yellow color; row of chevrons along midline of dorsum; costal grooves 19 .... Graybelly Salamander, *Eurycea multiplicata griseogaster* (p. 71).
15a Ground color brown or black, covered with flecks of white; red, orange or yellow dorsal stripe (sometimes absent) 16
15b Ground color tan, yellow or orange; no white flecks or dorsal stripe; with or without dark spots..........................17
16a Color jet black; dorsum of head, body and tail with numerous white or yellowish flecks; no dorsal stripe; belly gray; costal grooves 14–15... Slimy Salamander, *Plethodon glutinosus glutinosus* (p. 79).
16b Color brown; dorsum of body and tail with red or orange stripe; belly with black and white mottling 18

17a Color light tan; no markings; eyes sometimes covered with skin; tail rounded; costal grooves 16–19;............ Grotto Salamander, *Typhlotriton spelaeus* (p. 83).

17b Color greenish yellow, orange, or red-orange; dark spots on head and body; spots or bars on tail, tail long and slender; costal grooves 13–14...19

18a Dorsal stripe uniform in width, not widest at hind legs; stripe edges serrated or sawtoothed; serration points correspond to costal grooves; costal grooves 18–19 ...... Southern Redback Salamander, *Plethodon serratus* (Fig. 3A; p. 81)

18b Dorsal stripe narrow and broken or lobed; stripe widest at hind legs; costal grooves 17–19 (Fig. 3B) ..... Ozark Zigzag Salamander, *Plethodon dorsalis angusticlavius* (p. 77).

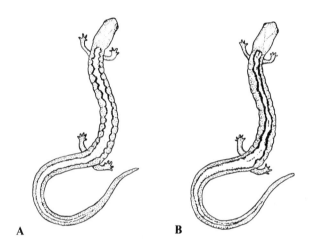

Fig. 3. *Dorsal view of redback salamanders: (A) southern (B) Ozark zigzag salamander.*

19a General color greenish yellow, yellow to orange-yellow; dark irregular spots on dorsum; dark markings on tail in the shape of bars or fused to form a dark lateral line on body and tail ... Longtailed and Dark-sided Salamander, *Eurycea longicauda* (p. 67).

19b General color bright orange or red-orange; numerous small black spots on body and tail; no dark lateral line on sides of body and tail .... Cave Salamander, *Eurycea lucifuga* (p. 69).

Key to the Toads and Frogs of Missouri

1a   One or two large spades on heel of hind feet; parotoid glands behind eyes; little webbing between toes of hind feet; skin relatively dry 2

1b   No spades on heel of hind feet; no parotoid glands behind eyes; weak to strongly webbed toes on hind feet; skin relatively moist 6

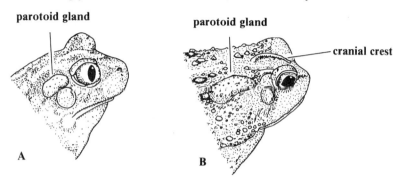

parotoid gland

parotoid gland

cranial crest

A

B

Fig. 4. Side view of heads of spadefoot (A), and true toad (B).

2a   Paratoid glands small and round; eye with vertical pupil when exposed to strong light (Fig. 4A); no bony cranial crest on head; only one spade per hind foot (Fig. 5A) 3

2b   Parotoid glands large; eye with horizontal or round pupil (Fig. 4B); bony cranial crest on head; one large and one small spade per hind foot (Fig. 5B); numerous warts 4

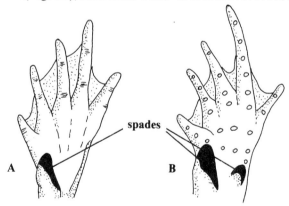

spades

A

B

Fig. 5. Underside of hind feet of (A) spadefoot and (B) true toad showing spades.

3a   Pronounced boss between eyes; spade on hind feet short and rounded; general color tan to greenish tan; red warts . . . . Plains Spadefoot, *Scaphiopus bombifrons* (p. 90).

3b   No boss between eyes; spade elongated and sickle-shaped; general color dull yellow, tan or brown; two or four yellowish longitudinal lines on dorsum; warts may be orange . . . . Eastern Spadefoot, *Scaphiopus holbrookii holbrookii* (p. 92).

4a   Parotoid glands oblong and connected to cranial crest; general color light gray to greenish gray; three or more warts per large dorsal spot; belly white or with one dark spot on chest 5

4b   Parotoid glands kidney-shaped, either separate from cranial crest or connected with a short spur; general color light brown to reddish brown; three or fewer warts per large dorsal spot; chest spotted with dusky markings. . . . American and Dwarf American toads, *Bufo americanus* (p. 95).

5a   Raised boss between eyes; large, paired dorsal blotches greenish brown bordered by white . . . . Great Plains Toad, *Bufo cognatus* (p. 98).

5b   No raised boss between eyes; usually with a single chest spot . . . Woodhouse's and Fowler's toads, *Bufo woodhousei* (p. 100).

6a   Tips of toes on front and hind feet expanded to form adhesive toe pads, which may be very small or large; if toe pads not present, with a V-shaped marking or small triangle between eyes; no dorso-lateral fold 7

6b   Tips of toes on front and hind feet without adhesive toe pads; no V-shaped marking or small triangle between eyes; with or without dorsolateral fold; if without dorsolateral fold, may have a transverse fold of skin behind head 12

7a   Tips of toes with adhesive toe pads; no V-shaped or small triangular marking between eyes 8

7b   Tips of toes without adhesive toe pads; V-shaped or small triangular marking between eyes 9

8a   Toe pads small; dorsal markings in the form of long stripes or lines of spots . . . . Upland and Western Chorus frogs, *Pseudacris triseriata* (p. 115).

8b   Toe pads medium to large size 10

9a   V-shaped marking between eyes; front legs large and muscular; no alternating light and dark bars on upper lip; a dark spot beneath each eye; no black stripe along inner thighs . . . Illinois Chorus Frog, *Pseudacris streckeri illinoensis* (p. 113).

9b   Dark triangle-shaped marking between eyes; front legs small and not muscular; alternating light and dark bars on upper lip; no dark spot below each eye; rough-edged black stripe along each inner thigh . . . . Blanchard's Cricket Frog, *Acris crepitans blanchardi* (p. 104).

10a   Toe pads prominent; no white spot beneath each eye; color yellow-green to emerald green; yellow or white line extending from snout to about midway to hind legs; dorsum may have a few small white or golden spots . . . . Green Treefrog, *Hyla cinerea* (p. 106).

10b   Toe pads small to large; with or without white spot below eyes; color gray, tan, green or greenish gray; no light lateral line; dorsum without white or golden spots 11

11a   Toe pads small; no white spot below eyes; color pinkish tan to grayish tan; dark line between eyes; X-shaped dorsal marking; no bright orange-yellow color on underside of thighs . . Northern Spring Peeper, *Hyla crucifer crucifer* (p. 108).

11b Toe pads prominent; large white spot below eyes; color may be light gray to green, with dark irregular blotches on dorsum; no dark line between eyes; underside of thighs bright orange-yellow .... Cope's and Eastern Gray treefrogs, *Hyla chrysoscelis* and *H. versicolor* (p. 110).

12a Transverse fold of skin behind head; no tympanum; no dorsolateral fold; head small (less than 1/4 snout–vent length) 13

12b No transverse fold of skin behind head; tympanum prominent; with or without dorsolateral folds; head large (greater than 1/4 snout–vent length) 14

13a Color uniform dark brown, two wide tan stripes along each side of dorsum; belly heavily marked with dark pigment .... Eastern Narrowmouth Toad, *Gastrophryne carolinensis* (p. 118).

13b Color uniform gray to olive tan; no markings or stripes on dorsum; belly light gray or creamy yellow without mottling ..... Great Plains Narrowmouth Toad, *Gastrophryne olivacea* (p. 120).

14a Large dark masklike marking on sides of head extending from snout through eye and nearly to front legs; with distinct dorsolateral folds; general color pinkish tan or grayish brown; no prominent dorsal markings .... Wood Frog, *Rana sylvatica* (p. 142).

14b No large dark masklike markings on sides of head; with or without dorsolateral folds; general color tan, brown, or greenish brown; with or without large dorsal spots or blotches 15

15a No light line along upper lip; tympanum same size or larger than eye; dorsal spots few and indistinct; with or without dorsolateral folds, but if present, never extending full length of body 16

15b With or without light line along upper lip; tympanum same size as eye; dorsal spots or blotches distinct; dorsolateral fold prominent, extending full length of body 17

16a No dorsolateral folds; prominent tympanal fold of skin from eye to shoulder; upper lip green; dorsal spots usually obscure if present .... Bullfrog, *Rana catesbeiana* (p. 128).

16b Dorsolateral folds extending halfway to hind legs; tympanal fold of skin from eye to shoulder not prominent; head greenish, with a few small dorsal spots..... Green and Bronze frogs, *Rana clamitans* (p. 131).

17a No light line on upper lip; dorsal spots numerous and closely set, interspaced with reticulations of dark brown or black......Northern Crawfish Frog, *Rana areolata circulosa* (p. 123).

17b Light line on upper lip; dorsal spots scattered or in two distinct rows down the dorsum, not interspaced with reticulations of dark brown or black 18

18a Dorsolateral folds wide and moderately raised; dorsal spots large and weakly to strongly ringed with white 19

18b Dorsolateral folds narrow and distinctly raised; dorsal spots small to medium and not ringed with white 20

19a Dorsal spots squarish or rectangular, set in two longitudinal rows, faintly ringed with white; dorsal ground color tan, never green; groin area and underside of hind legs bright yellow ... Pickerel Frog, *Rana palustris* (Fig. 6A; p. 134).

19b Dorsal spots round, not set in two longitudinal rows, strongly ringed with white; dorsal ground color often green; groin area and underside of hind legs white or pale green .. Northern Leopard Frog, *Rana pipiens* (Fig. 6B; p. 137).

20a Dorsolateral folds broken posteriorly and displaced toward midline; snout rounded, often with a dark spot; dorsal spots small, round, closely spaced and often greenish brown; dorsal ground color tan to light brown, never green .... Plains Leopard Frog, *Rana blairi* (Fig. 6C; p. 126).

20b Dorsolateral folds continuous, but, if broken posteriorly, broken sections not displaced toward midline; snout pointed, usually without a dark spot; dorsal spots small to medium, rounded and/or oblong, well spaced and brown to black; dorsal ground color usually green, or brown with some green... Southern Leopard Frog, *Rana sphenocephala* (Fig. 6D; p. 139).

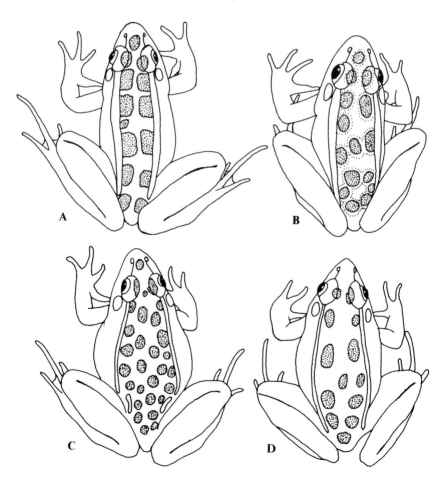

Fig. 6. *Dorsal view of (A) pickerel frog (B) northern leopard frog (C) plains leopard frog and (D) southern leopard frog.*

Key to the Turtles of Missouri

1a Carapace flat, soft, leathery and without scales; snout tube-shaped 2

1b Carapace dome-shaped, hard and covered with large scales; snout not tube-shaped 3

2a Anterior edge of carapace smooth, without bumps or spines; nostrils without projections from septum . . . Smooth Softshell, *Trionyx muticus* (p. 190).

2b Anterior edge of carapace rough, with short bumps or spines; nostrils with a projection on each side of septum . . . . Spiny Softshell, *Trionyx spinifer* (p. 193).

3a Tail long and at least half the length of carapace 4

3b Tail short and less than one-third the length of carapace 5

4a Top of head lacking large plates; beak moderately hooked; carapace without supramarginal scales . . . . Common Snapping Turtle, *Chelydra s. serpentina* (Fig. 7A; p. 147).

4b Top of head with large plates; beak strongly hooked; carapace with supramarginal plates . . . . .Alligator Snapping Turtle, *Macroclemys temminckii* (Fig. 7B; p. 150).

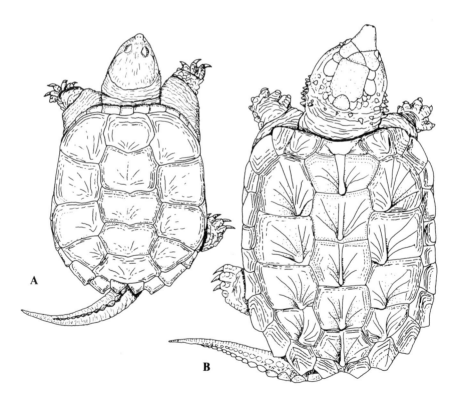

Fig. 7. *Dorsal view of common snapping turtle (A), and alligator snapping turtle (B).*

5a   Plastron with 11 plates (Fig. 8A), pectoral plates not connected to marginal plates or carapace; carapace smooth, dome-shaped, posterior marginal plates not serrated 6

5b   Plastron with 12 plates (Fig. 8B), pectoral plates connected to marginal plates of carapace; carapace smooth or with a mid-dorsal ridge, dome-shaped or low, posterior marginal plates slightly to heavily serrated 8

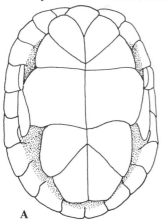 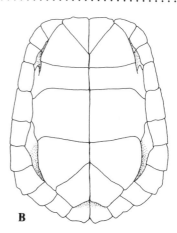

Fig. 8. Plastron with 11 plates (A), and with 12 plates (B).

6a   Plastron narrow, with one hinge, but incapable of closing; ninth marginal plate along edge of carapace same size as eighth marginal; tail without a horny, clawlike tip; head with two distinct, yellow lateral lines.............. Stinkpot, *Sternotherus odoratus* (p. 160).

6b   Plastron moderately wide, with two distinct hinges, capable of slightly closing; ninth marginal plate along edge of carapace same size or much higher than eighth; tail with horny, clawlike tip; head without distinct yellow, lateral lines 7

7a   Ninth marginal plate same size as eighth; head with two irregular rows of lateral, yellow markings; chin not yellow .. Mississippi Mud Turtle, *Kinosternon subrubrum hippocrepis* (p. 157).

7b   Ninth marginal plate higher than eighth; head gray, without two rows of yellow lateral markings, chin yellow .... Yellow and Illinois Mud turtles, *Kinosternon flavescens* (p. 154).

8a   First vertebral plate in broad contact with nuchal and four marginals...9

8b   First vertebral plate in broad contact with nuchal and only two marginals..10

9a   Carapace moderately dome-shaped, dark brown with numerous small, yellow spots; neck without yellow lines; plastron with transverse hinge that does not allow shell to completely close ..Blanding's Turtle, *Emydoidea blandingii* (p. 168).

9b   Carapace slightly dome-shaped, patterned with light colored network of lines on dark brown ground color; neck strongly patterned with yellow lines; plastron not hinged ..... Western Chicken Turtle, *Deirochelys reticularia miaria* (p. 166).

10a Plastron with transverse hinge that allows both anterior and posterior halves to completely close against carapace 11

10b Plastron without transverse hinge and immovable...............12

11a Each rear foot usually with three claws; plastron a uniform brownish yellow; carapace without keel or ridge .... Three-toed Box Turtle, *Terrapene carolina triunguis* (p. 180).

11b Each rear foot usually with four claws; plastron boldly marked with radiating yellow and brown lines; carapace with keel or ridge ....Ornate Box Turtle, *Terrapene o. ornata* (p. 183).

12a Carapace rounded and smooth, posterior edge not serrated, first marginal extends to or beyond ventral; numerous red markings along marginal plates 13

12b Carapace with or without a dorsal ridge, posterior edge moderate to strongly serrated, first marginal does not extend to or beyond ventral; no red color along marginal plates .,,..................14

13a Plastron with intricate dark markings which follow plate seams outward from center; carapace without a mid-dorsal stripe ....Western Painted Turtle, *Chrysemys picta bellii* (p. 163).

13b Plastron immaculate yellow; carapace with a distinct orange-red mid-dorsal stripe .... Southern Painted Turtle, *Chrysemys picta dorsalis* (p. 164).

14a Carapace without a mid-dorsal keel; head with large, reddish, lateral markings, or with thin, yellow, longitudinal lines and no yellow spot behind each eye 15

14b Carapace with low or prominent mid-dorsal keel; head with yellow triangular-shaped marking behind each eye, crescent-shaped, or large and globular; with at least some yellow transverse or vertical lines 16

15a Plastron yellow and boldly marked with 12 dark brown smudges; head usually with a wide reddish stripe behind each eye (adult males melanistic) ...... Red-eared Slider, *Trachemys scripta elegans* (p. 186).

15b Plastron yellow, with a few faint smudges anteriorly or without markings; head with numerous thin, yellow, lateral lines, widest yellow line begins below eye through angle of jaw (Fig. 9) .. Missouri River Cooter, *Pseudemys concinna metteri* (p. 178).

Fig. 9. *Head of Missouri river cooter.*

16a Carapace with low mid-dorsal ridge; yellow marking behind eye small and triangular (Fig. 10) .. Map Turtle, *Graptemys geographica* (p. 171).

16b Carapace with medium to high mid-dorsal ridge; yellow marking behind eye crescent or globular in shape 17

Fig. 10. Head of map turtle.

17a Carapace with medium mid-dorsal ridge; yellow marking behind eye, crescent-shaped which prevents the thin yellow lines of neck from reaching eye; no yellow spots below eye (Fig. 11A) .... Mississippi Map Turtle, *Graptemys kohnii* (p. 173).

17b Carapace with high mid-dorsal ridge; yellow marking behind eye globular-shaped; a few thin, yellow lines of neck touch each eye; one or two round or oblong, yellow spots below each eye (Fig. 11B)....... False Map Turtle and Ouachita Map Turtle, *Graptemys pseudogeographica* (p. 175).

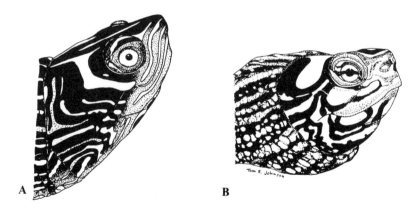

A   B

Fig. 11. Head of Mississippi map turtle (A), and false map turtle (B).

Key to the Lizards of Missouri

1a   Four limbs present 2

1b   Limbs absent .... Western Slender Glass Lizard, *Ophisaurus a. attenuatus* (p. 222).

2a   Dorsal and lateral scales large 3

2b   Dorsal and lateral scales small and granular 4

3a   Large, rough scales on body, limbs and tail 5

3b   Dorsal and lateral scales same size as ventrals; scales smooth and shiny 6

4a   Head large; dorsal and lateral scales small and granular; ventral scales hexagonal-shaped and in more than 15 rows across venter; a distinct black collar on neck .. Eastern Collared Lizard, *Crotaphytus c. collaris* (p. 198)

4b   Head long and narrow; dorsal and lateral scales small and granular; ventral scales large, transverse, and in fewer than 15 rows across venter; six or seven longitudinal light stripes on body; no distinct black collar on neck .... Six-lined and Prairie-lined racerunners, *Cnemidophorus sexlineatus* (p. 218).

5a   Back of head with large, pointed scales in the form of spines or "horns;" tail very short .... Texas Horned Lizard, *Phrynosoma cornutum* (p. 201).

5b   Back of head without spines; tail about same length as body; scales on body, limbs, head and tail strongly keeled; grayish brown to rusty brown color .... Northern Fence Lizard, *Sceloporus undulatus hyacinthinus* (p. 203).

6a   Frontal scale V-shaped; no supranasal scales present; lower eyelids with a transparent "window;" size small (maximum snout–vent length 52 mm) .... Ground Skink, *Scincella lateralis* (p. 215).

6b   Frontal scale rectangular-shaped; supranasal scales present; lower eyelids without a transparent "window" 7

7a   Dorsal and lateral scales form parallel rows with the long axis of body (Fig. 12A) 8

7b   Dorsal and lateral scale rows in oblique pattern to long axis of body (Fig. 12B); tan ground color with numerous black spots in longitudinal rows forming stripes ..... Great Plains Skink, *Eumeces obsoletus* (p. 213).

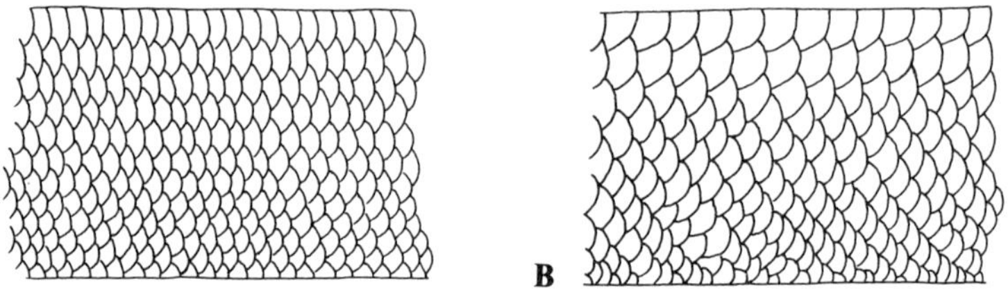

Fig. 12. *Five-lined skink showing parallel body scale rows (A), and Great Plains skink showing oblique body scale rows (B).*

8a Chin with one postmental scale (Fig. 13A); no light lines on head; dark lateral stripe along body black . . . . Southern Coal Skink, *Eumeces anthracinus pluvialis* (p. 207).

8b Chin with two postmental scales; light lines on head (Fig. 13B) 9

9a Eight or nine upper labials (Fig. 14A); no postlabial scales, or one or two small postlabials present; large lizard with a maximum snout–vent length over 85 mm . . Broadhead Skink, *Eumeces laticeps* (p. 211).

9b Seven upper labials (Fig. 14B); two large postlabial scales present; maximum snout–vent length under 88 mm . . . . Five-lined Skink, *Eumeces fasciatus* (p. 209).

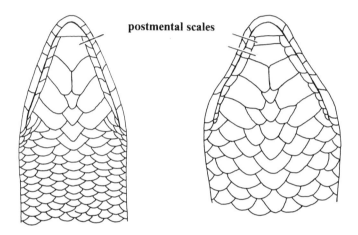

postmental scales

Fig. 13. *Underside of coal skink head showing one postmental scale (A), and of five-lined skink showing two postmental scales (B).*

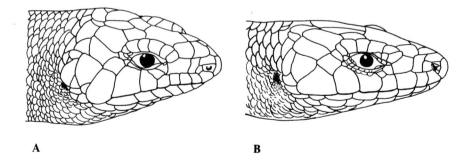

A   B

Fig. 14. *Lateral view of broadhead skink head with eight labial scales (A), and five-lined skink head with seven labial scales (B).*

Key to the Snakes of Missouri

1a A facial pit present between nostril and eye on each side of head; eyes with elliptical, vertical pupil (Fig. 15A); ventral surface of tail covered with one row of scales 2

1b No facial pit between nostrils and eye on each side of head; eyes with round pupil (Fig. 15B); ventral surface of tail covered with two rows of scales 6

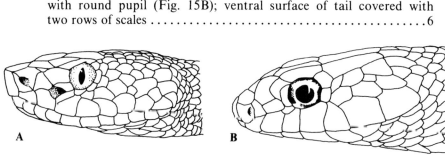

A   B

Fig. 15. *Head of pit viper showing facial pit and elliptical, vertical pupil of eye (A), and head of colubrid snake without facial pit; pupil is round (B).*

2a Tail ends with a rattle 3

2b Tail does not end with a rattle................................5

3a Head covered with small scales along with supraocular scales; dorsal markings crossbands and/or chevron-shaped; a rust colored dorsal stripe normally present; tail black; rattle size large.... Timber Rattlesnake, *Crotalus horridus* (p. 312).

3b Head covered with nine large scales; round, dark blotches along dorsum; with or without rust colored dorsal stripe; tail banded; rattle size small to medium 4

4a Dorsal blotches small, irregular-shaped, dark brown; ground color purple-gray; a rust colored dorsal stripe present; rattle size tiny ...... Western Pygmy Rattlesnake, *Sistrurus miliarius streckeri* (p. 319).

4b Dorsal blotches rounded, dark gray, brown or black, closely spaced; ground color gray or brownish gray; no rust colored dorsal stripe; rattle size medium ....Eastern and Western massasaugas, *Sistrurus catenatus* (p. 316).

5a Distinct, dark brown, hourglass-shaped dorsal markings over a pinkish-tan ground color; head without black stripe behind each eye; no white line along upper labials.......... Osage and Southern copperheads, *Agkistrodon contortrix* (p. 306).

5b Dorsal markings mostly obscured by dark brown or black; head with black stripe behind each eye; a white line present along upper labials ...Western Cottonmouth, *Agkistrodon piscivorus leucostoma* (p. 309).

6a Rostral scale pointed, projecting forward or upturned, or with a medial keel 7

6b Rostral scale rounded, not pointed or projecting forward, not upturned and without a medial keel 8

7a   Rostral scale pointed, slightly upturned; dorsal scale rows at mid-body number 25 (Fig. 16C); ventral coloration a mottled gray, underside of tail lighter in color than belly . . . . Eastern Hognose Snake, *Heterodon platyrhinos* (p. 250).

7b   Rostral scale strongly upturned; dorsal scale rows at mid-body number 23 or less; ventral coloration mostly black . . . . . . Plains and Dusty Hognose snakes, *Heterodon nasicus* (p. 248).

8a   Dorsal scales and at least some lateral scales weakly or strongly keeled (Fig. 16A) 9

8b   Dorsal and lateral scales smooth, without keels (Fig. 16B) 27

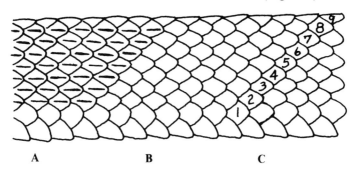

Fig. 16. *Diagram of snake body scales showing keeled scales (A), smooth scales (B) and method of counting scale rows (C).*

9a   Anal plate not divided (Fig. 17A) 10

9b   Anal plate divided (Fig. 17B) 14

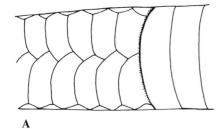 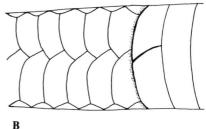

Fig. 17. *Snake anal plate not divided (A) and divided (B).*

10a   Rostral scale narrow and high, curving upward to tip of snout; four prefrontals present; dorsal scale rows at mid-body number 25 or more; ventral scales number 200 or more . . . . Bullsnake, *Pituophis melanoleucus sayi* (p. 277).

10b   Rostral scale wide and low, not curving upward to tip of snout; two prefrontals present; dorsal scale rows at mid-body number 24 or fewer; ventral scales number 190 or less 11

11a   Venter with two rows of black spots down the center; supralabial scales number six or less . . . . Central and Northern lined snakes, *Tropidoclonion lineatum* (p. 297).

11b   Venter with no black spots, or black spots present along lateral edges; supralabial scales number seven or more 12

12a Lateral light stripe includes scale rows two and three anteriorly (Fig. 18A); supralabial scales with narrow black bars; interspace between lateral body scales sometimes red .... Eastern and Red-sided garter snakes, *Thamnophis sirtalis* (p. 294).

12b Lateral stripe includes scale rows three and four (Fig. 18B) 13

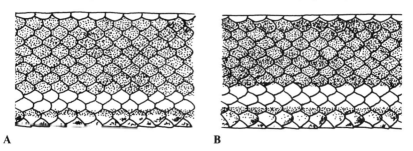

A   B

Fig. 18. *Lateral light stripe on scale rows 2 and 3 (A), and lateral light stripe on scale rows 3 and 4 (B).*

13a Supralabial scales white or pale green, without black bars; space between mid-dorsal light stripe and lateral light stripe uniformly dark; dorsal scale rows number at mid-body 19 or less; tail length usually more than 27 percent of total length ...... Western Ribbon Snake, *Thamnophis p. proximus* (p. 290).

13b Supralabial scales light in color, boldly marked with black bars; space between mid-dorsal light stripe and lateral light stripe marked with alternating round, dark spots; dorsal scale rows number at mid-body usually 21; tail length usually less than 27 percent of total length .... Eastern and Western Plains garter snakes, *Thamnophis radix* (p. 292).

14a Dorsal scale rows number at mid-body 19 or fewer 15

14b Dorsal scale rows number at mid-body 23 or more 20

15a Dorsal scale rows number at mid-body 15 to 17 16

15b Dorsal scale rows number at mid-body 19; light lateral stripe on scale rows one to three, along entire length of body; venter yellow and bordered by rows of small dark markings ... Graham's Crayfish Snake, *Regina grahamii* (p. 280).

16a Dorsal scale rows number at mid-body 15; one or more preocular scales present; supralabial scales number five or six; belly usually red-orange ...... Northern Redbelly Snake, *Storeria o. occipitomaculata* (p. 286).

16b Dorsal scale rows number at mid-body 17; no more than one preocular; belly not red-orange 17

17a Preocular scales present 18

17b Preocular scales absent 19

18a Light tan mid-dorsal stripe, usually bordered by small black dots; venter cream colored or pale pink with small, dark dots along each side .... Midland and Texas brown snakes, *Storeria dekayi* (p. 284).

18b No dorsal stripe; uniform color with no markings; dorsal green; venter yellow .... Rough Green Snake, *Opheodrys aestivus* (p. 273).

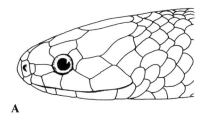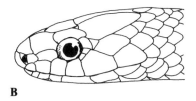

A   B

Fig. 19. *Head of rough earth snake with five labial scales (A), and head of western earth snake with six labial scales (B).*

19a	Supralabial scales number five, one postocular scale present; one internasal scale on snout; dorsal scales strongly keeled . . . . Rough Earth Snake, *Virginia striatula* (Fig. 19A; p. 300).
19b	Supralabial scales number six; two postocular scales present; usually two internasal scales on snout; dorsal scales weakly keeled . . . . Western Earth Snake, *Virginia valeriae elegans* (Fig. 19B; p. 302).
20a	Ventral scales number 159 or fewer; dorsal scales strongly keeled 21
20b	Ventral scales number 190 or more; dorsal scales weakly keeled . . . 25
21a	Dorsal scale rows number 25 or fewer 22
21b	Dorsal scale rows number 27 or more 24
22a	Venter boldly patterned with irregular dark markings 23
22b	Venter yellow and without markings, or with some light brown mottling; dorsal coloration uniformly dark brown to nearly black, or with obscure bands or blotches of brown . . . . Yellowbelly and Blotched water snakes, *Nerodia erythrogaster* (p. 263).
23a	Dorsal bands and blotches number 20 or less; ventral coloration yellow with irregular brown or reddish-brown markings that may cover parts of two or three scales, or may merge to form large ventral blotches . . . . . . Broad-banded Water Snake, *Nerodia fasciata confluens* (p. 266).
23b	Dorsal bands and blotches number more than 20; ventral coloration light yellow with irregularly spaced half-moons or spots of orange, red, brown or black . . . . Northern and Midland Water Snakes, *Nerodia sipedon* (p. 270).
24a	One or two subocular scales separating eye from supralabials; dorsal scale rows at mid-body number 27 to 29; dorsal coloration dark olive-brown; venter mottled brown with two or three yellow half-moons per scale . . . . . . Green Water Snake, *Nerodia c. cyclopion* (p. 261).
24b	No subocular scales between eye and supralabials; dorsal scale rows at mid-body number 25 to 29; dorsal coloration yellow-brown with narrow, dark brown, dorsal spots alternating, but connected to, narrow lateral spots; venter yellow with small half-moon shaped dark markings . . . Diamondback Water Snake, *Nerodia r. rhombifer* (p. 268).

25a Ventral scales number 220 or more; dorsal coloration uniform black or dark brown or with a faint pattern of 28 to 38 dark blotches; head dark, no marking between eyes; ventral coloration black-and-white checkerboard pattern anteriorly, gray mottling posteriorly .... Black and Gray rat snakes, *Elaphe obsoleta* (p. 240).

25b Ventral scales number less than 220; head light, with or without markings..26

26a Head orange to orange-brown with no "spearpoint" marking between eyes; ventral coloration yellow with large squarish, dark brown markings ......Western Fox Snake, *Elaphe vulpina* (p. 243).

26b Head gray or brownish gray with reddish-brown "spearpoint" marking between eyes; ventral coloration white with numerous small squarish, dark gray markings; dark gray stripes along venter of tail .... Great Plains Rat Snake, *Elaphe guttata emoryi* (p. 238).

27a Anal plate divided (Fig. 17B) 28

27b Anal plate single (Fig 17A) 35

28a Light colored ring around neck contrasting with dark brown or black dorsal color; venter yellow to orange with small black spots .... Prairie and Mississippi ringneck snakes, *Diadophis punctatus* (p. 235).

28b No light colored ring around neck 29

29a Dorsal scale rows at mid-body number 15 or less 30

29b Dorsal scale rows at mid-body number 17 or more 33

30a Dorsal scale rows at mid-body number 13; brownish-purple dorsal color in strong contrast to pink venter .... Western Worm Snake, *Carphophis amoenus vermis* (p. 230).

30b Dorsal scale rows at mid-body number 15 31

31a Venter cream colored; venter of tail with two broken rows of gray or black spots; dorsal color tan, orange or reddish brown, with or without saddle-shaped dark markings ...... Ground Snake, *Sonora semiannulata* (p. 282).

31b Venter yellow or salmon-pink; no gray or black spots along venter of tail 32

32a Yellow venter; dorsal color a plain bright green; head same color as body ....Western Smooth Green Snake, *Opheodrys vernalis blanchardi* (p. 275).

32b Venter salmon-pink; dorsal color a plain tan; head usually darker than body ....Flathead Snake, *Tantilla gracilis* (p. 288).

33a Dorsal scale rows at mid-body number 19; venter with red bands over black; tip of tail with pointed terminal scale......Western Mud Snake, *Farancia abacura reinwardtii* (p. 246).

33b Dorsal scale rows at mid-body number 17; venter without light and dark bands 34

34a Dorsal coloration dark brown to black anterior 2/3 of body, light tan to reddish posterior 1/3; 13 or fewer scale rows at end of body; venter coloration pale orange-brown, anterior ventral scales edged in gray ... Eastern Coachwhip, *Masticophis flagellum* (p. 259).

34

34b   Dorsal coloration uniform and varies from black to blue-green; 15 scale rows at end of body; ventral cream colored to yellow with some small random brown spots . . . . Eastern Yellowbelly and Southern Black racers, *Coluber constrictor* (p. 232).

35a   Dorsal coloration tan or cream with distinct red or orange-red blotches edged in black 36

35b   Dorsal coloration black with yellow spots or tan with brown blotches 37

36a   Snout pointed, venter white and without markings . . . . Northern Scarlet Snake, *Cemophora coccinea copei* (p. 230).

36b   Snout blunt, venter white with gray or black squarish or rectangular markings . . . . Red Milk Snake, *Lampropeltis triangulum syspila* (p. 257).

37a   Dorsum tan or brown with 45 to 80 mid-dorsal brown or dark brown blotches which are edged in black; dorsal scale rows at mid-body number 25 to 27 . . . . . . Prairie Kingsnake, *Lampropeltis c. calligaster* (p. 253).

37b   Dorsum black, each scale generally with a yellow spot; dorsal scale rows at mid-body number 19 to 21 . . . . Speckled Kingsnake, *Lampropeltis getulus holbrooki* (p. 255).

Part I—Amphibians

(Class Amphibia)

Salamanders, Toads and Frogs

Missouri has 42 species of amphibians, with an additional eight subspecies or geographic races. Amphibians are members of a group of vertebrate animals known as the Class Amphibia. There are presently 3,260 species of amphibians recognized by herpetologists. These animals are placed in three major groups: salamanders (Order Caudata), toads and frogs (Order Anura), and Caecilians (Order Apoda). Caecilians— long, legless wormlike animals—are represented by about 154 species; because they are found only in the tropics, they are not treated in this book.

Amphibians have played a vital role in the evolution of the vertebrates (animals with backbones). Some early amphibians were the first vertebrate animals to leave the security of their watery world and venture forth on land. This took place about 250 million years ago when some members of a group of fresh water fish called "lobed-finned" fish began moving over land to escape the drying-up of swamps. Some amphibians became established on land (if only during part of their lives), and eventually advanced to the point where they no longer needed to return to the swamps to breed and lay eggs. Some of these animals became the first reptiles.

Salamanders, toads and frogs generally have moist skin; none have scales. They require fresh water or a damp environment in which to live. The majority of Missouri's amphibians must return to water to reproduce; some species are totally aquatic or lay their eggs in moist places on land. Amphibians are poikilothermic or "cold blooded" animals—they are unable to internally control their own body temperatures. Skin secretions of amphibians are toxic or irritating to the mucus membranes of our eyes; thorough washing is recommended after handling specimens.

All Missouri amphibians lay eggs, either in the water or in moist areas. The eggs of toads and frogs hatch into tadpoles which have gills and eat aquatic plants, such as algae. Most salamander eggs hatch into aquatic larvae which have external gills and eat various small aquatic animals.

Adult salamanders may be distinguished from adult toads and frogs by the presence of a tail. The hind legs of toads and frogs are much larger than those of salamanders. Also, salamanders are voiceless; male toads and frogs produce a breeding call.

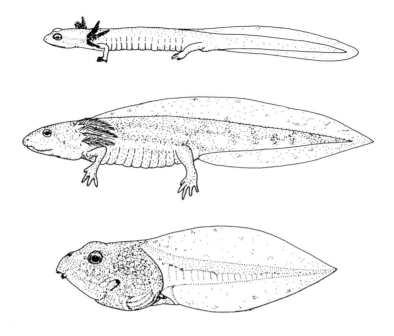

Typical stream-type salamander larva (top) *has small gills and low tail fin. A typical pond-type salamander larva* (center) *has large gills and high tail fin. A typical tadpole* (bottom).

Family Cryptobranchidae
Giant Salamanders

This family contains two genera, *Andrias* and *Cryptobranchus*. *Andrias* is strictly Asiatic, with two living forms, the Chinese and Japanese giant salamanders (*A. davidianus* and *A. japonicus*, respectively). The Japanese giant salamander is the largest living amphibian in the world, and has been reported up to five feet in length.

The other genus, *Cryptobranchus*, is restricted to the United States. Two subspecies, the eastern hellbender (*C. a. alleganiensis*) and the Ozark hellbender (*C. a. bishopi*), are recognized. Although primarily an eastern species, the hellbender is common in Missouri. The Ozark hellbender is endemic to southern Missouri and a small part of northern Arkansas. Missouri is the only state that contains both subspecies.

All members of this family are permanently aquatic salamanders.

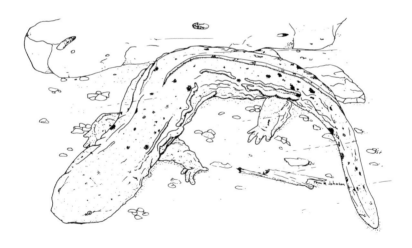

Eastern Hellbender

Adult Ozark hellbender from Howell County.

Hellbender
Cryptobranchus alleganiensis (Daudin)

Description: A large aquatic salamander. Its head is broad and flat, with very small, lidless eyes. Sides of body have soft, pronounced folds of skin with large flaps of skin on front and hind limbs. The tail is flattened and rudderlike. A single gill opening is usually present on one side of the head. Color varies from reddish brown to dull gray-brown. Some dark markings occur on the back and tail, but they do not have a distinct pattern. The belly is a uniform dark tan or gray-brown, and is lighter in color than the rest of the body.

Adult hellbenders range in total length from 29.3 to 51 cm (11 1/2 to 20 inches). Largest Missouri specimen recorded is 60 cm (24 inches; Powell *et al.*, 1982). The record size is 74 cm (29 inches; Conant, 1975).

Habits and Habitat: The hellbender is well suited for an aquatic existence. Its flat head and streamlined shape reduce water resistance. This salamander makes its home under flat rocks in large permanent streams and rivers. It is a slow swimmer, and often moves by walking along the bottom. It is normally a solitary animal, and usually only one will be found at a time, hiding under a rock (Nickerson and Mays, 1973).

In a study in Missouri (Nickerson and Mays, 1973), hellbenders were found to feed mainly on crawfish although other aquatic animals were occasionally eaten. Captive hellbenders will eat crawfish, minnows, earthworms and sliced beef liver.

*Freshly laid eggs of the eastern hellbender from the
Niangua River, Dallas County.*

Breeding: Hellbenders breed from late September to November; they
are the only salamander species in Missouri which fertilize their eggs
externally. From 200 to 700 eggs (each about 6 mm in diameter) are
deposited in depressions under flat rocks in rivers. The eggs are laid in
long strands, like a string of beads, and hatch in four to six weeks.
Female *C. a. alleganiensis* are reported to be sexually mature at a total
length of 380 mm (Taber *et al.,* 1975). The study by Topping and Ingersal
(1981) found that up to 24 percent of the gravid hellbenders examined
from the Niangua River (Laclede County) retained their eggs and eventually resorbed them.

I collected a clump of 165 hellbender eggs in the Niangua River on
September 19, and incubated them under artificial conditions. The eggs
began to hatch after 29 days. Hatchlings averaged 27.5 mm in total
length. The newly hatched larvae had large amounts of yolk in their
abdomen. They moved on the aquarium bottom with short, jerky swimming movements. From my observations of these larvae, I determined
that the yolk furnished nourishment to the young hellbenders for up to
three months. Once the larvae began to eat natural food, their color
became nearly black. Hellbender larvae lose their gills after about two
years, when they reach a length of 100 to 130 mm (4 to 5 1/2 inches;
Bishop, 1943).

Subspecies: There are two subspecies of hellbender in Missouri. The
Ozark hellbender (*Cryptobranchus alleganiensis bishopi* Grobman) is
found in southeast Missouri. One of the characteristics which distin-
guishes the two forms is the presence of black or dusky markings over a
large part of the chin of *C. a. bishopi,* which are usually lacking in the
other subspecies *C. a. alleganiensis.* Also, the dark brown markings on
the back are more numerous on the Ozark hellbender. Nickerson and
Mays (1973) found that the Ozark hellbender is smaller (largest Missouri
specimen 53.5 cm) and weighs less than *C. a. alleganiensis.*

Remarks: Hellbenders are often caught by fishermen in streams and rivers of southern Missouri, and are thought to be dangerous, poisonous and even deadly. None of this is true. The hellbender is a harmless amphibian which seldom, if ever, attempts to bite; if caught, it should be released unharmed.

Missouri Distribution: The hellbender is restricted to the Ozark Plateau in rivers which drain into the Missouri–Mississippi river system. The Ozark hellbender is found in the Black River system and the North Fork of the White River system (hatching).

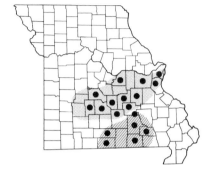

Family Sirenidae
Sirens and Lesser Sirens

This family of completely aquatic salamanders is restricted to North America. There are only three species represented by two genera: *Siren* (two species) and *Pseudobranchus* (one species). All members of this family have external gills, are somewhat eel-like in appearance, and have only front legs. The dwarf sirens (*Pseudobranchus*) are small, slender salamanders found in the extreme southeastern United States. The lesser siren and the greater siren (genus *Siren*) are much larger than *Pseudobranchus*, and are found throughout the southeast and south central United States and the Gulf Coast of Mexico. The greater siren (*Siren lacertina*) is one of the longest salamanders in the United States with a maximum length of over 90 cm (3 feet). In Missouri the family is represented by the western lesser siren (*Siren intermedia nettingi*).

Western Lesser Siren

42

Adult western lesser siren.

Western Lesser Siren
Siren intermedia nettingi Goin

Description: Characterized by external gills, small eyes, lack of hind legs and small front legs with four toes. The general shape of this animal is eel-like. The three pairs of external gills are red or grayish red and have a bushy appearance. Color varies from dark gray to brown to almost black. The belly is lighter than the back. Tiny dark brown or black flecks or spots are usually scattered over the back. Costal grooves vary from 34–36. There is no apparent external difference between the sexes except that males are larger than females.

Adult western lesser sirens range in length from 18 to 40.7 cm (7 to 16 inches). Largest Missouri specimen recorded is 419 mm (16 7/16 inches; Powell *et al.,* 1982).

Habits and Habitat: This completely aquatic salamander is found in sluggish streams, ditches, ponds, sloughs and swamps. By day it remains hidden under clumps of aquatic plants and submerged roots or branches, but becomes active at night to search for food. Its diet includes small crayfish, aquatic insects, snails and worms. Altig (1967) found that this species can apparently obtain food by "filter feeding" through bottom material and in aquatic vegetation. He reported that small crustaceans may account for up to 87 percent of the total number of food items eaten.

Western lesser sirens are known to produce two kinds of sounds, which may be used as means of communication between individuals. These include clicking sounds made by an individual when approached by another, and a "yelp" sound made when captured (Gehlbach and Walker, 1970).

If the pond or slough where a western lesser siren lives begins to dry up, the animal will burrow into the bottom mud. As the mud begins to dry out, the siren's skin glands produce a parchmentlike cocoon which covers the entire body except the head. This covering prevents the salamander from drying out, and allows it to aestivate many months until rains again flood the pond (Gehlbach *et al.,* 1973).

Head of a western lesser siren.

Breeding: Courtship and mating have not been observed in this species. In the spring each female lays up to 200 eggs in a small pocket in the bottom mud of a pond or ditch. The young at hatching are about 11 mm (3/8 inch) in total length. Maturity is reached after two years of development (Martof, 1973).

Remarks: Sirens produce a large amount of mucus on their skin. Add to this the ability to wriggle and squirm, and handling becomes next to impossible. These salamanders do not bite and are completely harmless to humans.

Missouri Distribution: The western lesser siren occurs in eastern and southeastern Missouri.

Family Ambystomatidae

Mole Salamanders

Members of this family (32 species in 4 genera) are found throughout most of the United States and parts of Canada and Mexico. The genus *Ambystoma* includes the majority of species and is the only genus of this family found in Missouri. There are six species of *Ambystoma* in our state.

The majority of Missouri species breed in early spring, courting and depositing their eggs in shallow ponds. Exceptions to this breeding behavior are discussed in the species accounts. The gilled larvae usually transform from aquatic to land animals in late summer, but some may spend the winter as larvae and transform the following summer.

Outside of the breeding season, adult *Ambystoma* spend most of their time burrowing in the soil or under logs and rocks. They may sometimes be seen wandering about at night, especially after a heavy rain.

Ringed Salamander

45

Adult ringed salamander from St. Louis County.

Ringed Salamander
Ambystoma annulatum Cope

Description: A slender and elongated salamander, usually with 15 costal grooves (J.D. Anderson, 1965). The head and neck are somewhat elongated compared to other members of the genus. The dorsal ground color ranges from dark brown to black; the belly is normally buff yellow. A series of pale rings usually extends over the back, but may be broken at the midline. The rings never completely encircle the body. Ring color may vary from dull white to yellow.

Adult ringed salamanders range in length from 140 to 180 mm (5 1/2 to 7 inches). Largest Missouri specimen recorded is 238 mm (9 3/8 inches; Powell *et al.*, 1982).

Habits and Habitat: Because of the secretive nature of this salamander, little is known about its habits. The ringed salamander probably lives much like other members of the genus—hiding under logs and rocks or burrowing in the soil, seldom venturing into the open and preferring heavily forested areas. Its food habits have not been studied in Missouri, but food probably includes earthworms, insects and land snails.

Breeding: The ringed salamander breeds in autumn, usually between September and early November. The salamanders are stimulated by heavy rains and cool temperatures to travel by night to fishless, woodland ponds, where they may congregate by the hundreds. The males arrive at the ponds before the females and can be distinguished by their slender bodies and swollen cloacas. Spotila and Beumer (1970) studied the ringed salamander in northwest Arkansas. They observed the courtship of this

46

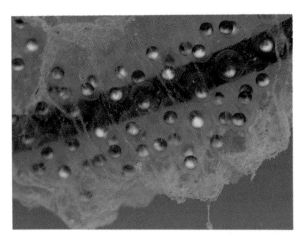

Fresly laid eggs of ringed salamander from a fishless pond in Warren County.

species to be similar to the *liebessipiel* (Bishop, 1941) of the spotted salamander (*Ambystoma maculatum*).

Courtship commences soon after females begin to arrive at the breeding pond, with from 2 or 3 to 25 males courting each gravid female. The spermatophore has a wide base and a short stalk that supports the sperm cap. Egg-laying begins on the night of courtship or the next night, and all egg-laying is completed within two days. The eggs are laid on submerged branches, aquatic plant stems, or on the bottom of shallow ponds. Each female may lay one or two clumps of eggs with from 75 to over 150 eggs per clump. The eggs may begin hatching in two to three weeks, depending on the water temperature. Newly hatched larvae are approximately 12 to 15 mm (7/16 to 5/8 inches) in length. The larvae remain in the ponds until the following summer.

Remarks: The ringed salamander and smallmouth salamander (*A. texanum*) were considered closely related due to the comparison of bone structure; both species were placed in the subgenus *Linguaelapus* by Tihen (1958). Spotila and Beumer (1970) suggested a close phylogenetic relationship between this species and the spotted salamander (*A. maculatum*) due to the similarity of the two species' courtship behavior, spermatophores, manner of egg deposition and egg masses. I elected to follow the J.D. Anderson (1965 and 1967a) arrangements of various species within the genus *Ambystoma*.

Missouri Distribution: This salamander occurs in the southwestern and central Missouri Ozarks, and in the river hills of the Missouri River in the eastern section of the state.

Adult spotted salamander from Warren County.

Spotted Salamander
Ambystoma maculatum (Shaw)

Description: Dorsum ground color slate black, belly dark gray. There are two irregular rows of rounded yellow spots from the head onto the tail. Number of yellow spots may range from 17 to 78 (Pierce and Shayevitz, 1982). Several specimens collected in Missouri lacked most or all yellow spots. Spots on the head may be bright orange. Sides of head, neck and body usually have small white flecks.

Adult spotted salamanders range in length from 150 to 200 mm (6 to 7 3/4 inches). Largest Missouri specimen recorded is 213 mm (8 7/16 inches; Powell *et al.,* 1982). The record length is 240 mm (9 inches; Conant, 1975).

Habits and Habitat: This species can be found in damp hardwood forests in the vicinity of shallow ponds, usually hidden under logs or rocks, inside piles of dead leaves, or burrowed in the soil. They venture forth at night in search of worms, insects, spiders and land snails, and are often seen crossing roads on warm rainy nights.

Breeding: The spotted salamander is an early spring breeder. During the first warm rains in late February to mid-March, they congregate in shallow, fishless, woodland ponds to court and lay eggs.

Sexton (pers. comm.) studied the breeding migration of a population of spotted salamanders in St. Louis County for six seasons. He found that there were slightly more males than females. Certain areas of the pond at the heads of valleys were used as entrance and exit points.

Spotted salamander eggs, Warren County.

Males appeared to be more consistent users of these pathways than females. The salamanders he studied traveled up to 172 meters to the pond.

During courtship two or more salamanders go through a series of movements somewhat like a nuptial dance (Johnson, 1983). They may number in the hundreds in a single pond, and their aquatic courtship, known as *liebesspiel* ("love play," Bishop, 1941) takes place at night in shallow water. The males walk and swim around, nudging the females. A male may swing his head from side to side near a female, or nudge her at the base of her tail. Eventually, the female will move forward and pick up a packet of sperm left by one of the males. The sperm are located on the top of a clear stalk of jelly, known as a spermatophore, which is about 6 mm (1/4 inch) high. These stalks of jelly may nearly cover the dead leaves and twigs on the pond bottom, and can be found the next day—evidence of the salamanders' breeding frenzy the night before.

The sperm are picked up by the cloaca of the female, stored in a chamber (*spermatheca*) in the roof of the cloaca. The eggs are fertilized as they are laid in a mass on submerged branches or aquatic plants, usually within one or two days after courtship. A female spotted salamander may lay up to three or four egg clumps, each up to 200 mm (4 inches) across, and produce a total of 300 to 400 eggs. Each egg mass may contain from a dozen to over 250 eggs (Bishop, 1943).

A green, single-celled algae (*Oophila*) is usually found in the egg clumps of spotted salamanders, as well as other salamander species. Gates (1973) was able to prove that the algae enters the eggs soon after they are laid; eggs inside gravid females do not contain algae. The egg masses take on a light green color due to the presence of the algae, but the color is not visible until the algae has had a week or more to grow. This may be an example of a symbiotic relationship—the algae provide oxygen to the embryos during the day, and the developing larvae provide carbon dioxide and waste products that can be used by the algae.

The gilled larvae hatch in about one month, average 13 mm (1/2 inch) in length, and remain in the water to feed and develop until the end of summer. Some larvae may overwinter in the pond and metamorphose during the next summer. Spotted salamanders take two years to reach maturity. Individuals may return to the same pond to breed year after year.

Missouri Distribution: The spotted salamander is found throughout the southern two thirds of the state.

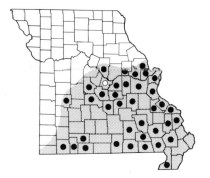

Adult marbled salamander from Warren County.

Marbled Salamander
Ambystoma opacum (Gravenhorst)

Description: This small, stout salamander has silvery or white saddle-shaped markings on its body from head to tail. These crossbands vary in shape and also in color, from silver-white to gray. The back is generally shiny jet black, while the belly is plain black. Adult male marbled salamanders have white or silver colored crossbands; adult females have dull gray crossbands.

Adult marbled salamanders range in length from 90 to 115 mm (3 1/2 to 4 1/2 inches). Largest Missouri specimen recorded is 124 mm (4 7/8 inches; Powell *et al.,* 1982). The record length is 127 mm (5 inches; Conant, 1975).

Habits and Habitat: The marbled salamander is secretive—it spends most of its time under rocks, logs, or forest debris. It prefers forested areas, but may also be found in open sandy woods and on rocky dry hillsides. Food probably consists of insects, worms, slugs and other invertebrates found under rocks or logs. These salamanders are seldom encountered except during the autumn breeding season.

Breeding: In this species, courtship and spermatophore deposition take place on land near fishless, woodland ponds or swamps. Fertilization is internal (eggs are fertilized as they move through the cloaca) and each female may lay from 50 to 200 eggs (Bishop, 1943). The eggs are laid in a small depression under logs, in leaf litter, or under vegetation at the edge of the water. The female remains with the eggs until they are covered by rising water levels caused by autumn rains.

*Adult female marbled salamander with a freshly laid
clutch of 175 eggs, from Warren County.*

I found a female near a small pond in Warren County on September 25, with 110 eggs. A gravid female was also found and retained in captivity. She eventually laid 175 eggs and was photographed. The larvae hatch and develop in the water, and metamorphosis takes place the following summer. At the time of transformation, the larvae range in length from 63 to 74 mm (2 7/16 to 2 7/8 inches; Bishop, 1943).

Remarks: The marbled salamander and many other Missouri amphibians require small, fishless, woodland ponds for reproduction. Their breeding habitat can be enhanced by providing logs along the edge of the water for egg-laying niches.

Missouri Distribution: The marbled salamander occurs in the Mississippi River lowlands and in the Ozark Plateau. It also occurs in the forested, river hills of the Missouri River in eastern Missouri.

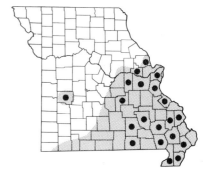

Adult mole salamander.

Mole Salamander
Ambystoma talpoideum (Holbrook)

Description: A salamander with a very large head, small body and tail, and large legs. There are 10 or 11 costal grooves. Color is usually dull gray or brown, and on most specimens there are whitish or light gray flecks over most of the body, legs and tail.

Adult mole salamanders may range in length from 80 to 100 mm (3 to 4 inches). Largest Missouri specimen recorded is 109 mm (4 1/4 inches; Powell *et al.*, 1982). The record length is 122 mm (4 13/16 inches; Conant, 1975).

Habits and Habitat: This species lives in lowland forests in association with marbled and smallmouth salamanders. It finds shelter under logs, leaf litter and in the soil. Mole salamanders are seldom encountered, since they rarely venture above ground except during the breeding season. A variety of small insects, worms and land snails make up their diet.

Breeding: No studies of the breeding habits of this species have been conducted in Missouri. Smith (1961) reported that the species may be an autumn breeder in Illinois, and this is probably true for the population in southeastern Missouri.

Data from other states indicates that leaf-littered, fishless, woodland ponds or swamp pools are utilized for breeding. Courtship takes place in water. Fertilization occurs as the eggs pass through the cloaca; each female may produce from 200 to 400 eggs. The eggs are loosely attached to submerged twigs or leaves in small clumps containing 4 to 20 eggs. The larval stage lasts from three to four months (Smith, 1961). Shoop (1964) reported that mole salamander larvae may live in crayfish burrows. Newly transformed mole salamanders may be from 50 to 65 mm (2 to 2 9/16 inches; Bishop, 1943) in total length.

Remarks: The mole salamander requires natural swamps and lowland forest to survive. This habitat has been greatly reduced in southeastern Missouri, and the remaining swamps and forests should be protected.

Missouri Distribution: The mole salamander was first reported in Missouri by Easterla (1967). It is restricted to the Mississippi River lowlands where it has been found in only a few locations.

Adult smallmouth salamander from Callaway County.

Smallmouth Salamander
Ambystoma texanum (Matthes)

Description: The smallmouth salamander is of moderate size, has a small head and mouth, and is usually black or dark brown in color. The body, limbs and tail may be mottled with small, irregular flecks of tan, grayish yellow or gray. The belly is usually black, but small flecks may be present.

Adult smallmouth salamanders range in total length from 110 to 140 mm (4 1/2 to 5 1/2 inches). Largest Missouri specimen recorded is 168 mm (6 5/8 inches; Powell *et al.,* 1982). The record length for this species is 178 mm (7 inches; Conant, 1975).

Habits and Habitat: The smallmouth salamander lives under rocks, rotten logs, piles of dead leaves, or in burrows in the soil. They are found in a wide variety of habitats including rocky hillsides, swamps, woodlands, prairies, river floodplains and even farmlands. In Missouri they have been observed living in mole burrows (Bursewicz, pers. comm.).

As with other species in this genus, the food of smallmouth salamanders consists of earthworms, slugs and insects.

Breeding: In Missouri the smallmouth salamander breeds from late February to early April. Large numbers of them may congregate at a suitable breeding pond, slough, stream or flooded ditch. Petranka (1982 a and b) showed that this species has diverged into two distinct reproductive forms that utilize different breeding habitats. One form uses streams for breeding; it deposits its eggs singly on the undersides of flat limestone rocks or submerged logs or leaves. The form of smallmouth salamander

Smallmouth salamander larva from Stoddard County.

that breeds in ponds (small woodland ponds or roadside ditches) lays its eggs in clumps on leaves or twigs. Courtship involves a male nudging a female with his snout, then moving or swimming a short distance from the female. Wyman (1971) reported an observation of male *texanum* from an Illinois population which included the clasping (amplexus) of females during courtship. The male deposits a spermatophore on the bottom, and the female follows and picks up the sperm located on the top of the spermatophore with her cloaca (Garton, 1972; and Keen, 1975).

Each gravid female may deposit from 300 to over 800 eggs (Plummer, 1977). Eggs may take several weeks to hatch into gilled, pond-type larvae. The larvae take about two months to transform into young adults and begin life on land.

Remarks: Easterla (1970) reported finding an albino smallmouth salamander in Stoddard County, Missouri. Also see Remarks section in the ringed salamander species account.

Missouri Distribution: This species occurs throughout most of Missouri except for the Ozark Plateau and the extreme northwestern corner of the state.

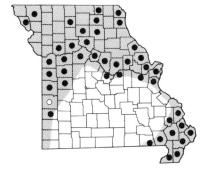

Eastern tiger salamander from Lincoln County.

Eastern Tiger Salamander
Ambystoma tigrinum tigrinum (Green)

Description: A dark, medium to large salamander with yellow or olive blotches. Ground color is black or dark brown. The large spots or blotches vary greatly in size and shape, and are found over the head, body and tail. Blotch color ranges from bright yellow to dull olive-brown. The belly is dark gray or black with yellow mottling. The number of costal grooves ranges from 11 to 14. As with all members of the genus *Ambystoma*, males usually have longer tails than females, and during the breeding season have a swollen cloaca.

Adult eastern tiger salamanders range in total length from 180 to 210 mm (7 to 8 1/4 inches). Largest Missouri specimen recorded is 238 mm (9 3/8 inches; Powell *et al.,* 1982). The record length is 330 mm (13 inches; Conant, 1975).

Habits and Habitat: Eastern tiger salamanders are found in a wide variety of habitats including woodlands, swamps, prairies, farmlands (in the vicinity of farm ponds), and may sometimes be found in wells, basements and root cellars. They spend most of their time in burrows under logs and rocks and are active only at night. Eastern tiger salamanders become migratory during autumn rains, moving to ponds where breeding will take place the following spring.

Prey of this species includes any animal small enough for them to swallow. Common foods include earthworms, insects, spiders, slugs and snails.

Breeding: Males can be observed migrating to fishless ponds or marshes during rainy autumn weather. Females may also move toward the ponds in autumn or early spring. Courtship and egg-laying take place in the water between February and April. Courtship usually involves males and females rubbing together, with much tail thrashing and some nipping. Eventually the male moves away and the female follows, keeping her head close to the cloaca of the male. He then deposits a spermatophore on the bottom which is quickly picked up by the female's cloaca, and her eggs are fertilized as they pass through the cloaca.

Each female may lay up to 1,000 eggs (Collins, 1982), which are deposited in small clumps containing from 18 to 110 eggs (Vogt, 1981). The eggs hatch in a few weeks, and the pond-type gilled larvae develop throughout the summer, feeding on a variety of aquatic invertebrates. Transformation to a land-dwelling sub-adult takes place between late July and early September. Neoteny (the condition of gilled adults) has been reported for this species, but to date this has not been found in Missouri.

Eastern tiger salamander larva from Linn County.

Remarks: The larvae of this species are often erroneously called "water-dogs." The term waterdog is a local name for the mudpuppy.

Missouri Distribution: The eastern tiger salamander is presumed to occur statewide, but is more commonly found in the northern half of the state than in the Ozarks.

Family Salamandridae

Newts

This salamander group has about 42 species occurring in Europe, Asia, northwest Africa and North America. In North America it is represented by two genera: *Taricha* with species on the west coast, and *Notophthalmus* with species occurring from the east coast to the Great Plains.

Unlike most salamanders which have smooth skin, newts have rough, almost bumpy skin. Adults of the West Coast newts (*Taricha*) spend their lives on land in mosses and under logs, while adult *Notophthalmus* are usually aquatic.

The central newt (*Notophthalmus viridescens louisianensis*) is the only representative of this family in Missouri.

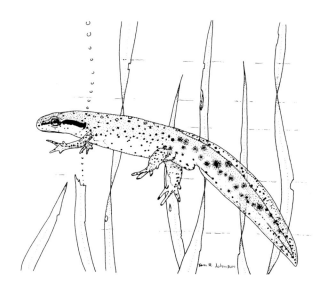

Central Newt

Adult central newt from Warren County.

Central Newt
Notophthalmus viridescens louisianensis (Wolterstorff)

Description: The adult is a small, aquatic salamander without costal grooves or gills. It has an olive-brown back and a bright orange-yellow belly. The dark color of the back and the yellow of the belly are distinctly separated along the sides of the body. A number of very small red spots ringed with black may be present along the back on both sides of the spine. Usually the entire body is covered with numerous small black spots that may be somewhat larger on the belly than on the back. A dark brown or black line is present from the nostril through the eye to the forelimbs. The eyes are often orange-yellow in color.

During the breeding season, adult males can be distinguished by the presence of very high fins on the tail, large, swollen hind limbs and cloacal lips; females appear heavy-bodied. The "eft" or middle stage of this salamander lives on land. Its dull brown color, rounded tail, rough skin and lack of any secondary sexual characteristics distinguish it from the adult.

Adult central newts may range in length from 70 to 100 mm (2 7/8 to 4 inches). Largest Missouri specimen recorded is 125 mm (4 15/16 inches; Powell *et al.,* 1982) which may also be the record for this subspecies. Efts range in length from 35 to 86 mm (1 3/8 to 3 3/8 inches).

Habits and Habitat: The food of adult newts consists of small aquatic invertebrates such as insects, small molluscs, crayfish and various worms. The terrestrial efts feed on small insects and tiny snails found under logs and rocks. The aquatic larvae eat smaller aquatic invertebrates.

Central newt larva (left) *from Pulaski County, and eft* (right) *from Boone County.*

Adult central newts are found in woodland ponds, swamps and occasionally water-filled ditches. They are seldom numerous in ponds that harbor fish or that lack aquatic plants. The efts take shelter under logs, rocks, or piles of dead leaves in wooded areas near ponds inhabited by the adults. Efts eat small land snails and a variety of small insects (Burton, 1976). A small, undisturbed pond may contain a surprisingly high number of adult newts. They are active by day or night, and may be observed from shore as they swim near the surface, come up for air or remain still in mid-water. They remain active throughout the year and have been observed in winter swimming about under the ice (Conant, 1975).

Breeding: The courtship and life cycle of the central newt is more complex than that of most salamander species. Breeding takes place in the spring. A male will swim after a female, mount her back, clasp her body with his hind legs, and then will fan his tail toward the female. Tail fanning may help to propel a sexually stimulating odor secreted from the male's cloaca to the female; this induces the female to allow the courtship to continue toward completion. Eventually the female will begin fanning her tail, which induces the male to begin swimming about. At this time, the male's cloaca becomes more swollen, he leaves the female, and, moving forward, begins more rapid undulations. The female follows him; if she touches his tail with her head, the male can then complete his courtship act by depositing a spermatophore. This sperm packet is then picked up by the female with her cloacal lips as she moves over the spot where it was deposited.

After the eggs are internally fertilized, they are laid singly on aquatic plants and hatch between three and five weeks later. From 200 to 375 eggs may be laid by a single female during May and June (Bishop, 1943). The gilled, pond-type larvae average from 7 to 9 mm (1/4 to 3/8 inches) in length at hatching, and remain in the water until late July or early August. They then metamorphose into rough-skinned, land-dwelling efts. These small salamanders live from two to three years on land, hiding in leaf litter, under logs, or in rotten stumps. Here they find shelter, moisture and food. Gilled adult central newts have been found in southern Illinois (Brandon and Bremer, 1966), but this condition has not been reported in Missouri.

Remarks: The presence of fishless, woodland ponds, swamps and small sloughs is vital to the existence of this species. Efts require downed logs, brushpiles and other forest floor debris to survive their sojourn on land. Concerned landowners and land managers are encouraged to provide or protect these habitat elements.

Missouri Distribution: The central newt is found throughout most of Missouri with the exception of the northwest corner of the glaciated region.

Family Amphiumidae
Amphiumas

This strictly North American family is represented by only one genus, *Amphiuma,* consisting of three recognized species: the one-toed amphiuma (*Amphiuma pholeter*), the two-toed amphiuma (*A. means*) and the three-toed amphiuma (*A. tridactylum*). Their combined range covers the southeastern and southern United States from North Carolina to east Texas. The three-toed amphiuma ranges northward into southeastern Missouri.

In general amphiumas are the longest salamander in North America, and have been known to reach over 116 cm (45 inches; Conant, 1975). They have tiny, almost useless legs, small eyes (which lack eyelids) and smooth skin.

Three-toed Amphiuma

Adult three-toed amphiuma.

Three-toed Amphiuma
Amphiuma tridactylum Cuvier

Description: A completely aquatic salamander shaped like a long cylinder with a somewhat pointed head; it has tiny gray eyes, and very small front and hind limbs. Each limb has three very small toes. Dorsal color is dark brown or black; belly is lighter brown or gray. Adults do not have gills, but a gill slit is present on each side of the head. Amphiumas have lungs and must breathe air at the surface of the water.

Adult three-toed amphiumas range in length from 46 to 76 cm (18 to 30 inches). Largest Missouri specimen recorded is 81 cm (32 inches; Powell *et al.*, 1982).

Habits and Habitat: Three-toed amphiumas spend the daylight hours buried in silt or hiding under submerged roots, debris, or aquatic plants. Their heads and necks may be exposed, and periodically they must come to the surface for air. They venture forth at night in search of small fish, crayfish, tadpoles, snails, aquatic insects, earthworms and other aquatic animals.

This salamander makes its home in still water, such as ditches, sloughs and swamps. In Missouri, cypress swamps are the favorite haunt of this species.

These animals are difficult to collect in the wild because they are alert, fast, slippery and may bite viciously. The western mud snake (*Farancia abacura reinwardtii*) is known to prey on amphiumas.

Breeding: Very little is known about the breeding habits of the three-toed amphiuma in Missouri. In areas where it has been studied (western

Tennessee) it is known to breed in late summer and early autumn. A female lays an average of 200 eggs (Salthe, 1973). The eggs are laid on land, usually under a rotten log near water. Once water from autumn rains covers the eggs, they complete development and hatch. Larvae have gills and are between 63 and 75 mm (2 1/2 to 3 inches) long.

Remarks: Local common names for this salamander are "congo eel" and "blue eel." The cypress swamps of southeastern Missouri are important to the survival of this interesting amphibian and should be protected. Fishermen who catch amphiumas on hook-and-line should cut their line and release them unharmed.

Missouri Distribution: The three-toed amphiuma is found in a few counties in the Mississippi lowlands of southeastern Missouri.

Family Plethodontidae

Lungless Salamanders

This successful family of salamanders is represented by 18 genera containing about 80 species. The family probably originated in the southern Appalachian Mountains of the eastern United States. Plethodontid salamanders occur over the eastern half of North America, the west coast, and into Mexico, Central America and northern South America. A few species also occur in southern Europe.

The adults lack lungs and most lack gills; the oxygen they require is taken from their environment through the skin and the mucous membrane of the mouth. One characteristic exclusive to this family is the presence of a groove in the skin running from each nostril down to the lip. In some species, associated with this groove (called the naso-labial groove) is a projection of skin which extends the groove below the upper lip. These projections are called *cirri* and are more pronounced on adult males. The groove and cirri may be associated with the sense of smell.

Lungless salamanders are found in a wide variety of moist habitats. Woodlands, springs, caves, cold streams and rock outcroppings with seepage are habitats commonly associated with this group.

This family is represented in Missouri by four genera with nine species.

Southern Redback Salamander

Adult longtail salamander from Scott County.

Longtail Salamander
Eurycea longicauda (Green)

Description: A medium-size salamander with a long tail. It is usually yellow in color, but may vary from greenish yellow to orange-yellow. The belly is plain yellow. Dark brown or black markings and spots are found along the back and sides. Prominent vertical bars are present on the tail. There are 13 or 14 costal grooves. Young of this species have fewer and smaller dark markings and a proportionately shorter tail.

Adult longtail salamanders range in length from 102 to 160 mm (4 to 6 1/4 inches). Largest Missouri specimen recorded is 150 mm (5 15/16 inches; Powell *et al.,* 1982). The record length is 197 mm (7 3/4 inches; Conant, 1975).

Habits and Habitat: The longtail salamander is nocturnal, but may emerge from hiding during the day after a heavy rain. It is usually found under rocks near streams, springs and seepages in forested areas; it has also been found in caves. These salamanders are quite agile, and are able to escape predators by using their tails for quick jumps. If grasped by the tail, they will twist it off. Tail waving is used to distract a predator's attention away from the salamander's head. Specimens without tails or with partially regrown tails are often found. Food consists mainly of various small arthropods.

Breeding: Courtship and breeding take place in or near springs or cool, rocky creeks between November and April. The eggs are fertilized internally and each female may produce up to 90 eggs (Collins, 1982).

The eggs are laid in small clumps or in a single row on the underside of rocks along the edge of springs or creeks, or in shallow water. The larvae are dark-colored, stream-type and may require up to two years to metamorphose into juveniles (Smith, 1961). Length at metamorphosis ranges from 65 to 75 mm (2 1/2 to 3 inches).

Adult dark-sided salamander from Howell County.

Subspecies: The dark-sided salamander, *Eurycea longicauda melanopleura* (Cope), is common in Missouri. This subspecies has larger and more numerous dark spots on the back, and large amounts of dark pigment along the sides of the body from the head onto the tail. The sides are often spotted with white flecks. Vertical bars on the tail are more irregular in shape and may form dark vermiculations. Ground color may vary from a yellowish green to yellowish brown. The belly is a dull yellow with numerous dark flecks.

The dark-sided salamander is slightly smaller than the longtail salamander, with a length from 90 to 150 mm (3 5/8 to 5 7/8 inches; Conant, 1975). Intergradation between these subspecies is known from many areas of southeastern Missouri (see map).

Missouri Distribution: The longtail salamander is restricted to southeastern Missouri exclusive of the Mississippi River lowlands. The dark-sided salamander is found throughout most of southern and eastern Missouri.

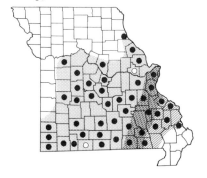

Adult cave salamander from Crawford County.

Cave Salamander
Eurycea lucifuga Rafinesque

Description: This species is of medium size with a long tail. It is normally bright orange, but can vary in color from yellow-brown to orange-red. Distinct dark brown or black spots cover most of the body. The belly is usually yellow-orange and without spots. There are 13 or 14 costal grooves. The end of the tail is often black.

Adult cave salamanders range in length from 100 to 150 mm (4 to 6 inches). Largest Missouri specimen reported is 177 mm (7 inches; Powell *et al.,* 1982). The record is 181 mm (7 1/8 inches; Conant, 1975).

Young cave salamanders are yellow in color and have shorter tails. Adult females are often larger than males, and males have a more prominent cirrus. Males can also be distinguished from females by the presence of a swollen cloaca.

Habits and Habitat: The range of this species is confined to areas having limestone outcroppings. Although usually found in caves, the cave salamander can also be found in wooded areas, along rocky streams and springs, and even in wells and swamps. Cave-dwelling individuals live in the twilight zone, but also occur far back in areas of permanent darkness. They are good climbers, able to cling to walls with their wet bodies; their long tails help support them on stalactites or stalagmites. When found away from caves, this species is nocturnal and spends daylight hours under rocks or rotten logs. It may be seen during the day on rocks or boulders after a heavy rain. If pursued, these salamanders will jump and scamper away with remarkable agility. A cave salamander will wave its tail in an effort to distract a predator's attention away from its head.

The food of this species consists of a variety of small arthropods.

Breeding: Reproduction in this species has not been studied in detail in Missouri, but breeding generally takes place in early summer. A female lays from 50 to 90 eggs, either in cave streams, springs, or rocky streams outside of caves. The eggs are laid singly under rocks or on the stream bottom. The larvae are gilled, stream-type and live from one to two years in the water. When ready to leave the water, the young may be from 51 to 65 mm (2 to 2 1/2 inches; Barbour, 1971; Collins, 1982).

Remarks: As with all animals living in caves, the cave salamander should never be disturbed. The ecological balance in a cave is extremely fragile, and any disturbance could be dangerous to this balance.

Missouri Distribution: The cave salamander is found throughout most of the southern half of Missouri, with the exception of the Mississippi River lowlands. It is a common amphibian of the Ozark Plateau.

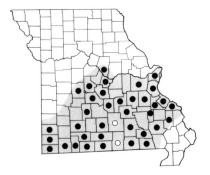

Adult graybelly salamander from Stone County, Arkansas.

Graybelly Salamander
Eurycea multiplicata griseogaster Moore and Hughes

Description: A small, dark, slender salamander, generally yellowish-tan to dark brown or gray in color. The dorsal stripe may be yellow-tan to brown, and is bordered by dark brown lines. There may be a medial row of dark brown chevrons along the dorsum corresponding to each costal groove. There are 19 to 20 costal grooves. Small white flecks are present along the sides and tail. The belly is gray, but may have some yellow color.

Adult graybelly salamanders range in length from 48 to 83 mm (1 7/8 to 3 1/4 inches). Largest Missouri specimen recorded is 102 mm (4 inches; Powell *et al.,* 1982). Neotenic individuals may reach a larger size than metamorphosed individuals (Dundee, 1965a).

Habits and Habitat: The graybelly salamander hides under rocks and logs in or near cave springs or cold, clear streams. In Missouri, it is most often encountered in cave twilight zones and streams. When outside caves, these salamanders are nocturnal and may venture away from streams on rainy nights. Neoteny is common in this species, and Dundee (1965) reports that entire cave populations may be neotenic. Small arthropods are the primary food of both adults and larvae.

Breeding: Little is known about the reproduction of this species in Missouri. In general, fertilization is internal and the eggs are laid along the undersurface of rocks in cave streams and springs. The larvae are gilled stream-type. Larvae either metamorphose into adults or retain the gills and mature as neotenic individuals. Ireland (1976) studied this species in Arkansas, and found that breeding lasts from September to April. Females lay from 3 to 21 eggs in strands and the larvae metamorphose in five to eight months.

Missouri Distribution: The gray-belly salamander occurs in the central and southwestern portions of the Ozark Plateau.

Adult Oklahoma salamander from McDonald County.

Oklahoma Salamander
Eurycea tynerensis Moore and Hughes

Description: A small, slender, gilled salamander that is permanently aquatic. The back and sides are cream or light tan covered with extensive gray stippling. The amount of stippling may vary between individuals. The belly is pale and without markings. There are one or two lines of small white spots along the sides. There are 19 to 21 costal grooves. Poorly developed dorsal and ventral fins are present on the tail. A broad, dark stripe is usually found on each side of the tail.

The Oklahoma salamander ranges in length from 44 to 79 mm (1 3/4 to 3 1/8 inches; Conant, 1975). Largest Missouri specimen recorded is 73 mm (2 7/8 inches; Powell *et al.*, 1982).

Habits and Habitat: The Oklahoma salamander lives in cool, clear creeks and springs where there is a large amount of gravel. When surface water is present, this species may be found under rocks in shallow water or in aquatic plants. During dry periods, and presumably during the winter, it follows the water level down into the creek bed gravel; using this type of aquatic habitat allows it to remain active all year. Its diet is composed of small aquatic arthropods.

Dodd (1980) reported on laboratory observations of the feeding behavior of this species. He observed a salamander approach a prey item (pieces of tubifex worms), slowly and deliberately arch its pectoral region, then snap or suck up the prey with rapid movements.

Breeding: Little is known about the reproduction of this salamander. Dundee (1965a) reports that the eggs are attached to stones in the water. The larvae are said to resemble the adults in shape and color (Bishop, 1943).

Remarks: This neotenic salamander has been artificially induced to metamorphose and acquire adult characteristics (Kezer, 1952).

The Oklahoma salamander has a restricted distribution in Missouri, Oklahoma and Arkansas. Its requirements for clean creeks, springs and an abundance of clean gravel make it vulnerable to water pollution and habitat loss. This species is listed as rare in the Missouri rare and endangered species list.

Missouri Distribution: Known from five counties in the extreme southwestern corner of the state.

Adult four-toed salamander from Reynolds County, photographed on mirror to show belly.

Four-toed Salamander
Hemidactylium scutatum (Schlegel)

Description: A small, delicate salamander with a thick, round tail and four toes on both front and hind feet. The snout appears short and blunt. General color is yellowish tan to brown on the back with many faint, irregular black spots. Sides of the body are grayish brown with black stippling and the belly is pure white with numerous large, irregular black spots. The tail is distinctly constricted near its base. There are 12 to 14 costal grooves. Males of this species are smaller, more slender and have longer tails than females (Bishop, 1943).

Adult four-toed salamanders range in length from 51 to 89 mm (2 to 3 1/4 inches). Largest Missouri specimen recorded is 81 mm (3 3/16 inches; Powell *et al.,* 1982). The record length is 102 mm (4 inches; Conant, 1975).

Habits and Habitat: This salamander is commonly associated with sphagnum (peat) bogs across most of its range. In Missouri, however, the four-toed salamander is found in mosses along heavily forested, spring-fed creeks associated with igneous (Precambrian) rock, and also in and near natural sinkhole ponds. Away from permanent water it may be found under rotten logs, in leaf litter or under rocks in seepage areas. This species preys on a variety of small arthropods and molluscs. If captured, a specimen can easily break off its tail and escape.

Breeding: Four-toed salamanders breed in autumn. Sperm are stored in a chamber (*spermatheca*) inside the cloaca of females. Females move to

Female four-toed salamander with egg clutch (left) *in a clump of moss, and four-toed salamander larva* (right), *both from Iron County.*

a creek or sinkhole pond in the spring, soon after ending their winter dormancy. The eggs are fertilized as they pass through the female's cloaca. About 30 eggs are laid in a protected pocket of moss, usually overhanging the water. The eggs are usually attached to strands or roots of mosses (Bishop, 1943). The female will remain with the eggs and protect them from other salamanders; she will also eat eggs that spoil. The presence of a female attending a clutch of eggs increases embryonic survival (Harris and Gill, 1980).

Communal nesting (two or more complements of eggs in one site) may occur, especially where there are few ideal nesting sites. Breitenbach (1982) reported that communal nesting in this species was observed in 12 percent of the nests he examined. He also found that the majority of females deserted their nest just prior to egg hatching. I have found what appeared to be communal nests (60 or more eggs) on several occasions in Iron County. Most of the nests I have observed were along small, fishless creeks in thick mats of mosses, *Thuidium delicatulum vardelicatulum* or *Climacium americanus* (Redfearn, pers. comm.). Upon hatching, the gilled larvae find their way to water, where they remain for a period of up to two months. The larvae have a high fin or keel which begins on the back and extends down the entire length of the tail. After metamorphosing, the juveniles, which average 20 mm, (3/4 inch) become terrestrial. They may take over two years to reach sexual maturity (Bishop, 1943).

Remarks: This species is listed as rare in Missouri principally because of its unique habitat requirements and the small number of known populations.

Missouri Distribution: Occurs in eastern Missouri, with a concentration in the St. Francois Mountains. A single, isolated population occurs in Lincoln County; it is the only recorded population in the state north of the Missouri River (Schuette, 1979).

Adult Ozark zigzag salamander from McDonald County.

Ozark Zigzag Salamander
Plethodon dorsalis angusticlavius Grobman

Description: A small, dark, slender, woodland salamander with a narrow, somewhat lobed mid-dorsal stripe. The dorsal stripe usually has irregular or wavy edges, especially closer to the head. Color of the dorsal stripe may range from yellow to yellow-orange, orange or red. Dark brown or black pigment may invade the dorsal stripe causing it to appear lobed, or may cover a large part of the stripe. Normally the width of the dorsal stripe is less than one-third the width of the body; it is widest near the hind legs. Some specimens may lack a dorsal stripe. The belly has white and black mottling. The sides of the body are generally dark gray or brownish gray, containing some orange or red, and small white flecks. There are 17 to 19 costal grooves. The sexes are difficult to distinguish, but males are smaller and more slender than females.

Adult Ozark zigzag salamanders range in length from 60 to 98 mm (2 3/8 to 3 7/8 inches). Largest Missouri specimen recorded is 81 mm (3 3/16 inches; Powell *et al.,* 1982).

Habits and Habitats: Conant (1975) stated that the Ozark zigzag salamander is found "usually in or near caves of the Central Highlands." Myers (1958) also found this species in Missouri caves. I have found this salamander living in or under rotten logs, under rocks and leaf litter in seepages near small streams, and on steep hillsides. The Ozark zigzag salamander may have a preference for living in cooler and damper habitats than the closely related southern redback salamander (*P. serratus*). Food consists of very small arthropods.

Breeding: No study has been made of the reproductive biology of this salamander in Missouri. Females deposit their eggs in a small cavity in rotten logs or under rocks, and remain with the eggs until they hatch. As with all members of the genus *Plethodon*, the young go through their complete development in the egg, and hatch into tiny replicas of the adults. Newly hatched Ozark zigzag salamanders have proportionately shorter tails than adults, and average 22 mm (7/8 inch) in total length.

Remarks: See Remarks section under the southern redback salamander account.

Missouri Distribution: The Ozark zigzag salamander is found in the south central and southwestern portion of the Missouri Ozarks.

78

Adult slimy salamander from Douglas County.

Slimy Salamander
Plethodon glutinosus glutinosus (Green)

Description: A black, medium-size woodland salamander with a long rounded tail and numerous silver flecks irregularly distributed over the head, back, limbs and tail. The chin and belly are dark gray in color. There are usually 16 costal grooves. Males can be distinguished from females by the presence of a light colored swelling (mental gland) under the chin during the breeding season.

This is the largest plethodontid salamander found in Missouri. Adult slimy salamanders range in length from 122 to 172 mm (4 3/4 to 6 3/4 inches). Largest Missouri specimen recorded is 169 mm (6 5/8 inches; Powell *et al.,* 1982).

Habits and Habitat: The slimy salamander is commonly found under rocks or logs in damp ravines and moist wooded hillsides. During dry summer weather they may retreat underground or burrow into large piles of leaf litter to find a damp place to live. They venture out of hiding at night or after heavy rains. This species has been found in the twilight zone of Missouri caves (Myers, 1958). Food includes small arthropods and worms.

Skin glands of the slimy salamander secrete a thick, very sticky substance that adheres to human skin like glue and is difficult to remove.

Breeding: The reproductive biology of the slimy salamander has not been studied in Missouri. Barbour (1971) found that 10 to 20 eggs are laid in early summer. Females select cool, damp retreats deep in the ground or under rotten logs. The eggs are attached to a thin stalk and suspended from the "ceiling" of the cavity. As with other members of the genus *Plethodon,* females remain with the eggs during the incubation period. Hatching probably takes place in late summer or early autumn. As with all *Plethodon* species, there is no aquatic larval stage; the hatchlings resemble adults but have proportionately shorter tails.

Remarks: It is important that landowners and land managers understand the significance of fallen logs on the forest floor. Missouri's three species of woodland salamanders (genus *Plethodon*) require rotten logs for their survival. Fallen logs located along steep, north facing, forested hillsides in the southern half of the state are especially valuable to these salamanders.

Missouri Distribution: The slimy salamander is found throughout the southern half of the state, but is generally absent from the Mississippi River lowlands.

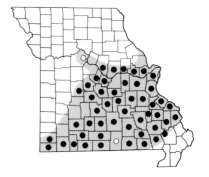

Adult southern redback salamander from Madison County.

Southern Redback Salamander
Plethodon serratus Grobman

Description: A small, dark, slender salamander with a long, rounded tail. A distinct, narrow, red or orange mid-dorsal stripe with saw-toothed edges that correspond with the costal grooves is usually present. The sides are brownish gray, with some red pigment. The belly is covered with gray mottling. There are 18 or 19 costal grooves. Sexes are difficult to distinguish, but males are normally smaller and more slender than females.

Adult southern redback salamanders range in length from 70 to 102 mm (2 3/4 to 4 inches). Largest Missouri specimen recorded is 103 mm (4 1/16 inches; Powell *et al.,* 1982).

Habits and Habitat: This terrestrial salamander is commonly found in forests where it hides under rocks, clumps of mosses, and rotten logs. During dry parts of the summer it may be found near seepages, springs or in damp soil. Myers (1958) found this species in the twilight zone of Missouri caves, but this is not a common occurrence. A variety of small arthropods are eaten by this species.

Breeding: The reproductive biology of this species has not been studied in Missouri. I can only presume it is similar to that of the redback salamander, *Plethodon cinereus* (Green), a species common to the north and east of Missouri. Until we gain information on the breeding of *Plethodon serratus* in Missouri, I offer the following information on the redback salamander studied in Wisconsin (Vogt, 1981): Courtship and the transfer of sperm to females take place in autumn. Sperm are retained inside the female's cloaca until the following summer. From 6 to 14 eggs are produced; fertilization occurs as they pass through the cloaca. The eggs are attached to a thin stalk suspended from the top of a cavity under rotten logs or in a clump of moss. Females remain with the eggs until they hatch, sometime during August. Hatchlings are small replicas of adults and average 20 mm (6/8 inch) in length.

Remarks: The redback salamander of south central and southeastern Missouri has been identified as *Plethodon cinereus cinereus* by most authors (Highton, 1962a; Smith, 1961; Johnson and Bader, 1974; Conant, 1975). Investigations by Highton and Webster (1976) have shown that the Missouri population is more closely associated with the Arkansas population (*P. serratus*), as well as other southern isolated populations, and has been elevated to species level.

The two species of redback salamander found in Missouri may be easily confused. The southern redback salamander's dorsal stripe is usually uniform in width and has serrated edges. The dorsal stripe of the Ozark zigzag salamander is usually very thin (less than one third of the body width); it may be broken up into lobes, and is always widest near the hind legs. These two species may be found together in several Missouri counties, but the possibility of hybridization between the two forms is remote (Highton, pers. comm.).

Missouri Distribution: The southern redback salamander is found in the south central and southeastern section of the state, with the exception of the Mississippi River lowlands.

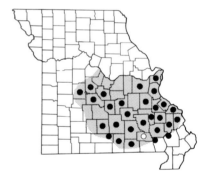

Adult grotto salamander from Camden County.

Grotto Salamander
Typhlotriton spelaeus Stejneger

Description: Adults of this species range from beige to pink in color. These *troglobitic* salamanders lack gills as adults. They are partly or completely blind. The head is rather wide and flat, the eyes are small, and the tail is long, rounded and finless. There are 16 to 19 costal grooves.

Males can be distinguished from females by the presence of fleshy projections on the upper lip (*cirri*), and a larger, swollen vent (cloaca). Adults of both sexes have reduced eyes which are covered or partially covered by a fusion of the eyelids. Their eyes may appear sunken into the head.

The larvae of this species have gills, functional eyes and broad tail fins. Their legs are thin and weak. Larvae have more pigment than adults and color varies from brown to dark gray. Dark pigmentation may form spots or streaking along the sides and tail.

Adult grotto salamanders range in length from 80 to 120 mm (3 to 4 3/4 inches). Largest Missouri specimen is 109 mm (4 5/16 inches; Powell *et al.,* 1982). The record length is 135 mm (5 5/16 inches; Conant, 1975).

Habits and Habitat: This is the only species of blind salamander living in Missouri. Adults of the grotto salamander are true troglobites; they are found in wet caves and underground streams where they live in total darkness. This species requires caves which have a spring or stream running through them. They are found in greater abundance in caves that have a large number of bats (due likely to a plentiful supply of insects which feed upon bat guano). The food of adults is made up of various small insects found in caves (Smith, 1948; Brandon, 1971).

Grotto salamander larva from Phelps County.

Breeding: More is known about the reproduction of this species in Missouri than anywhere else. Brandon (1971) correlates the breeding of the grotto salamander with the period of greatest food supply (late spring and early summer). The eggs have not yet been observed. Fertilization is internal, and the eggs are probably attached to stones in or near water in caves. The larvae are stream-type and normally inhabit cave streams, though they are occasionally found in springs or streams that flow out of caves or grottoes.

Brandon (1970) found that the larvae may take from two to three years to transform into adults. During this time they range from 36 to 56 mm in snout–vent length (Brandon, 1966). Larvae probably eat tiny freshwater shrimp (*Gammaris*) and other small aquatic invertebrates. Some populations in Missouri are known to be neotenic (Brandon, 1966).

Remarks: Because of the delicate balance of cave ecosystems, the grotto salamander should be protected from any form of disturbance, including alteration of caves or their water supplies. The type locality for this species is in Barry County, Missouri.

Missouri Distribution: This species is found in wet caves of the Ozark Plateau.

Family Proteidae

Mudpuppies

This family contains only two genera. The first, *Proteus,* contains only one species, the European olm. The European olm is a slender, white, blind cave salamander. This species has bright red gills and three toes on each of its four limbs; it inhabits cave streams.

The other genus of this family is *Necturus,* which consists of four species, all exclusively North American. They are commonly known as mudpuppies or "waterdogs;" together their ranges cover most of the eastern United States. These salamanders are aquatic. They have permanent gills and can be found in a variety of habitats, including streams, rivers, sloughs and lakes. In larger lakes in the northern part of its range, the mudpuppy has been netted at a depth of several hundred feet.

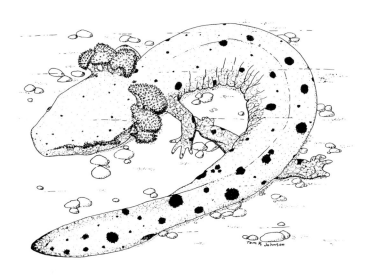

Mudpuppy

Adult mudpuppy from the Lake of the Ozarks, Miller County.

Mudpuppy
Necturus maculosus (Rafinesque)

Description: The mudpuppy is a completely aquatic species. It has a gray-brown back and pale gray belly. Most of the body has numerous small, irregular dark brown to black spots which sometimes appear on the belly. Behind the head are plumes of red gills. These gills vary in size, depending on the oxygen content of the salamander's aquatic habitat. There are four toes on both the front and hind limbs. The eyes are small and lack eyelids. All *Necturus* are neotenic gilled adults.

Adult mudpuppies range in length from 200 to 300 mm (8 to 13 inches). Largest Missouri specimen recorded is 420 mm (16 1/2 inches; Johnson, 1975a). The record length is 432 mm (17 inches; Conant, 1975).

Habits and Habitat: In Missouri this species is found in large creeks, rivers, or reservoirs. Mudpuppies are inactive during the day; they usually remain hidden in deep pools under submerged logs, rocks, or tree roots. Mudpuppies are known to remain active throughout the year. I have received a number of reports of these salamanders being caught on hook-and-line at the Lake of the Ozarks during the fall and winter. They feed at night on any aquatic animal small enough to be captured and swallowed, including crayfish, molluscs, small fish, worms and aquatic insects and their larvae.

Breeding: The breeding habits of the mudpuppy have not been investigated in Missouri, but the species has been studied elsewhere. Mating takes place in the fall; fertilization is internal, but the eggs are not laid

Head of adult mudpuppy.

until the following spring or summer. Between 75 and 100 eggs are laid by each female and are attached to the underside of a submerged rock (Smith, 1961). The female remains with the eggs until hatching, which may take from a few weeks to more than 30 days. The average length of larvae at hatching is 22 mm (7/8 inch; Bishop, 1943). Mudpuppy larvae have gills, a tail fin of medium height, a dark brown mid-dorsal stripe which is bordered by pale yellow lines and a broad, dark brown stripe on each side from the head to the tip of the tail. Sexual maturity is reached in four to six years (Collins, 1982).

Subspecies: There are two subspecies of *Necturus maculosus* found in Missouri—the mudpuppy (*N. m. maculosus*) described above, and the Red River mudpuppy (*Necturus maculosus louisianensis* Viosca). The latter may be distinguished from the mudpuppy by a lighter gray-brown or red-brown ground color. Dark spots on the upper part of the body are more distinct and more numerous. The belly has a wide, light, unspotted area down the center which may be light gray with edges of pale pink. The Red River mudpuppy is somewhat smaller than the mudpuppy; it has a maximum length of about 280 mm (11 inches; Conant, 1975).

Remarks: Mudpuppies are the only host for the larvae of the salamander mussel (*Simpsonaias ambigus*). The small, dark larvae (*glochidia*) attach themselves to the mudpuppy's gills as external parasites. This freshwater mussel averages 1 to 1 1/2 inches in length. Its range in Missouri is restricted to a small section of the Bourbeuse River in Gasconade County (Buchanan, 1980).

Mudpuppies are harmless to humans and to natural fish populations; they are an integral part of the aquatic fauna of Missouri. Fishermen often catch this species on baited hook-and-line or in minnow traps. Individuals may live for 20 years or more.

Missouri Distribution: The mudpuppy is found throughout most of Missouri except the northwestern corner of the state. It is replaced by the Red River mudpuppy in the extreme southern part of the state (hatch lines).

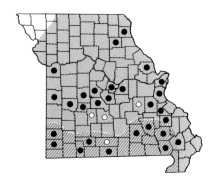

Family Pelobatidae
Spadefoots

Members of this family have been divided into two subfamilies: the Megophryinae of Asia, and the Pelobatinae of Europe, North Africa and North America.

Spadefoots, often called spadefoot toads, are not true toads (Family Bufonidae), but resemble them in general appearance and habits. The name spadefoot is derived from a special tubercle found on the hind feet which is spade-shaped and used to dig into soil. Spadefoots are highly fossorial. They have smoother skin than true toads, and the pupils of their eyes are vertical in shape when exposed to light.

In North America this family is represented by only one genus, *Scaphiopus,* with five species, two of which occur in Missouri.

Eastern Spadefoot Toad

Adult plains spadefoot toad from Callaway County.

Plains Spadefoot
Scaphiopus bombifrons Cope

Description: The plains spadefoot can be distinguished from the eastern spadefoot by the presence of a raised area ("boss") between the eyes, and by the wedge-shaped spade at the base of each hind foot. The color of the plains spadefoot ranges from gray to tannish gray to brown; some green may be mixed into the background color. A number of irregular dark brown markings are usually present on the back and hind legs. Two or four faint light stripes may be found on the back. The belly is white. Small, round warts, often reddish in color, are usually found on the back and sides. Males can be distinguished from females by their swollen forelimbs and dark throats.

Adult plains spadefoots range in snout–vent length from 38 to 51 mm (1 1/2 to 2 inches). Largest Missouri specimen recorded is 52 mm (2 1/16 inches; Powell *et al.,* 1982). The record length is 57 mm (2 1/4 inches; Conant, 1975).

Habits and Habitat: This species is at home on the Great Plains, where it can be found in prairie or open floodplain environments. By day it remains hidden in burrows, usually in sandy soil. It emerges at night, especially after heavy rains. A variety of insects makes up its diet.

Breeding: The plains spadefoot is stimulated to breed only after warm, heavy rains. This is an "explosive" breeder—great numbers of plains spadefoots appear suddenly after a heavy rain and breed in one or two nights. The males congregate at temporary pools in flooded fields. If a

"Calling" male plains spadefoot from Callaway County.

female approaches a calling male, he will clasp her just forward of her hind legs and they will enter the water. The female can produce up to 2,000 eggs; they are fertilized by the male as they are laid. The eggs are usually attached to submerged vegetation in clumps of 10 to 250 (Collins, 1982). If conditions are favorable, the eggs hatch in one or two days. The rate of hatching and transformation is regulated by water temperature, amount of dissolved oxygen and food supply. Spadefoot tadpoles are carnivorous; if the temporary pool in which they hatch evaporates too fast, the tadpoles become overcrowded and cannibalism may result.

The voice of the breeding plains spadefoot can be described as a long rasping or nasal *"garvank,"* called at intervals of one-half to one second.

Missouri Distribution: The plains spadefoot has been collected in northwestern Missouri and in a number of counties along the Missouri River.

Adult eastern spadefoot toad from Mississippi County.

Eastern Spadefoot
Scaphiopus holbrookii holbrookii (Harlan)

Description: A stout, toadlike amphibian with large protruding eyes, vertically elliptical pupils, short legs and large feet. Small, inconspicuous parotoid glands are present. There is no "boss" between the eyes. The general ground color is light brown to yellow-brown. Head, back and upper parts of legs are mottled with dark brown. The amount of dark brown on the dorsum may be great enough to form two or three light yellow-brown longitudinal stripes. Belly is pale white to gray. The inner surface of each hind foot has a sickle-shaped spur or spade.

Males can be distinguished during the breeding season by swollen forefeet and by the presence of a dark, horny covering on the inner surface of each forefoot.

Adult eastern spadefoot toads range in snout–vent length from 44 to 57 mm (1 3/4 to 2 1/4 inches). Largest Missouri specimen recorded is 69 mm (2 3/4 inches; Powell *et al.*, 1982). The record length is 73 mm (2 7/8 inches; Conant, 1975).

Habits and Habitat: Eastern spadefoots spend most of their time in burrows dug with their hind feet. They are nocturnal and become active on warm, damp or rainy nights. They are occasionally found in wooded areas, but seem to prefer open fields where loose sand and soil facilitates burrowing. Food includes a variety of insects.

Breeding: Breeding takes place after heavy rains, usually between April and August in southeastern Missouri. Rain must be sufficiently heavy to stimulate breeding aggregations.

Eastern spadefoots breed in temporarily flooded fields or ditches. During amplexus the eggs are fertilized by the male as they are laid. Eggs are laid in short strands attached to submerged vegetation. Hatching takes place in only a few days and the tadpoles usually transform in less than three weeks (Smith, 1961).

The voice of the male eastern spadefoot can be described as a quick series of coarse "*wank, wank, wank*" sounds. Wright and Wright (1949), describes their call as sounding like a "young crow."

Missouri Distribution: This species occurs in southeastern Missouri.

Family Bufonidae
True Toads

Members of this family are found almost all over the world. They are absent only from New Zealand, Australia, Madagascar and the polar regions. There are approximately 15 species of true toads in the United States, and all are members of the genus *Bufo*. Missouri has five types of true toads comprised of three species and two subspecies.

Toads have dry skin compared to frogs; they lack extensive webbing on the hind feet and have large parotoid glands behind their eyes. Numerous "warts" over most of their bodies produce toxic skin secretions that are irritating to a predator's mucous membrane. All species of toads found in Missouri are primarily nocturnal, seeking shelter during the day among piles of dead leaves, under rocks and logs, or in loose soil. These amphibians are well known for their consumption of large numbers of insects. Contrary to popular belief, toads do not cause warts.

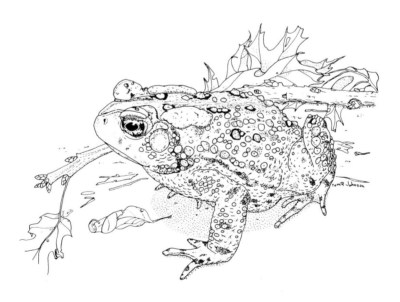

Eastern American Toad

Adult dwarf American toad from Pulaski County.

Eastern American Toad
Bufo americanus Holbrook

Description: A medium-size toad with kidney-shaped parotoid glands behind the eyes. The bony cranial ridges between the eyes usually do not touch the parotoid glands but may be connected by a small spur. Large black or dark brown spots on the back usually encircle from one to three warts. A narrow, light stripe down the back may be present. The general color may be gray, light brown, brown, or reddish brown. The belly is white with dark gray mottling. Adult males can be distinguished from adult females during the breeding season by an enlarged, horny pad on the inside of each forelimb, and the presence of a dark gray throat. Females are generally larger than males.

Adult American toads range in snout–vent length from 51 to 89 mm (2 to 3 1/2 inches). Largest Missouri specimen recorded is 105 mm (4 1/8 inches; Powell *et al.,* 1982). Record length is 111 mm (4 3/8 inches; Conant, 1975).

Habits and Habitat: The American toad prefers rocky wooded areas and is often found along the edge of hardwood forests. They hide during the day under rocks where there is loose, moist dirt or burrow into a depression where dead leaves have accumulated. Like most toads, the American toad becomes active at dusk; it feeds at night on earthworms and insects.

Breeding: In Missouri, male American toads begin calling during mid- to late March. Breeding sites are usually ditches, small temporary ponds, or slow, shallow streams. The male grasps the female behind her front

"Calling" male American toad from Callaway County (left), *and American toad eggs* (right) *from Cole County.*

legs; while they float on the water, the female begins laying eggs in long, double strands. As the eggs emerge they are fertilized by the male. From 2,000 to over 20,000 eggs may be laid by one female. The eggs hatch in about one week into tiny black tadpoles. The tadpoles remain in the water until early to mid-June, at which time they metamorphose into small toadlets 7 to 12 mm in length (1/4 to 1/2 inch; Wright and Wright, 1949). In Missouri, the peak breeding period is mid-April.

The call of the male American toad is described as a sustained high-pitched musical trill (Smith, 1961).

Subspecies: There are two subspecies of *Bufo americanus* in Missouri: the eastern American toad (*Bufo americanus americanus* Holbrook) as described above, and the dwarf American toad (*Bufo americanus charlesmithi* Bragg).

The dwarf American toad is a generally smaller race of the American toad. The ground color is deep reddish brown and the size and number of dark spots on the back are reduced or absent. The belly is cream colored with a small number of dark gray spots on the breast. The call of a male *B. a. charlesmithi* is similar to the American toad but higher in pitch.

After examining a number of specimens of both races of American toads from many parts of Missouri, it is apparent that there is a wide band of intergradation between these two subspecies along a line from St. Louis to below Kansas City (see distribution map).

Remarks: The two subspecies of the American toad in Missouri have been known to hybridize with the Fowler's toad (*Bufo woodhousei fowleri*) in some parts of the state. The offspring of this crossbreeding are very difficult to identify because they often have characteristics of both species. Generally, hybridization occurs when there is an overlap of breeding activity or where human activity has caused extensive habitat disturbance.

Missouri Distribution: Statewide. The eastern American toad (stippling) occurs in the northern half of the state, while the dwarf American toad (hatch lines) occurs in the southern half.

Adult Great Plains toad.

Great Plains Toad
Bufo cognatus Say

Description: A medium-size toad with large dark blotches on the back and sides of the body. Each blotch is usually encircled with white or light tan and contains many warts. Blotch color may vary from gray to brown, dark green, green or yellowish. A light, narrow stripe may run down the back of some individuals. The parotoid glands are kidney-shaped and are connected to the bony cranial crest. The bony crests unite between the eyes and form a raised boss on the snout. The belly is cream colored with little or no gray spotting. Adult male *Bufo cognatus* are smaller than adult females. A dark throat and the presence of horny pads on the inside of each foreleg distinguish males from females during the breeding season.

Adult Great Plains toads range in snout–vent length from 48 to 89 mm (1 7/8 to 3 1/2 inches). Largest Missouri specimen recorded is 74 mm (2 7/8 inches; Powell *et al.,* 1982). The record length is 114 mm (4 1/2 inches; Conant, 1975).

Habits and Habitat: This species has a limited distribution in Missouri; its natural history has not been studied in this state. In other states it has been reported to occur in mixed grass and short-grass prairies. It frequents open floodplains of rivers and avoids forested areas. As with most species of toads, the Great Plains toad hides in underground burrows by day but emerges at night to feed. Ants, beetles and other insects make up the bulk of its diet.

*"Calling" male Great Plains toad from Callaway
County.*

Breeding: Rain-filled ditches and temporary pools are selected as breeding sites. Males begin their chorus in late April. Breeding aggregations may form as late as June. Breeding takes place after a female has been mounted by the male (amplexed) in the water. The eggs are laid in long strands in the water; they are fertilized by the male as they are laid. A single female may lay up to 20,000 eggs. The eggs hatch in about a week and the tadpoles usually metamorphose to tiny toadlets (average 10 mm; 3/8 inch) by early June.

   The call of the Great Plains toad can be described as a loud, rapid, piercing, metallic, chugging sound: *chee-ga, chee-ga, chee-ga,* lasting from 20 to 50 seconds. The inflated vocal sac of calling males is sausage-shaped, and extends forward and above the snout (see photo).

Missouri Distribution: The range of the Great Plains toad in Missouri is restricted to the floodplain of the Missouri River from the northwestern corner to St. Charles and St. Louis counties.

Adult Fowler's toad from Montgomery County. Fowler's toads are a subspecies of Woodhouse's toads.

Woodhouse's Toad
Bufo woodhousei Girard

Description: This medium-size toad has a number of irregular dark brown or black spots on the back, containing from one to six warts inside each spot. The general color varies from gray, greenish or tan-gray, to brown. The belly is white and usually unspotted, although a single "breast" spot may be present on some individuals. A tan or white stripe is usually present down the back. The parotoid gland is oblong in shape; it is connected to a rather shallow, bony cranial crest. Adult males are smaller than adult females. Males can be distinguished during the breeding season by dark throats and dark, horny pads on the inside of each foreleg.

Adult Woodhouse's toads range in snout–vent length from 60 to 100 mm (2 1/2 to 4 inches). Largest Missouri specimen recorded is 96 mm (3 3/4 inches; Powell *et al.,* 1982). The record is 127 mm (5 inches; Conant, 1975).

Habits and Habitat: This species prefers sandy lowlands, particularly river bottoms, and open, dry areas adjacent to marshes. As with other toads, they remain hidden in burrows by day, becoming active at night to hunt for insects and other prey.

Breeding: Although individuals can become active in late March, this species will not begin to breed until late April or early May; breeding activity peaks in mid-May. In general, the Woodhouse's toad breeds

"Calling" male Fowler's toad from Clark County.

later and at warmer temperatures than the American toad. Small groups of males congregate and call from the shore of shallow bodies of water (river sloughs, shallow ditches, ponds and flooded fields). They produce their distinct call until a female is attracted. The eggs are laid in long strands during amplexus and are fertilized by the male. Up to 25,000 eggs can be laid by a female (Collins, 1982). The eggs hatch in about a week; the black tadpoles begin to metamorphose into toadlets by late June or mid-July.

The call of the male Woodhouse's toad is a short, nasal "w-a-a-a-h," lasting from one to two and one-half seconds (Conant, 1975).

Subspecies: Two subspecies of *Bufo woodhousei* occur in Missouri: the nominate race, Woodhouse's toad (*Bufo woodhousei woodhousei* Girard), described above; and Fowler's toad (*Bufo woodhousei fowleri* Hinckley). Fowler's toad is very similar to Woodhouse's toad, especially in its habits, habitat requirements and breeding. However, it can be distinguished from *Bufo w. woodhousei* by the presence of dark spots on the back which are usually larger and more uniform in shape and arranged in pairs down the back. Each spot contains three or more warts. General color is gray, green-gray, or tan-gray. The light line down the back is white. The bony cranial crest of Fowler's toad seems to be slightly more developed than in Woodhouse's toad, but not as well developed as in the American toad. The belly is white and a breast spot is often present. The voice of a male Fowler's toad is very similar to Woodhouse's toad, but has a slightly higher pitch (Conant, 1975).

Remarks: Both subspecies of *Bufo woodhousei* have been known to hybridize with the American toad (see species account for the American toad).

Missouri Distribution: Fowler's toad is the more widespread sub-species in the state; it ranges over all of eastern and southern Missouri. Woodhouse's toad is restricted to the west central and northwestern part of the state. Conant (1975) did not show an area of intergradation between the two subspecies in Missouri, and only a few specimens were available from counties where intergradation may occur. The area of intergradation shown on the map is based on these few specimens; it is included to stimulate others to study the relationship of these toads in Missouri.

Family Hylidae
Treefrogs, Chorus Frogs and Cricket Frogs

This family contains over 450 species found on all continents where suitable habitats are present. Hylids are most numerous in Central America and northern South America. The family seems to have originated in the tropics and spread northward and southward toward the temperate regions. Most treefrog species are small, secretive creatures.

Of the six genera of treefrogs and their allies found in North America, three are native to Missouri: *Hyla* (treefrogs), *Pseudacris* (chorus frogs) and *Acris* (cricket frogs). A total of seven species occurs in Missouri.

Several of Missouri's treefrogs have the ability to change color; this characteristic seems to be associated with temperature, humidity, light and even the temperament of the frog. The majority of species have adhesive pads on their fingers and toes, which are helpful in climbing. In this family, females are usually larger than males.

Northern Spring Peeper

103

Adult Blanchard's cricket frog from Pulaski County.

Blanchard's Cricket Frog
Acris crepitans blanchardi (Harper)

Description: A small, non-climbing, warty frog that exhibits a variety of colors. Three important color patterns are always present: a series of light and dark bars on the upper jaw, a dark triangle between the eyes and an irregular black or brown stripe along the inside of the thigh. The general color may vary from gray to tan, greenish tan, brown, or almost black. An irregular stripe usually present down the back may be green, yellow, orange, or red. The belly is white. The feet are strongly webbed, but the adhesive pads are small and poorly developed on the fingers and toes. During the breeding season the chin of males may be spotted with gray and the throat may be yellow in color.

Adult Blanchard's cricket frogs range in snout–vent length from 16 to 38 mm (5/8 to 1 1/2 inches). Largest Missouri specimen recorded is 33 mm (1 1/8 inches; Powell *et al.*, 1982).

Habits and Habitat: This frog is usually active from late March to early November. During the spring and autumn, Blanchard's cricket frogs are active only during the day, but in warmer weather they are active both day and night. These alert little frogs will avoid their enemies by a series of quick, erratic hops. When approached, cricket frogs jump into the water but return quickly to shore. They prefer the open, sandy, or muddy edges of streams and ponds. The bulk of their food consists of a variety of small terrestrial insects (Johnson and Christiansen, 1976).

Breeding: In Missouri Blanchard's cricket frogs breed between late April and mid-July. They select the shallow water of ponds and river back-

"Calling" male Blanchard's cricket frog (left) *from Bollinger County, and a pair of Blanchard's cricket frogs in amplexus* (right) *from Pulaski County. Male is on top.*

waters where there is an abundance of aquatic plants. Warm air and water temperatures are needed to stimulate males to chorus. Amplexus, egg-laying and fertilization of the eggs take place in shallow water. A female may lay up to 400 eggs, either singly or in small packets of up to seven; they are laid on the surface of a pond or shallow pool. The eggs hatch in a few days, and the small tadpoles begin metamorphosis five to ten weeks later. Burkett (1969) speculated that some females may lay two clutches of eggs during the species' breeding season.

The call of the male Blanchard's cricket frog is a metallic *"gick, gick, gick,"* somewhat like the sound of small pebbles being struck rapidly together. Although their breeding season may last until mid-July, the males can be heard calling day and night throughout the summer.

Missouri Distribution: Blanchard's cricket frog is presumed to be state-wide in occurrence.

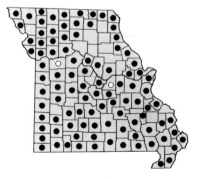

105

Adult green treefrog from Bollinger County.

Green Treefrog
Hyla cinerea (Schneider)

Description: A large member of the treefrog family, usually light to dark green in color. A white or pale yellow stripe running from the upper lip and down the side is always present. In most of the green treefrogs in Missouri, this stripe stops halfway down the side, seldom reaching the groin. It may be outlined with a thin black line in some individuals. Another white or pale yellow stripe is present on the inside of the hind legs. The smooth back may have a few small gold spots. The belly is white or yellow. Males calling at night are light green to yellow in color. Distinct, round adhesive pads are present on all digits. Adult males are smaller than females and have loose skin over their throats; the skin is inflated while they call.

Adult green treefrogs range in snout–vent length from 32 to 57 mm (1 1/4 to 2 1/4 inches). Largest Missouri specimen recorded is 58 mm (2 6/16 inches; Powell *et al.,* 1982). The record size is 64 mm (2 1/2 inches; Conant, 1975).

Habits and Habitat: This species prefers permanent bodies of water, especially cattail marshes, cypress swamps, or river sloughs. Green tree-frogs often spend the day resting among the long blades of cattails where they are camouflaged by their light green color. They are active on warm nights, climbing among vegetation in search of insects.

Breeding: Male green treefrogs can be heard in chorus from early May until early August, but egg-laying probably occurs in June or early July (Garton and Brandon, 1975). Males call from plants, bushes and trees

A pair of green treefrogs (left) *in amplexus (male is on top) from Bollinger County, and a "calling" male green treefrog* (right).

along the water's edge, or while sitting on floating plants. They begin calling after dark, and may continue until just before midnight. Amplexus will only occur when a female approaches and actually touches a calling male. Females lay from 500 to 1,000 eggs. The eggs are fertilized by the male as they are released by the female, and are laid near the water's surface on floating vegetation. Hatching takes place in two to three days; transformation to froglets occurs between late June and early September (Garton and Brandon, 1975).

The call of a male green treefrog is a series of measured nasal *"guank, guank, guank"* sounds with a ringing or metallic character. A chorus of frogs resembles the sound of distant Canada geese (Resetarits, pers. comm.).

Remarks: Populations of the green treefrog in Missouri represent the northwest limit of this species' total range. Swamp and marsh draining, and channelization of streams in southeastern Missouri have destroyed a large part of the suitable habitat of this species. Large areas of swamps should be preserved so that this species can remain a part of the natural wildlife heritage of Missouri.

Missouri Distribution: The green treefrog occurs in the southeastern corner of the state. An introduced population of this species has been established in Camden County at a private fish farm (Metter, 1982; pers. comm.).

Adult northern spring peeper from Warren County.

Northern Spring Peeper
Hyla crucifer crucifer Wied

Description: A small, slender treefrog with a dark X-mark on the back. General color varies from pink to tan, light brown, or gray. The dark X-mark may be very faint in light colored individuals or prominent in darker frogs. There is a dark line running across the top of the head and between the eyes; dark bars are found on the legs. The belly is a plain cream color. The tips of the fingers and toes all have distinct adhesive pads. Males are smaller than females; during the breeding season they have darker throats than females.

The northern spring peeper ranges in snout–vent length from 19 to 32 mm (3/4 to 1 1/4 inches). Largest Missouri specimen recorded is 32 mm (1 1/4 inches; Powell *et al.,* 1982). The record length is 35 mm (1 3/8 inches; Conant, 1975).

Habits and Habitat: This is a woodland species, living near ponds, streams or swamps where there is thick undergrowth. The northern spring peeper usually remains hidden during the day, becoming active at dusk; however, it may become active during the day if heavy rains persist. This species is active from early spring to late autumn in Missouri. It eats a variety of small insects.

Breeding: The northern spring peeper begins calling and breeding in early spring. The breeding season normally lasts from early March to mid-May in Missouri. Woodland ponds, temporary pools, water-filled ditches or semi-permanent fishless swamps are favorite breeding sites, especially if brush, branches and rooted plants are standing in the water.

"Calling" male northern spring peeper (left) *and northern spring peeper eggs from a fishless pond* (right), *both from Warren County.*

The males emit their calls from sites at the edge of the water or from dead leaves or branches sticking out of the water. While in amplexus, the female will lay up to several hundred eggs which are fertilized by the male as they are laid. The eggs are 1 mm in size; they are laid singly or in small clusters and are attached to dead leaves, grasses or sticks in shallow water. The eggs hatch in three or four days; tadpoles metamorphose in about two months.

The call of male northern spring peepers is a clear, high-pitched peep, with a slight rise at the end. The peeping call is repeated about one per second (Conant, 1975). This frog is one of the first species to begin calling in the spring. After the breeding season their call may be heard during the day or night from wooded areas. Smith (1961) reported that males may be heard calling in the autumn in Illinois. Johnson (1975) heard several choruses of northern spring peepers calling on a rainy November night in eastern Missouri.

Missouri Distribution: The northern spring peeper is found throughout Missouri except in the extreme northwestern corner.

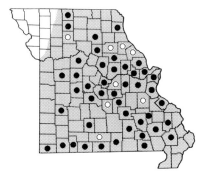

Adult eastern gray treefrog from St. Louis County.

Gray Treefrog
Hyla chrysoscelis - *Hyla versicolor* Complex

Description: Both species of gray treefrogs can be described together due to the extreme similarity of external characteristics. These frogs have warty skin and prominent adhesive pads on their fingers and toes. Color varies from green to light greenish gray, gray, brown, or dark brown. Except for very light individuals, a few large, irregular dark blotches are usually present on the back. A large white spot is always present below each eye. The belly is white. The inside of the hind legs is yellow or orange-yellow. Although both species of gray treefrogs found in Missouri are morphologically identical, the Cope's gray treefrog (*H. chrysoscelis*) has a tendency to be slightly smaller in size and is more often green in color than the eastern gray treefrog (*H. versicolor*; Vogt, 1981). During the breeding season, females usually appear more heavy-bodied, while males have dark throats.

Adult gray treefrogs range in snout–vent length from 32 to 51 mm (1 1/4 to 2 inches). Largest Missouri specimen recorded is 51 mm (2 inches; Powell *et al.*, 1982). The record length is 60 mm (2 3/8 inches; Conant, 1975).

Habits and Habitat: These look-alike species of treefrogs appear to have the same habits and habitat preference in Missouri. Gray treefrogs may be found in small wood lots, in trees along prairie streams, in large tracks of mixed hardwood forest, and in bottomland forests along rivers and swamps. These frogs can also be observed hiding in nooks and crannies of farm buildings and on porches or decks of homes. In Missouri, gray treefrogs are normally active between April and October.

110

During the breeding season they may be seen on the ground at night en route to a breeding pond. During the day gray treefrogs hide on or beneath rough tree bark, in hollow trees and on leaves. Green (1981) described how the toe pads of gray treefrogs enable them to climb or rest on vertical surfaces. He found that treefrog toe pads are "sticky" because of surface tension between a mucous layer produced by toe pad cells and the surface. A meniscus is produced all around the edge of the "interface" between each toe pad and the surface, causing surface tension which in turn causes a relatively strong bond.

Insects, spiders and other invertebrates are eaten by gray treefrogs.

"Calling" male eastern gray treefrog from Pulaski County (left), *and an eastern gray treefrog tadpole from a fishless pond in Warren County* (right).

Breeding: In Missouri, gray treefrogs breed from early April to early June. Males gather and begin calling at breeding sites when the night air temperature is 16°C (60°F) or more. Preferred breeding sites include fishless sloughs, woodland ponds and swamps. Vocalizing males may sit at the water's edge or station themselves on a log or branch above the water. A male will grasp a female with his front legs when she comes near him. As they float in the water, the female will begin laying eggs. The male fertilizes the eggs while they are being laid. Each female produces up to 1,800 eggs, which are attached to floating vegetation in clumps of 30 to 40 eggs. Each egg is a little over 1 mm (1/25 inch) in diameter and a light brown color. The protective jelly is weak and indistinct. Hatching takes place in about four or five days. Gray treefrog tadpoles have a high tail membrane which may be red or orange-red, and bordered with black blotches. The tadpoles transform into froglets in about two months. The newly transformed gray treefrogs average 13 mm (1/2 inch) in length and are usually green. They spend most of the remainder of the summer in low vegetation near the breeding pond.

Calls of the two gray treefrogs found in Missouri are described in the Remarks section of this account. Males can be heard calling away from breeding sites until early October.

Sonograms are "voice prints" that can be used to distinguish between species that are identical in appearance. The sonogram, left, of Hyla chrysoscelis *indicates 42 pulses per second, contrasted with sonogram on right of* Hyla versicolor *with 19 pulses per second. The calls were recorded May 5, 1975, two miles north of Higginsville in Lafayette County. The two species were calling sympatrically at an air temperature of 22.2 degrees C. The recordings were analyzed with a Kay model 6061A SonoGraph (narrow band).*

Remarks: The eastern gray treefrog (*Hyla versicolor*) and Cope's gray treefrog (*Hyla chrysoscelis*), can be distinguished in the field by comparing the calls of the males. In *Hyla versicolor*, the call is a musical, birdlike trill, which may vary from 17 to 35 pulses per second (depending on the frog's temperature). The call of *Hyla chrysoscelis* can be described as a high pitched buzzing trill, with from 34 to 69 pulses per second depending on the frog's temperature. For proper identification of gray treefrog calls, a tape recording of the call must be analyzed in the laboratory using sophisticated equipment; the results then must be correlated with the treefrog's temperature when recorded. These two treefrogs also differ in the number of chromosomes: tetraploid in *Hyla versicolor* and diploid in *Hyla chrysoscelis*. In addition, the red blood cells of *Hyla versicolor* are larger than those of *Hyla chrysoscelis*. Johnson (1966) reported that the two gray treefrog species were genetically incompatible throughout their distribution.

Missouri Distribution: The eastern gray treefrog (*Hyla versicolor*; solid circles) occurs throughout eastern and central Missouri. The Cope's gray treefrog (*Hyla chrysoscelis*; solid squares) occurs in southeastern, southwestern and western Missouri. Both species have been found sympatrically in a number of counties.

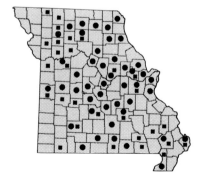

Adult Illinois chorus frog from Scott County.

Illinois Chorus Frog
Pseudacris streckeri illinoiensis (Smith)

Description: A medium-size member of the treefrog family and our largest chorus frog. This species has a "chubby" appearance, with large, muscular, almost toadlike forelimbs. The general ground color may vary from light tan to tannish gray. There is a distinct V-shaped marking between the eyes, a dark stripe from the snout to the shoulder, and a dark spot below the eye. A pair of large, dark, irregular V-shaped markings are present on the back behind the head. These markings are dark gray to brownish gray in color. The skin is rough or granular. The belly is white. Toe pads are small and round, and the webbing of the hind feet is poorly developed.

Adult Illinois chorus frogs range in snout–vent length from 25 to 41 mm (1 to 1 5/8 inches). Largest Missouri specimen recorded is 38 mm (1 1/2 inches; Powell *et al.,* 1982). The record length is 48 mm (1 7/8 inches; Conant, 1975).

Habits and Habitat: In Missouri this species prefers flat, sandy areas. Originally, Illinois chorus frogs were denizens of the sand prairies of southeast Missouri, but this unique habitat has been totally eliminated. The species continues to survive in soybean and cotton fields in the former sand prairie area. Unlike other fossorial species, such as members of the genera *Bufo* and *Scaphiopus*, these frogs enter the soil head first using their strong forelimbs and hands for digging (Brown *et al.,* 1972). Their strong hands seem to have good grasping ability; I have observed them hanging onto grasses as they sit in the water during the breeding season. This species eats various small insects and possibly burrowing larvae.

Breeding: The Illinois chorus frog breeds early in the spring. Depending on local weather conditions, they may begin in late February or early March and continue until early April. Usual breeding sites are flooded fields, ditches, or other temporary bodies of water. The males can be seen calling while floating in the water. A male will clasp a female about mid-body; while they are floating in shallow water, the female will begin laying from 200 to 400 eggs. Females can be observed using their hands to grasp onto twigs or grass for support. As the female lays the eggs they are fertilized by the male. Once the eggs have hatched, the tadpoles will take up to 60 days to transform into froglets. Smith (1961) reported that newly metamorphosed Illinois chorus frogs are dull gray in color and have inconspicuous markings.

The call of the male Illinois chorus frog is a clear, quick series of high-pitched birdlike whistles.

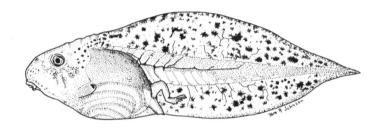

Illinois Chorus Frog tadpole.

Remarks: Continued draining and clearing of bottomlands in southeastern Missouri have greatly reduced the habitat of this species. Although this frog is still present in the highly cultivated areas of southeastern Missouri, there is concern whether these amphibians can withstand the wide use of herbicides and pesticides. An analysis for pesticides was recently carried out on four adult Illinois chorus frogs collected in Scott County. The analysis showed a significant residue of heptachlor epoxide and traces of dieldrin and DDE (Whitley, 1979, pers. comm.). These chemicals may in time cause the species to further decline in numbers.

Missouri Distribution: The Illinois chorus frog is restricted to the southeastern corner of Missouri.

Adult western chorus frog from Cole County.

Western Chorus Frog
Pseudacris triseriata (Wied)

Description: A small gray or tan frog with dark stripes down the back. Another dark brown or black stripe extends from the snout through the eye and down each side of the groin. The head, body and legs may be gray, tan or brown. The three dark stripes on the back may be broad and continuous from head to back of legs, or they may be broken into three rows of spots. A dark triangle is usually found on the top of the head between the eyes. The upper lip is white. Dark markings are gray or brown. The belly is white and there may be a few gray spots on the throat and chest. Adult females are larger than adult males; during the breeding season the males have dark throats.

Adult western chorus frogs range in snout–vent length from 19 to 38 mm (3/4 to 1 1/2 inches; Conant, 1975). Largest Missouri specimen recorded is 38 mm (1 1/2 inches; Powell *et al.,* 1982).

Habits and Habitat: This frog is more abundant in prairies, but may also be found on agricultural lands. Other habitats include damp woods, grassy areas along ditches, streams and farm ponds, and the edges of marshes. Because they take shelter in animal burrows, under boards, logs or rocks, in clumps of grass or in loose soil they are seldom seen after the breeding season. Breeding sites are generally temporary bodies of water: flooded grain fields, ditches, woodland ponds, marshes, or river sloughs. In Missouri, the western chorus frog is probably the first frog to become active in the spring.

This species eats a variety of small insects and insect larvae.

"Calling" male western chorus frog (left), *and western chorus frog eggs from a flooded ditch* (right), *both from Callaway County.*

Breeding: Western chorus frogs begin breeding activities in late February or early March, with peak activity during April. Males have been heard in chorus at air temperatures as low as 35° F (Collins, 1982). Eggs are laid during amplexus; they are fertilized by the male as they are laid. The eggs are attached to submerged grasses in clutches containing from 20 to 300 eggs. A total of 500 to 1,500 eggs may be produced per female (Collins, 1982). Hatching takes place from a few days to nearly a week after being laid, depending on the water temperature. Transformation to froglets occurs from six to eight weeks after hatching.

The call of the male western chorus frog is a vibrating *"prrreeep"* with a rise in pitch at the end; it lasts one to two seconds. The sound is similar to running a fingernail over the small teeth of a pocket comb (Conant, 1975).

Subspecies: Two subspecies of chorus frogs occur in Missouri: the western chorus frog, *Pseudacris triseriata triseriata* (Wied), described above, and the upland chorus frog, *Pseudacris triseriata feriarum* (Baird). In the latter, the size, body color and shape are like *P. t. triseriata*, but the dark stripes on the back are generally narrow or are broken up into three rows of spots. These markings may be rather faint on some individuals and the stripe along each side tends to be dark gray rather than black. Breeding habits are the same, but the upland chorus frog seems to prefer forested habitats such as swamps, moist woods or edges of marshes.

Due to the variation of markings in both *Pseudacris t. triseriata* and *P. t. feriarum*, it is difficult to distinguish the two races in specimens from southeastern Missouri. A large area of intergradation seems to occur in that part of the state.

Missouri Distribution: The western chorus frog (stippling) is found statewide except in southeastern Missouri where it intergrades with and is subsequently replaced by the upland chorus frog (hatch lines).

Family Microhylidae
Narrowmouth Toads

This large family of burrowing, secretive frogs has representatives in Asia, Africa, northern Australia, New Guinea, Madagascar, and North and South America. The group probably originated in Asia. The family contains 55 genera and covers 215 species. In the United States this group is represented by two genera and three species; of these, two species of one genus (*Gastrophryne*) are found in Missouri. Most members of this group are fossorial, spending a great part of the time in burrows or under rocks or logs. They tend to be small, plump and squatty in appearance. All species found in the United States have a characteristic fold of skin behind a small, narrow, pointed head. Although many types of small insects may be eaten, these amphibians are mostly ant eaters.

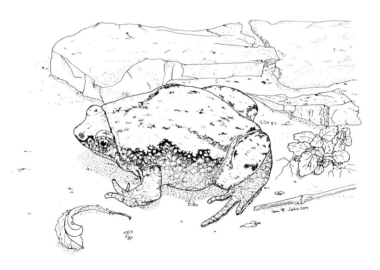

Eastern Narrowmouth Toad

Adult eastern narrowmouth toad from Jasper County.

Eastern Narrowmouth Toad
Gastrophryne carolinensis (Holbrook)

Description: A small, plump amphibian with a distinct fold of skin behind a narrow, pointed head. General color may be tan, brown, or reddish brown. The color pattern on the back forms a long dark wedge with the narrow end at the head. This dark wedge is bordered by a wide lateral stripe of lighter color. There is also a dark stripe running from the snout to the side of the hind legs. Much of this pattern will be obscured by the presence of numerous small, irregular dark brown or black markings. The belly is mottled with dark gray. Characteristics of this burrowing species include a small, pointed head, a fold of skin across the back of the head, short legs, and absence of both an external eardrum (tympanum) and webbing between the toes. Males can be distinguished from females by their deeply pigmented throat.

Adult eastern narrowmouth toads range in snout–vent length from 22 to 32 mm (7/8 to 1 1/4 inches). Largest Missouri specimen recorded is 36 mm (1 1/2 inches; Powell *et al.,* 1982). Record length for the species is 38 mm (1 1/2 inches; Conant, 1975).

Habits and Habitat: This toad spends most of its time in loose, damp soil under rocks, logs or boards. It prefers a habitat where shelter and moist soil are available, usually in the vicinity of ponds and streams. However, in the Ozarks, specimens have been found under flat rocks in relatively dry cedar glades. Once an eastern narrowmouth toad is uncovered, it tries to escape with a series of quick hops and a scramble into leaf litter or a nearby hiding place. The primary food of this species is ants, although termites and small beetles are also eaten.

118

Breeding: The eastern narrowmouth toad selects permanent or semi-permanent bodies of water in which to breed, including ponds, lakes, swamps, or ditches. In Missouri, choruses of males are not usually heard until late May or June. The males usually hide under leaves or other debris at the water's edge as they call. Once a male has attracted a female, he will clasp her with his front legs and may continue to call during amplexus. Special glands on the belly of the male secrete a substance which causes the male and female to become firmly stuck together. It is possible that these special "breeding glands" evolved in the eastern narrowmouth toads due to their rounded bodies and the male's short arms, which makes amplexus difficult (Conway and Metter, 1967).

The female will lay up to 850 eggs (Wright and Wright, 1949) in a film on the surface of the water. The eggs are fertilized by the male as they are laid. The eggs hatch in less than two days; the tadpoles metamorphose from 30 to 60 days later.

The call of a male eastern narrowmouth toad is a bleating nasal "*baaaaa*;" it lasts from one to four seconds, sounding like the cry of a forlorn lamb.

Remarks: In western Missouri this species is known to occur in sympatry with the Great Plains narrowmouth toad (*Gastrophryne olivacea*; see *G. olivacea* account for ways to distinguish the two species).

Missouri Distribution: The eastern narrowmouth toad is found in the southern half of Missouri.

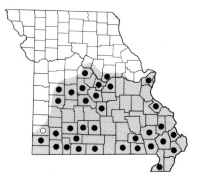

Adult Great Plains narrowmouth toad.

Great Plains Narrowmouth Toad
Gastrophryne olivacea (Hallowell)

Description: This small toad can be identified by its plump body, short legs, uniform color, small pointed head and a fold of skin across the back of the head. The general color is gray, tan or olive-tan. Small black spots may be scattered over the back and hind legs. There is no webbing between the toes. The belly is white. Adult females are larger than males; during breeding season the males have dark throats.

This species can best be distinguished from the eastern narrowmouth toad by its lighter overall color and the absence of any prominent dorsal markings.

Adult Great Plains narrowmouth toads range in snout–vent length from 22 to 38 mm (7/8 to 1 1/2 inches). Largest Missouri specimen recorded is 37 mm (1 7/16 inches; Powell *et al.,* 1982). Record length for the species is 41 mm (1 5/8 inches; Conant, 1975).

Habits and Habitat: This species prefers grasslands, rocky and wooded hills, and areas along the edge of marshes. These frogs spend most of their time hiding in loose soil, under rocks, boards, logs, or other objects; they have been known to take shelter in animal burrows (Blair, 1936). This species has evolved a toxic skin secretion which may protect it from ant bites, since it is known to sit on ant hills while eating its preferred food.

Breeding: Usual breeding sites are ditches, temporary ponds, flooded fields, or pools in wooded areas. Warm, heavy rains will stimulate males to congregate at breeding sites and begin calling. A male clasps a female just behind her front legs. Special skin glands on the male's belly secrete a gluelike substance which helps hold them together (Fitch, 1956a; Conway and Metter, 1967). During amplexus the female lays over 600 eggs (Collins, 1982); the male fertilizes them as they are laid. The eggs hatch in two to three days, and the tadpoles metamorphose from 20 to 30 days later (Collins, 1982). In Missouri, breeding takes place from late May to early July.

The call of a male Great Plains narrowmouth toad is a high-pitched short *"peet"* followed by a nasal buzz, which lasts from one to four seconds. The sound is similar to the buzz of an angry bee (Conant, 1975).

Remarks: Both *Gastrophryne carolinensis* and *G. olivacea* are known to occur in several western counties in Missouri, and sympatric populations may be found in that area. However, the calls of both species are different enough to keep the populations isolated from hybridization (Nelson, 1972b).

Missouri Distribution: The Great Plains narrowmouth toad has been reported from counties primarily in northwestern and western Missouri. Metter *et al.,* (1970) reported breeding populations in Boone and Callaway counties in central Missouri.

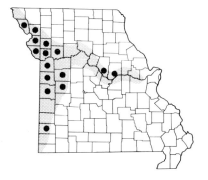

Family Ranidae
True Frogs

The family Ranidae is the largest and most widespread family of frogs. It contains 586 species in 45 genera (Duellman, 1979), and probably has its origin in Africa. Representatives of this cosmopolitan family are found on every major land mass except New Zealand, central and southern Australia, and southern South America. The largest genus in the family is *Rana*, with over 250 species. It is the only genus of this family which occurs in the United States; there are over 19 species found in the United States.

In Missouri the genus *Rana* is represented by eight species. Members of this family are commonly called "true frogs;" they are typically of medium to large size, have long legs, smooth skin, and well developed webbing between the toes. Another common characteristic is a glandular dorsolateral fold or ridge of skin along each side of the back. The largest member of the group in the United States, the bullfrog (*Rana catesbeiana*), does not have this ridge of skin.

Natural food of true frogs consists of nearly any animal small enough to be swallowed, including insects, spiders, crayfish, other frogs, fish and earthworms. The tadpoles of most species of true frogs are herbivorous, but may occasionally eat dead animal matter.

Pickerel Frog

Adult northern crawfish frog from Montgomery County.

Northern Crawfish Frog
Rana areolata circulosa (Rice and Davis)

Description: This is a large frog with a light ground color and numerous, closely-set dark spots. The head is disproportionately large in this species. A prominent dorsolateral fold extends from the eye to the thigh. Ground color may vary from light tan to light gray; the dark spots may be dark brown, gray, or nearly black, and are sometimes edged in white. A fine network pattern or spotting of dark pigment is usually present between the dark spots. The belly is white. Males can be distinguished from females by their smaller size, enlarged thumbs, and (during the breeding season) presence of a pair of saclike vocal pouches behind and below each eardrum (*tympanum*).

The northern crawfish frog ranges in snout–vent length from 65 to 104 mm (2 1/2 to 4 inches). Largest Missouri specimen recorded is 99 mm (3 7/8 inches; Powell *et al.,* 1982). Record length for the species is 114 mm (4 1/2 inches; Conant, 1975).

Habits and Habitat: Northern crawfish frogs are active from March to October in Missouri. The species is restricted to native prairie or former prairie areas in this state. Populations occur in or near low-lying hay fields, native grass pastures, prairies and occasionally in river floodplains. Although nearly all of the true native prairie regions of the state have undergone intensive cultivation, this species has been able to persist.

Crawfish frogs are known to use crawfish burrows for retreats but also use burrows of other animals as well. A crawfish burrow being used by this frog will have a noticeably flattened and denuded platform at the entrance. Because the crawfish burrows can run from 3 to 5 feet deep and are often at or below ground water level, the frogs are probably able to use them as winter retreats.

This is a very secretive species, spending most of its time hidden in burrows or under logs or boards. Crawfish frogs become active at night especially after warm, heavy summer rains. However, they are seldom encountered except during their short breeding season.

Food of this species consists of a variety of invertebrates, including small crawfish.

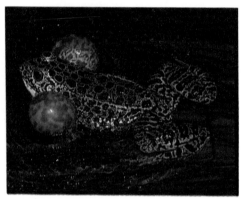

"Calling" male northern crawfish frog from Callaway County (left), and a newly transformed northern crawfish frog (44 mm long) from a native prairie in Newton County (right).

Breeding: In Missouri northern crawfish frogs breed from late February to early May. Males congregate in flooded ditches, semi-permanent pools, and fishless ponds. Heavy rains and moderate temperatures seem to stimulate the males to chorus. Soon after the males begin to call, the egg-laden females begin to arrive at the breeding site. A male will clasp a female behind her front legs and while in amplexus in shallow water, the eggs are laid and fertilized. The large clumps of eggs are usually deposited on a submerged plant stem or branch. Each female may lay up to 7,000 eggs (Collins, 1982). The eggs take from a week to ten days to hatch; the tadpoles metamorphose from mid-May to early June.

The call of a male northern crawfish frog may be described as a deep, loud, snoring *"gwwaaa,"* which can be heard from a considerable distance. A number of males calling in chorus sound like pigs during feeding time (Conant, 1975). The males call while floating in open water, and have been reported to call while submerged in the water (Barbour, 1971).

Remarks: The last remaining native prairies in Missouri are valuable for many reasons, but they are particularly valuable as habitat for northern crawfish frogs. Protecting, properly managing and re-establishing prairies is encouraged. Because this species requires fishless ponds for breeding, the addition of ponds in or near native prairies would be advantageous. Protecting the water table from excessive use is also important. When the water table becomes too low, burrowing crawfish may be eliminated, reducing the available habitat for crawfish frogs.

Missouri Distribution: This species occurs in the rolling hills, prairies and meadows of north central and extreme western and eastern Missouri.

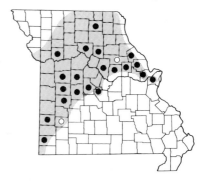

Adult plains leopard frog from Cooper County.

Plains Leopard Frog
Rana blairi Mecham, Littlejohn, Oldham, Brown and Brown

Description: A medium-size frog with light tan ground color and numerous rounded spots on the back. The head is wide and blunt, giving this species a stocky appearance. There is always a distinct light line along the upper jaw. A white spot is present on the tympanum. The dorsolateral folds are broken near the groin and a small posterior section of it is displaced further toward the midline. The numerous brown or greenish-brown spots on the back and legs are usually circular, and uniform in shape. A dark spot is usually present on the snout. The belly is white with pale yellow near the groin and lower inner thighs.

This species can be distinguished from other leopard frogs and the pickerel frog by the narrow, dorsolateral fold which is broken and displaced dorsally, and by the absence of distinct white rings around each dorsal spot. See species accounts for the pickerel frog (*Rana palustris*), northern leopard frog (*R. pipiens*) and southern leopard frog (*R. sphenocephala*).

Adult plains leopard frogs range in snout–vent length from 51 to 95 mm (2 to 3 3/4 inches). Largest Missouri specimen reported is 89 mm (3 1/2 inches; Powell *et al.*, 1982). The record is 111 mm (4 3/8 inches; Conant, 1975).

Habits and Habitat: The plains leopard frog is active from March to October. It occurs in the grasslands of the Midwest. In Missouri, this species may be found in the former prairie regions and associated river floodplains. It utilizes a variety of aquatic habitats, including water-filled

126

ditches, farm ponds, river sloughs, small streams, temporary pools and marshes. During the summer, specimens will venture into grassy areas well away from water. These frogs will retreat into the mud and dead leaves at the bottom of ponds and streams during winter. The plains leopard frog eats a variety of insects and spiders.

Breeding: This species breeds from mid-April to early June. Males will gather at a marsh, pond, or temporary pools and begin calling after sunset. Females with eggs are attracted by the males' call; amplexus takes place in the water. The eggs are fertilized by the males as they are laid. Each egg mass is attached to submerged stems or branches in shallow water. Each female may produce between 4,000 and 6,500 eggs. It takes between two and three weeks for the eggs to hatch. Metamorphosis from tadpoles to froglets usually occurs during mid-summer, but the tadpoles which hatched late in the breeding season may overwinter in the water and transform the next spring. Newly metamorphosed plains leopard frogs average 27 mm (1 1/16 inches) in length. In some years this species may breed during autumn.

The call of male plains leopard frogs can be described as a rapid series of guttural "*chuck-chuck-chuck*" sounds at a pulse rate of three per second (Mecham *et al.*, 1973).

Remarks: The plains leopard frog is known to occur sympatrically with the southern leopard frog (*R. sphenocephala*) in a number of Missouri counties. Hybridization between the two species may occur, but this is usually caused by habitat alteration due to human activity. When a breeding habitat is changed, the environmental barriers which would normally isolate the two species during their breeding season are lost, and the two species may hybridize.

Missouri Distribution: The plains leopard frog occurs throughout most of Missouri, but is not present in the Ozarks.

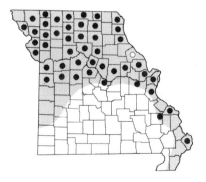

Adult male bullfrog (top) *from Cole County, and adult female bullfrog* (bottom) *from Pulaski County.*

Bullfrog
Rana catesbeiana (Shaw)

Description: This is Missouri's largest frog. General color ranges from green to olive to brown. Some dark markings may be present on the back in the form of small brown spots or indistinct irregular blotches. The hind legs are marked with distinct, dark brown bars. The belly is white, and the throat may have some gray mottling. The external eardrum is large and round. Adult male bullfrogs have a tympanum much larger than the eye. Adult females have a tympanum the same size or smaller than the eye. Bullfrogs lack a dorsolateral fold. During the breeding season, adult males have bright yellow throats.

Adult bullfrogs range in snout–vent length from 90 to 150 mm (3 1/2 to 6 inches). Largest Missouri specimen recorded is 151 mm (6 inches; Powell *et al.*, 1982). The record is 203 mm (8 inches; Conant, 1975).

Habits and Habitat: In Missouri, bullfrogs are active from late March to October. This is our most aquatic species of frog. Bullfrogs spend most of their time in or very near aquatic habitats such as lakes, ponds, rivers, large creeks, sloughs and permanent swamps or marshes. Because permanent water is required, this species may suffer a population decline during a drought year.

A bullfrog is easily disturbed during the day and escapes by powerful jumps into the water. However, it can be approached at night with the aid of a flashlight. At night during heavy summer rains, adult bullfrogs will move overland and may be seen crossing roads.

This species burrows into the mud at the bottom of rivers or ponds to avoid winter temperatures. In Missouri, adults usually enter winter retreats in late October; young bullfrogs follow a week later (Willis, Moyle and Baskett, 1956).

A number of studies have been conducted on the food consumed by bullfrogs. The size or age of the bullfrog, time of year, and type of habitat are factors which influence the kinds of prey eaten. Frogs living in farm ponds in central Missouri ate the following foods (in diminishing frequency): insects, crayfish, amphibians, small mammals, fish and birds (Korschgen and Moyle, 1955). A slight difference was noted between the prey of an impoundment (large pond) population, and bullfrogs living along rivers. Pond bullfrogs were found to eat dragonflies, spiders, ground beetles, crayfish, caterpillars and moths, and to a lesser extent other invertebrates and a few vertebrates. Bullfrogs from rivers were reported to eat scarab beetles, ground beetles, caterpillars and moths, crayfish, cicadas, spiders, and dragonflies, as well as a variety of other invertebrates and a few vertebrates (Korschgen and Baskett, 1963). Bullfrogs are opportunistic feeders, and generally speaking, their voracious appetite and size allow them to eat nearly any animal small enough to be captured and swallowed.

Breeding: In Missouri bullfrogs breed between mid-May and early July. Males are territorial during the breeding season and aggressively defend a calling station by mounting, pushing, kicking, bumping or biting intruding males. In marshes, large ponds, or sloughs, the choruses of males are usually in one or two sections of the area while egg-laying takes place in a different section. A male will mount a gravid female and begin amplexus. As the female begins to lay her eggs they are fertilized by the male. The eggs are laid as a large, wide floating mass, one egg deep, on the surface. Each egg is quite small, around 1 mm in diameter. Female bullfrogs can lay over 20,000 eggs per clutch; some

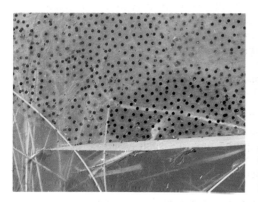

Freshly laid bullfrog eggs (left) *from Linn County, and a bullfrog tadpole* (right) *from Pulaski County.*

produce two clutches of eggs during the summer. The eggs hatch in four or five days and the tadpoles, which feed on algae, grow quickly. In Missouri, the tadpoles usually metamorphose in 11 to 14 months (Willis *et al.*, 1956). Bullfrog froglets take an additional two or three years before adult size is reached. Female bullfrogs become sexually mature between 123 to 125 mm (4 13/16 to 4 7/8 inches) snout–vent length (Willis *et al.*, 1956), while males attain sexual maturity at about 120 mm (4 3/4 inches) snout–vent length (Schroeder, 1975).

The call of a male bullfrog can be described as a deep sonorous "*ger-a-a-rum*," which can carry for a distance of half a mile or more. Males may be heard calling during the day, but more vocalization takes place at night.

Remarks: Bullfrogs (and green frogs) are classed as game animals in Missouri and are protected by a season and bag limit under the Wildlife Code. The legs of these frogs are edible and considered by many people to be a delicacy.

Missouri Distribution: This familiar amphibian occurs statewide in Missouri.

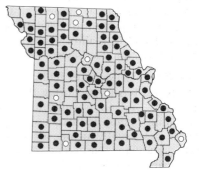

Adult green frog from Warren County.

Green Frog
Rana clamitans Latreille

Description: This is a medium-size frog. General color varies from green to greenish tan to brown. The upper lip and head are usually green. Faint dark spots may be present on the back, and the legs usually have indistinct dark spots or bars. Sides of the belly are often marked with dark gray vermiculation. The belly is white with some dusky markings. Adult males have a bright yellow throat. A distinct dorsolateral fold is present, but extends only to mid-body, not to the groin. The external eardrum (tympanum) is large and conspicuous, larger than the eye in males. During the breeding season, males have swollen thumbs and heavier front legs. This species can be confused with the bullfrog, (*Rana catesbeiana*) but is smaller and has a prominent dorsolateral fold, which bullfrogs lack.

Adult green frogs range in snout–vent length from 57 to 89 mm (2 1/2 to 3 1/2 inches). Largest Missouri specimen recorded is 91 mm (3 5/8 inches; Powell *et al.*, 1982). The record is 102 mm (4 inches; Conant, 1975).

Habits and Habitat: This species is active between April and mid-October. I have noticed young green frogs active into early December during a mild autumn.

Green frogs are rather solitary animals, especially in small stream habitats, where each deep pool may have a single adult in residence. In Missouri this species is likely to be found in creeks and streams, especially in the Ozarks. Other habitats include river sloughs, swamps, marshes and farm ponds. When disturbed, a green frog will quickly jump into the water, often emitting a high-pitched squawk as it jumps (Smith, 1961). This species presumably eats a variety of insects and small crawfish. Green frogs in southern Illinois were found to eat beetles, spiders, millipedes, snails, true bugs and flies (Jenssen and Klimstra, 1966). A Boone County population of green frogs was observed residing in a wet cave (Resetarits, pers. comm.).

Adult bronze frog from Bollinger County (right), *and freshly laid green frog eggs from Warren County.*

Breeding: The reproductive biology of this frog has not been studied in Missouri. Generally speaking, the green frog breeds from late April until late August, but June is probably the peak breeding month. Any permanent standing water is used as a breeding site, including ponds, swamps and sloughs. There is usually intense competition for choice calling areas, and the male with the best breeding site (one which has an abundance of emergent plants) has a better chance to attract gravid females (Wells, 1977). Once a male has engaged a female in amplexus, the female will begin depositing her eggs in a wide, floating mass on the surface of the water. Each female can lay over 4,000 eggs (Wright and Wright, 1949). The small, dark tadpoles begin hatching in several days, depending on the water temperature, but metamorphosis will not occur until the following summer. Newly transformed green frogs average 28 mm (1 1/8 inches) in body length.

The call of a male green frog can be described as an explosive "*bong,*" that sounds like a loose banjo string. The sound may be emitted once, or repeated three to four times (Conant, 1975).

Subspecies: Missouri has two subspecies of *Rana clamitans*. The green frog, *Rana clamitans melanota* (Rafinesque), was described in detail in the above account. The other subspecies, the bronze frog (*Rana clamitans clamitans* Latreille), has a restricted distribution in the state. It can be distinguished from the green frog by its smaller size, 54 to 76 mm (2 1/8 to 3 inches), by its brown or bronze body, and by the yellow color on the upper lip and head. Bronze frogs may have more distinct dark markings on the back and limbs.

Remarks: Green frogs are classed as a game species. See Remarks section in the bullfrog account.

Missouri Distribution: The green frog (stippling) is found over most of Missouri with the exception of the northwest part of the state. The bronze frog (hatch lines) is known only from extreme southeastern Missouri. Intergradation between the two subspecies may occur in several southeastern counties.

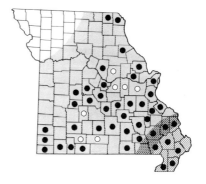

Adult pickerel frog from Miller County.

Pickerel Frog
Rana palustris Le Conte

Description: A medium-size frog with prominent dorsolateral folds and two parallel rows of squarish or rectangular spots running down the back between the folds. General color is gray, tan or brown. A white line is present along the upper lip. The distinct dorsolateral fold extends down to the groin, and may be white, cream, gray, yellow or golden. Spots on the back are reddish brown, dark brown or black. Dark bars on the hind legs are prominent. The underside of the hind legs and groin area are washed with bright yellow, orange-yellow, or pinkish yellow. The belly is white. During the breeding season males can be distinguished from females by their enlarged thumbs with dark, thick pads. Adult males are generally smaller than adult females.

The pickerel frog may be confused with the three species of leopard frogs which occur in Missouri. This species can be distinguished from the leopard frog by the wide, unbroken dorsolateral fold, the two distinct rows of square or rectangular dorsal spots, and the presence of yellow or orange-yellow color along the underside of the hind legs and groin area. See species accounts for the plains leopard frog (*Rana blairi*), northern leopard frog (*R. pipiens*) and southern leopard frog (*R. sphenocephala*).

Adult pickerel frogs range in snout–vent length from 44 to 80 mm (1 3/4 to 3 inches). Largest Missouri specimen recorded is 86 mm (3 3/8 inches; Resetarits, pers. comm.). The record is 87 mm (3 7/16 inches; Conant, 1975).

Habits and Habitat: This species is generally associated with springs, cold streams and cool, shaded woodland ponds. In Missouri, it occurs along Ozark streams; it can be found under rocks along the water's edge. Pickerel frogs live along streams in grassy areas, pastures and near farm ponds. In eastern Missouri along the Mississippi River, this species is associated with springs and creeks which flow from limestone bluffs.

A Boone County population of this species was intensely studied for several years; some of that information is provided below (Resetarits, pers. comm.). Pickerel frogs apparently use wet caves as a refuge from hot weather during late summer and cold temperatures during winter. This is the only species of frog in Missouri which takes shelter in caves with regularity and in high numbers. A single cave may harbor hundreds of pickerel frogs. The relatively constant temperature and moisture in a wet cave provide an ideal site for overwintering. The frogs may exit for short periods of time to feed, but as early as late September or early October or by November, they will have moved to a deeper section of the cave where the temperature is more stable; here they remain until spring. During March or early April, the frogs leave the cave and locate a pond or slough for breeding. The frogs feed during the spring and summer; some begin to return to the cave in July. Young-of-the-year pickerel frogs were found to have the greatest mortality during the winter. In some areas this species may overwinter in mud at the bottom of streams or ponds.

Pickerel frogs consume a variety of insects and spiders.

Breeding: Woodland ponds, sloughs and even water-filled ditches are used as breeding sites. In Missouri, this species breeds between March and May. Males usually form a chorus at one or two sites in a pond; over a dozen may call from a relatively small area (Wright and Wright, 1949). Amplexus will take place as soon as a male is approached by a female. The female lays her eggs in shallow water in the form of a globular mass which is attached to a submerged stick or stem. The eggs are fertilized by the male as they are being laid. From 700 to 2,900 eggs were produced by each female in a Missouri population (Resetarits, pers. comm.). The small tadpoles begin hatching in ten days or more, depending on the water temperature, metamorphosis into froglets will begin after three months. Pickerel frog tadpoles collected in late April in Pulaski County and kept at 70° F transformed into froglets by mid-July.

The call of male pickerel frogs can be described as a low-pitched, descending snore lasting one to two seconds. A number of authors have reported this frog vocalizing while under water (Morris, 1944; Wright and Wright, 1949; Barbour, 1971; Conant, 1975).

Remarks: Skin secretions of pickerel frogs are known to be irritating or even toxic to small animals. If newly captured pickerel frogs are placed in the same container with other frog species, the latter will die within a short time due to these skin secretions (Morris, 1944; Mulcare, 1965). Most frog-eating snakes will not eat pickerel frogs.

Missouri Distribution: Pickerel
frogs are common in southern and
eastern Missouri.

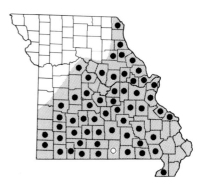

Northern leopard frog from Atchison County.

Northern Leopard Frog
Rana pipiens Schreber

Description: A medium-size frog with brown or green ground color and large, round, black dorsal spots. The head is wide with a short, blunt snout. There is a prominent white line along the upper lip. Tympanum color is rust-brown; there is no light spot present. The dorsolateral folds are wide, continuous to groin, and cream or fawn colored. Dark spots along the back and on the limbs are reddish brown to black, prominently ringed with white. The large round spots on the sides are black and are also ringed with white or pale green. The snout usually has a large round black spot. The belly is white. The groin area and the underside of hind legs are white or pale green.

This species can be distinguished from the southern leopard frog and plains leopard frog (*Rana sphenocephala* and *R. blairi*) by the wider and continuous dorsolateral folds, and the distinct white rings around each dark spot (see southern and plains leopard frog accounts). During the breeding season male northern leopard frogs can be distinguished from females by the enlarged thumbs.

Adult northern leopard frogs range in snout–vent length from 51 to 89 mm (2 to 3 1/2 inches). The record is 111 mm (4 3/8 inches; Conant, 1975).

Habits and Habitat: The northern leopard frog is active from March to October. This species occurs in marshes, flooded ditches and small ponds and lakes in northern and eastern United States and Canada. In Missouri it has been found along the edge of small marshes and shallow drainage ditches. Like other leopard frog species, northern leopard frogs move into grassy areas during summer where they feed on insects. A variety of insects and spiders are included in the natural diet of this species. In autumn leopard frogs move to permanent water where they retreat to the bottom or into the mud, remaining there throughout the winter.

Breeding: The reproductive biology of the northern leopard frog has not been studied in Missouri. Information gathered on the northern leopard frog in other states indicates that this species breeds in March or April. Males call from small areas of open water in marshes or shallow ponds; they begin calling at dusk. Gravid females are attracted to the calling males; once amplexus occurs, each pair of frogs moves to shallow water where the eggs are laid. The eggs are fertilized during amplexus. Several globular masses of eggs are produced with a maximum of 6,000 eggs per female (Vogt, 1981). The egg masses are attached to submerged sticks, cattails, or grasses. Hatching takes place within 10 to 15 days, depending on water temperature. Metamorphosis from tadpole to young frog occurs after 2 to 2 1/2 months of development (late May to mid-June).

The breeding call of male northern leopard frogs can be described as a deep rattling snore with occasional clucking grunts (Conant, 1975). The call has been compared to the sound made by rubbing a wet thumb slowly along the surface of an inflated balloon.

Remarks: Northern leopard frogs have been called "meadow frogs" because they often move into pastures and lawns during the summer.

Males of this species usually have Mullerian ducts (vestigial oviducts) present along each kidney. These vestigial organs are not found in males of other leopard frog species.

This species and the plains leopard frog (*Rana blairi*) have been found sympatrically in the northwest corner of Missouri. Field work is needed in this area to determine the voices, habitat use and breeding behavior of the two related species.

Missouri Distribution: The northern leopard frog was first discovered in this state in the spring of 1985. I had listed this species as "of possible occurrence in Missouri" in previous work (Johnson, 1977). A small population is known to occur in the extreme northwestern corner of Atchison County; it is also presumed to occur in other northwest Missouri counties due to populations in nearby southeastern Nebraska (Lynch, 1978) and southwestern Iowa (Christiansen, pers. comm.)

Adult southern leopard frog from Miller County.

Southern Leopard Frog
Rana sphenocephala Cope

Description: A medium-size frog with a variable number of rounded or oblong dark spots on the back. The dorsolateral fold is narrow and distinctly raised, yellow or tan in color, and extends to the groin. The head appears long and the snout is pointed. General color is green, greenish brown, or light brown with some green on the dorsum. Dark markings on the hind legs appear as broken bars or elongated spots. There is usually no dark spot on the snout. A white line is present along the upper lip; the center of the tympanum (external ear drum) usually has a distinct white spot. The belly is white. During the breeding season males can be distinguished from females by their smaller size, enlarged thumbs and vocal sacs on either side of the head.

The southern leopard frog can be distinguished from the pickerel frog and other species of leopard frogs by the narrow and continuous dorsolateral fold, pointed snout, the absence of a snout spot (in most specimens), the lack of any yellow color along the groin area and inner thighs, and the absence of white rings around each dorsal spot. See species accounts for the plains leopard frog (*Rana blairi*), pickerel frog (*R. palustris*) and northern leopard frog (*R. pipiens*).

Adult southern leopard frogs range in snout–vent length from 51 to 89 mm (2 to 3 1/2 inches). Largest Missouri specimen recorded is 81 mm (3 3/16 inches; Powell *et al.*, 1982). The record length is 127 mm (5 inches; Conant, 1975).

Habits and Habitat: The southern leopard frog is normally active between late February and mid-October in Missouri. During the summer months, southern leopard frogs may venture far from water into pastures, meadows, or wooded areas where they search for insect prey. When near an aquatic habitat, leopard frogs sit at the water's edge, but quickly enter the water with a powerful jump if alarmed. This species utilizes a wide variety of aquatic habitats including creeks, rivers, sloughs, swamps, marshes, ponds and lakes. A variety of insects and other invertebrates are eaten by this species.

"Calling" male southern leopard frog (left), *and a pair of southern leopard frogs in amplexus* (right), *both from Cole County.*

Breeding: In Missouri, the southern leopard frog breeds from mid-March to early May. Ponds, sloughs and flooded ditches are used as breeding sites. Males will call while floating in the water, or more often will hide themselves among grasses or stems in shallow water. The eggs are laid and fertilized during amplexus. Up to 5,000 eggs are normally laid in several clumps or masses which are loosely attached to submerged sticks or stems. The eggs will take up to two weeks to hatch, depending on the water temperature; the tadpoles metamorphose from mid-June to late July. In some years, southern leopard frogs are known to breed during the autumn.

The call of the male southern leopard frog can be described as a series of abrupt, chucklelike "quacking" sounds, repeated at a rate of 12 pulses per second (Illinois population, Mecham *et al.*, 1973).

Remarks: This species can be found sympatrically with the plains leopard frog (*Rana blairi*) in a number of Missouri counties; they are known to hybridize. To better understand the relationship between the two species of leopard frogs, research is needed to study their calls, time of breeding, breeding site and habitat preference, and egg and tadpole identification.

Missouri Distribution: The southern leopard frog occurs throughout
most of Missouri, except for the
northwest corner of the state.

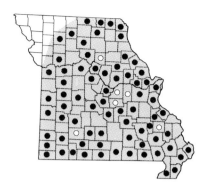

Adult wood frog from Warren County.

Wood Frog
Rana sylvatica Le Conte

Description: The wood frog is a medium-size tan amphibian with a distinct dark brown "mask" on each side of the head, extending from the snout to behind the tympanum. General color varies from pinkish tan, light brown, reddish brown, to dark brown. Scattered small dark markings may be present on the dorsum, and the hind legs usually have brown or dark brown longitudinal bars. There is a prominent white line along the upper lip. The dorsolateral fold is distinct and extends to the groin. The belly is white with scattered dusky markings.

During the breeding season adult male wood frogs can be distinguished from females by their smaller size, darker color, enlarged thumbs and a vocal sac found just above each forelimb.

The only other frogs native to Missouri which may be confused with the wood frog are young bronze frogs and green frogs which may have similar color but lack the distinctive dark brown "mask" through each eye.

Adult wood frogs found in Missouri range in snout–vent length from 45 to 76 mm (1 1/2 to 3 inches). The record length is 83 mm (3 1/2 inches; Conant, 1975).

Habits and Habitat: This species is active between February and October. It is a secretive and solitary species, and can be difficult to observe at the end of the short breeding season. During the summer, wood frogs live along shady ravines in deep accumulations of dead leaves, or in small openings along north-facing rock outcroppings and bluffs. In Missouri, this species is generally associated with the cooler, north-facing wooded hillsides, where there is ample shade and some moisture. This type of habitat often has sugar maple (*Acer saccharum*) as a common tree species. A wood frog among dead oak and maple leaves is nearly invisible. This species overwinters on land under a deep layer of leaves, or in the damp soil under brushpiles and logs.

Wood frogs eat a variety of insects and other invertebrates. Several young wood frogs were captured during early June in Warren County and observed for a few weeks; they ate small grasshoppers, leafhoppers and small crickets. As with other frogs in Missouri, wood frogs are preyed upon by snakes, fish, raccoons, mink and skunks. An adult wood frog was observed being eaten by an eastern yellowbelly racer in a forest habitat in Warren County on May 26 (John Karel, pers. comm.).

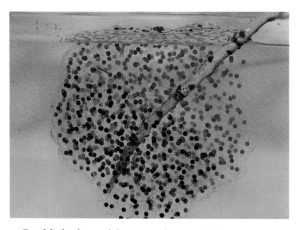

Freshly laid wood frog eggs from a fishless pond in Warren County.

Breeding: The wood frog is an explosive, early spring breeder. Small, fishless, woodland ponds and pools are utilized for breeding. In Missouri, breeding takes place between early February and late March, depending on local weather conditions. This species requires warm spring rains and an air temperature of at least 10°C (50°F) to stimulate breeding. Males move to a breeding pool as soon as the sun is down, and normally vocalize until midnight. During ideal weather conditions (warm and moist) I have seen and heard wood frogs calling during the day. The northern spring peeper (*Hyla crucifer crucifer*) choruses and breeds along with wood frogs; their loud, high-pitched voices can easily overpower the muted call of wood frogs. Gravid females begin arriving at the breeding pond on the first night the males begin to call. By the second or third night, all the eggs are laid and few wood frogs remain at the pond. The males normally call while floating in open water. Their paired vocal sacs expand and contract rapidly each time a call is produced. A

143

gravid female will swim toward a calling male and amplexus will commence. While in amplexus the pair swims to a shallow area where there is an abundance of submerged branches or stems; the eggs are attached to a branch just below the surface of the water. The eggs are fertilized by the male as they are laid. Most wood frog eggs I have observed were laid along the northern and northwestern section of each breeding pond, where the water temperature is warmest. A study of wood frog breeding in Pennsylvania revealed that the frogs were from two to three years of age when they bred for the first time (Seale, 1982).

Wood frog egg masses measure up to 11.5 cm (4 1/2 inches) across, and contain from 500 to over 1,000 eggs. Individual eggs are encased in a large amount of clear jelly which causes them to be widely separated. Newly laid eggs are black with a small white dot on the bottom, and average 2 mm (1/16 inch) in diameter. Wood frog eggs hatch within ten days to two weeks. Development is rapid and metamorphosis takes place in May to early June. Newly transformed wood frogs average 17 mm (5/8 inch) in body length; they are tannish gray in color, and have the distinct, dark brown "mask."

The call of a male wood frog is a rapid, hoarse "*waaaduck*" sound that lasts about one second, and may be quickly repeated three or four times; put simply, they sound like quacking ducks. The sound of a small chorus of this species carries only a short distance.

Remarks: Hurter (1911) first reported the presence of this species in Missouri.

In 1973, the wood frog was classified as an endangered species in this state. During June, 1978, a population was discovered in Warren County by Louise Mathis and reported to the Missouri Department of Conservation. A number of populations were subsequently reported in eastern and southeastern sections of the state and it was determined that the species could be reclassified as rare (1982).

Missouri Distribution: The wood frog occurs in eastern, southeastern and southwestern sections of Missouri.

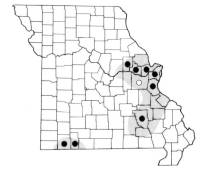

Part II—Reptiles

(Class Reptilia)

Turtles

Turtles and tortoises represent the oldest living group of reptiles on earth. These generally hard-shelled reptiles are known from fossils as far back as the Triassic Period—over 200 million years ago—and have changed very little since they became established. All turtles and tortoises belong to the Order Testudinata, containing over 230 living species.

Most people are familiar with the general characteristics of turtles, and they are seldom confused with other animals. However, few people are aware of the natural history, habitat requirements or distribution of even the most common species of turtles.

The turtles of Missouri can be divided into three groups: hard-shelled aquatic turtles, hard-shelled land turtles (box turtles) and softshells. The hard-shelled aquatic group has the largest number of species; it includes some of the smallest species, as well as the largest freshwater turtle on earth. Box turtles of Missouri are represented by only two species. Although many people call them "tortoises," these reptiles are actually more closely related to basking turtles (sliders and painted turtles). Missouri has only two softshell species.

Turtles have another unique feature besides their shells. They lost their teeth through evolution, and instead have a tough, horny beak.

Turtle shells can be divided into two sections: the upper shell known as the "carapace," and the lower shell called the "plastron." The shell of most turtles is composed of bony plates covered by a layer of horny scales called "scutes." Softshell turtles have reduced bony plates which are covered by tough skin instead of scutes.

All of our turtles lay their eggs on land. Females are particular about where they lay and bury their eggs; they may travel long distances over land to locate a suitable site. Most turtles select well-drained, sandy or loose soil to deposit their eggs. The site usually faces south or southeast in order to gain the sun's warmth. The eggs of the softshell and stinkpot are hard-shelled, while snapping turtles, painted, map and the rest of Missouri's turtles lay leathery-shelled eggs.

A total of 22 species and subspecies representing four families of turtles are native to Missouri. Turtles have been around for a very long time, but their long heritage and stability may, in part, cause their decline. The swamps, marshes and rivers where turtles make their homes are all being rapidly altered by man. These changes in habitat include pollution, channelization, and elimination of basking and nesting areas. Many of our native turtles do not have the ability to change or alter lifestyles in order to survive in a rapidly changing environment. Several of Missouri's turtles are on Missouri's rare and endangered species list. As long as our wetlands, clean rivers and other habitats diminish to make way for human "progress," we will continue to see more species decline in numbers. Persecution of turtles by needless (and unlawful) shooting is another reason turtle populations are declining. Some turtles are used as human food, but all our turtles play a role in the overall check-and-balance system we call nature. But now these long-lived, interesting animals need our help. It is time people began to care about the various animals native to our state, and to let others know that turtles have as much right to a healthy environment and a chance to survive as any other creature.

Family Chelydridae
Snapping Turtles

This family is composed of two species representing two genera (*Chelydra* and *Macroclemys*); it is restricted to North and South America. The common snapping turtle (*Chelydra serpentina*) and its subspecies range from Canada through the eastern and central United States, and south to Ecuador. The alligator snapping turtle (*Macroclemys temminckii*) ranges from northern Florida to east Texas, and northward to southeast Kansas, Missouri and Illinois. It is the largest freshwater turtle in the world. Both species are aquatic, and are seldom seen on land except when females search for a nesting site.

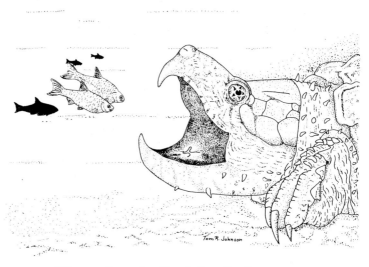

Alligator Snapping Turtle "angling"

Adult common snapping turtle from Cole County.

Common Snapping Turtle
Chelydra serpentina serpentina (Linnaeus)

Description: A large aquatic turtle with a big pointed head, long thick tail and small plastron. The carapace may be tan, brown or nearly black; it is often covered with mud or algae. Head, tail and limbs are brown. The head is often covered with numerous small black lines or spots. The plastron and underside of limbs are yellowish white. Upper part of the tail has a row of large sawtooth scales. The carapace has three rows of low keels which are prominent in young turtles, but become less apparent in old specimens. Adult males can be distinguished from adult females by their slightly smaller size; their cloacal opening is further out from the edge of the plastron than that of females. The young of this species have very rough shells and long tails.

Adult snapping turtles range in carapace length from 200 to 300 mm (8 to 12 inches). Largest Missouri specimen recorded is 326 mm (12 7/8 inches; Powell *et al.*, 1982). The record length is 470 mm (18 1/2 inches; Conant, 1975). An average adult may weigh from 4.5 to 16 kg (10 to 35 pounds).

Habits and Habitat: The common snapping turtle is primarily aquatic and seldom basks in the sun. Adult females may be seen crossing roads and traveling overland when the egg-laying season begins. Many common snapping turtles are killed by cars and trucks at this time. Turtles of either sex may travel overland if the pond in which they are living dries up.

A common snapping turtle plastron (left), *and a hatchling common snapping turtle from St. Louis County* (right).

Snapping turtles will vigorously defend themselves when taken out of water; they will even become aggressive and lunge at any adversary. Once in the water, however, they usually do not bite and will try to hide or escape rather than defend themselves.

This large turtle makes its home in a wide variety of aquatic habitats. It can commonly be found in farm ponds, marshes, swamps, sloughs, rivers and reservoirs—anywhere there is permanent water. Snapping turtles prefer bodies of water with a mud bottom, abundant aquatic vegetation and submerged logs and snags. They tend to spend a lot of time hidden in the mud in shallow water; they become more active at night when they forage for food (Collins, 1982).

Snapping turtles are active between March and November. They overwinter by burying themselves in deep mud at the bottom of ponds or rivers. Natural food of this species includes insects, crayfish, fish, snails, earthworms, amphibians, snakes, small mammals, birds and aquatic vegetation. Up to 36 percent of a snapping turtle's diet may consist of plant material (Ernst and Barbour, 1972). Carrion may also be consumed (Ernst and Barbour, 1972; Collins, 1982).

Breeding: Courtship and mating may take place any time between April and November, but most breeding activity occurs in late spring and early summer when water temperatures are warm. Mating takes place in the water. Courtship between a pair of snapping turtles usually involves the two turtles facing each other and waving their heads from side-to-side in opposite directions. Actual mating begins when a male mounts a female and grips her carapace with his claws. The male's tail moves beneath the female's tail so that their cloacal openings touch. The male then inserts his penis for sperm transmission. Like many species of turtles, the female snapping turtle is able to retain viable sperm for a number of years (Collins, 1982).

June is the usual month for egg-laying. The female selects an area with deep sand or loose soil where she will dig out a nest 4 to 7 inches deep with her hind legs. A single female may lay from 20 to 30 eggs; in

Missouri, more than one clutch may be laid per season. The eggs are cream colored and about the same shape and size as a ping-pong ball. Hatching will occur between 55 and 125 days after the eggs are laid, depending on nest temperature and humidity (Collins, 1982). Hatchling common snapping turtles are from 25 to 38 mm (1 to 1 1/2 inches) in carapace length. Males reach sexual maturity in four or five years at a plastral length of 149 to 155 mm (5 15/16 to 6 3/16 inches); females mature at four to seven years at a plastral length of 123 to 175 mm (5 to 7 1/8 inches; Christiansen and Burken, 1979).

Remarks: The common snapping turtle is one of the few economically valuable species in the state. Many people actively pursue this species for their meat, which is reported to make a fine stew and an excellent soup.

Over the years many people have developed an intense hatred of this species caused by misinformation and a lack of understanding. Field studies have proven that this turtle will not harm game fish populations in natural bodies of water, and that a large part of its diet consists of aquatic vegetation, rough fish, crayfish and dead animals (carrion). Contrary to popular belief, snapping turtles do not cause substantial damage to waterfowl young under natural conditions (Lagler, 1943). However, in artificial ponds where fish or waterfowl production is enhanced, this species may become a serious nuisance and require control measures such as trapping.

Extreme care must be taken when handling large snapping turtles. They have strong jaws and long necks, so the only safe way to carry a specimen is to grasp it at the base of the tail and keep it away from your legs.

Missouri Distribution: The common snapping turtle occurs statewide and is common throughout Missouri.

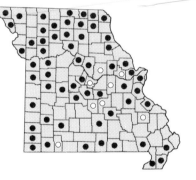

Adult alligator snapping turtle from Mississippi County.

Alligator Snapping Turtle
Macroclemys temminckii (Troost)

Description: This is a huge aquatic species with a noticeably large head. The carapace has three prominent ridges—one along the center line and one on either side. The large head terminates in a sharp, strongly hooked beak. The tail is long and muscular. Skin on the head, neck and front legs has a number of fleshy projections or tubercles. The plastron is reduced in size and affords little protection to the ventral area. Adults have dark brown heads, legs and shells; skin on neck and other areas may be yellowish brown. Males have longer tails than females.

Adult alligator snapping turtles range in carapace length from 38 to 66 cm (15 to 26 inches; Conant, 1975). Largest Missouri specimen recorded is 42.5 cm (16 9/16 inches; Powell *et al.*, 1982). Weight may range from 16 to 68 kg (35 to 105 pounds). Record weight is 99.3 kg (219 pounds; Conant, 1975).

Habits and Habitat: The alligator snapping turtle is totally aquatic and seldom climbs out of the water onto objects to bask in the sun. Most specimens seen out of water are apparently females in search of an egg-laying site. The majority of their time is spent in deep water in mud and other hiding places such as root snags. They spend daylight hours in hiding and become active at night. This species seldom attempts to swim; it normally moves about by slowly walking on the bottom.

According to Ernst and Barbour (1972), the alligator snapping turtle cannot remain submerged for long periods of time as other species can,

Head of adult alligator snapping turtle.

especially in warm water. At a water temperature of 21°C (70°F), specimens were unable to remain underwater for longer than 50 minutes without surfacing to take in air.

This species is unique among North American turtles in having the ability to lure fish to its mouth. The tongue of this species has a special appendage shaped like a stout worm; it can be moved at will by the turtle while it lies motionless on the bottom of a river or slough. Nearby fish are attracted to the wriggling "worm" and are captured and eaten when they venture too close.

Preferred habitat of this species includes deep sloughs, oxbow lakes and deep, muddy pools of large rivers.

The alligator snapping turtle feeds mainly on fish, but may at times capture and eat small turtles. Young of the species presumably eat small fish, aquatic insects, molluscs and snails.

Breeding: A study of the growth and reproductive biology of the alligator snapping turtle was conducted in Louisiana by Dobie (1971). He found that individuals become sexually mature between 11 and 13 years of age. Males were determined to be mature at a skull length of 115 mm (4 5/8 inches). Sperm were found in the *vasa deferentia* throughout the year in the Louisiana population, suggesting a prolonged breeding season. Females were determined to mature at a skull length of approximately 112 mm (4 1/2 inches); larger females produce more eggs than smaller females. Courtship and breeding take place in the water. It is presumed to occur in late spring. Females emerge from the water during May and June to dig a nest and lay eggs. Dobie (1971) estimated that from 16 to 52 eggs may be laid by a single female. The eggs are round, white and hard-shelled. Their diameter may be 30 to 44 mm (Ernst and Barbour, 1972). Hatching probably takes place in late summer. Louisiana turtles laid one clutch of eggs per season, but there were indications that some adult females produce eggs only every other year

A sub-adult alligator snapping turtle plastron (left) *and a young alligator snapping turtle* (right).

(Dobie, 1971). Shell length of a newly-hatched alligator snapping turtle averages 44 mm (1 3/4 inches; Allen and Neill, 1950); they normally have a brown or black shell and dark gray skin.

Remarks: A reduction in the number of this large aquatic turtle in the waters of Missouri has prompted the Missouri Department of Conservation to list it as a rare species. It is unlawful to capture or kill alligator snapping turtles in this state. Water pollution, habitat alteration, a reduction in egg-laying sites and over-harvesting have probably all had a part in causing the decline of this species.

Missouri Distribution: Presumed to occur in the large rivers, sloughs and oxbow lakes of southern, southeastern and eastern Missouri.

Family Kinosternidae

Mud and Musk Turtles

Kinosternidae is a strictly New World family comprised of 23 species. Species within this family occur from Canada to Argentina, and have been classified into four genera: *Staurotypus, Claudius, Sternotherus* and *Kinosternon*. The last two, *Sternotherus* and *Kinosternon*, contain nine species and are widely distributed in the United States. Both genera have representatives in Missouri.

This family is made up of rather small dull colored turtles. Indeed, one of the smallest turtles in the world, the stinkpot (*Sternotherus odoratus*), is a member of the Kinosternidae. Stinkpots have a very small plastron which affords little protection; only the front portion is movable. Mud turtles (*Kinosternon*), by comparison, have larger plastrons and the front and hind parts are both movable.

Illinois Mud Turtle

Adult yellow mud turtle.

Yellow Mud Turtle
Kinosternon flavescens (Agassiz)

Description: A small, uniformly colored turtle of the Great Plains. Color of the chin and throat is normally yellow. Upper shell is somewhat flattened and usually olive-brown. Scutes on the carapace are outlined in dark brown. Plastron is yellow-brown; scutes normally have dark brown margins. The legs and upper parts of the head and neck are olive. The tail of the yellow mud turtle ends in a clawlike, horny tip. Adult males can be distinguished from females by concave plastrons, and long, thick tails. An important characteristic which may be used to distinguish this species from other members of the family is the height of the ninth marginal scale on the upper shell. This scale is much higher toward the middle of the upper shell than the eighth marginal.

Adult yellow mud turtles range in carapace length from 100 to 125 mm (4 to 5 inches; Conant, 1975). Largest Missouri specimen recorded is 131 mm (5 1/8 inches; Powell *et al.*, 1982). Record length is 162 mm (6 3/8 inches; Conant, 1975).

Habits and Habitat: Yellow mud turtles are active between April and October. Specimens can be seen basking on logs or other stationary objects sticking out of the water, or along the bank. Turtles can be observed moving overland between ponds, especially during the summer. A variety of aquatic habitats may be used by this species: rivers, sloughs, oxbow lakes, ponds and water-filled ditches. Streams or ponds with muddy or sandy bottoms are preferred. Overwintering normally takes place in burrows on land, in mud or sandbanks, or in natural depressions where dead leaves and other debris have accumulated.

Yellow mud turtles eat a variety of aquatic animals, including insects, snails, crayfish, tadpoles and dead fish. Aquatic plants are occasionally consumed by mud turtles.

Breeding: Courtship and mating take place in shallow water between late April and mid-May. A male mud turtle will mount a receptive female and hold onto her upper shell with both front and hind legs. During copulation the male may nudge, rub or bite the head of the female.

Eggs are laid in a hole dug by the female in well drained sand or soil. Nesting sites usually have plenty of exposure to the sun. From two to six white, hard-shelled eggs are produced per female. Nests of the Illinois mud turtle were observed in June and July (Kangas and Palmer, 1982) during field studies of this subspecies in Clark County. Hatching occurs from late August to mid-September; hatchlings are known to remain in the nest until the next spring. Hatchlings average 25 mm (15/16 inch) in carapace length. Little is known about the aquatic activity, habitat requirements and feeding habits of hatchlings in Missouri.

Adult Illinois mud turtle from Clark County, Missouri (left) *and an Illinois mud turtle plastron* (right).

Subspecies: Two subspecies of *Kinosternon flavescens* occur in Missouri, both of which have limited distribution: the nominate race, the yellow mud turtle, *Kinosternon flavescens flavescens* (Agassiz), described above; and the Illinois mud turtle, *Kinosternon flavescens spooneri* (Smith). The Illinois mud turtle is similar in size and general appearance to the yellow mud turtle, but is much darker in color. The carapace is usually dark brown, while the head and limbs range from dark gray to black. Some yellow is present along the lower jaw and neck, and occasionally along the edge of the carapace. The plastron has yellow patches on the outer surface, and dark brown toward the center.

The occurrence of the Illinois mud turtle in northeast Missouri was first reported by Anderson (1957). The population in extreme northeastern Missouri occurs in natural marshes, oxbow lakes and in flooded fields associated with sandy soil. This population is located close to the

Mississippi River, but the turtles presumably do not use that aquatic habitat. In recent years, Illinois mud turtle populations in Clark County have been intensely studied (Kangas, Miller and Noll, 1980; Kangas and Palmer, 1982; Kofron and Schreiber, 1982); much of the natural history data for the subspecies has been gleaned from these study reports.

The Illinois mud turtle is normally active approximately 100 days during the warm season, with two periods of activity and feeding: April to mid-June, and early September to mid-October. When inactive, these turtles remain buried in loose sand at a depth of approximately 25.5 cm (10 inches). Overland movement is common during the active periods; most terrestrial activity takes place in early morning, evening and at night. Aquatic activity is primarily involved with locating available food. Turtles move into natural marshes or temporary flooded pools in search of prey. A study of Illinois mud turtle feeding habits revealed the following: snails 81 percent, insects 7 percent, fish 7 percent, crayfish 3 percent and freshwater mussels 2 percent (Kofron and Schreiber, 1982). Moll (1979) reported captive Illinois mud turtles were found to eat night crawlers while they were buried in an aquarium filled with moist sand.

Remarks: Both subspecies of *Kinosternon flavescens* are listed as endangered in *Rare and Endangered Species of Missouri*, published by the Missouri Department of Conservation in 1984.

A recent paper proposed that the Illinois mud turtle (*Kinosternon flavescens spooneri*) is not a valid subspecies, and indicated that it has a close affinity to the *K. flavescens* population in western Nebraska (Houseal, Bickham and Springer, 1982). Until more data is available, I prefer to recognize the original taxonomic name for the population in northeast Missouri.

Missouri Distribution: The yellow mud turtle is restricted to the extreme southwestern corner of Missouri (stippling); the Illinois mud turtle is restricted to the northeastern corner (hatch lines).

Adult male Mississippi mud turtle from Stoddard County.

Mississippi Mud Turtle
Kinosternon subrubrum hippocrepis (Gray)

Description: This is a small, dark turtle with yellow stripes along the side of the head and neck. The carapace is brown, dark brown or nearly black (especially when the shell is wet). The plastron is yellow-brown with brown extending along the margins of scutes and along the center. Exposed fleshy parts are normally gray-brown. On most specimens there are usually two yellow stripes along the side of the head and neck; they may appear as a series of spots rather than stripes. Small, irregular yellow spots may cover parts of the head and neck on lighter colored specimens. The ninth marginal scute on the carapace is not enlarged as in *Kinosternon flavescens*. Adult males can be distinguished from females by concave plastrons and by longer, thicker tails terminating in a clawlike process.

Adult Mississippi mud turtles range in carapace length from 75 to 121 mm (3 to 4 inches; Conant, 1975). Largest Missouri specimen recorded is 95 mm (3 11/16 inches; Powell *et al.*, 1982). Record size is 124 mm (4 7/8 inches; Conant, 1975).

Habits and Habitat: Although well equipped for an aquatic existence, this mud turtle spends as much time wandering about on land as it does in water. In a study of this turtle in Oklahoma, Mahmoud (1968) observed two daily activity periods from June through August; between 4 and 9 a.m., and again between 4:40 and 10 p.m. This species overwinters in mud at the bottom of ponds, oxbow lakes or swamps, or digs a burrow in soil or organic matter well away from water (Ernst and

Mississippi mud turtle plastron.

Barbour, 1972). A study in Illinois found that this species spent a considerable amount of time in underground burrows (Skorepa and Ozment, 1968). In Missouri, the Mississippi mud turtle probably enters its overwintering retreat in late October. This species is found in or near swamps, sloughs, oxbow lakes and canals. It is most often observed in shallow water and seems to avoid flowing rivers.

A wide variety of aquatic animals and plants is eaten. Mahmoud (1968) reported insects, crayfish, mussels and various amphibians were consumed by members of a population of *K. s. hippocrepis* studied in Oklahoma.

Breeding: Anderson (1965) observed a pair copulating in shallow water in Stoddard County on May 12. This species is presumed to breed from late April to early June. Females lay from one to six eggs. Mud turtles studied in Arkansas laid up to three clutches of eggs in one season (Iverson, 1979b). The eggs are normally laid in well drained sandy soil. Mississippi mud turtle eggs range in length from 22 to 30.5 mm (7/8 to 1 3/16 inches); incubation time averages 105 days (Iverson, *ibid.*). The eggs are elliptical, pinkish white and have a brittle, granular shell. Females were found to reach sexual maturity between six and eight years of age at a carapace length of between 80 to 85 mm (3 1/8 to 3 3/8 inches), while males mature at a carapace length of from 76.6 to 95.4 mm (3 to 3 3/4 inches; Iverson, 1979).

Remarks: Although the population of Mississippi mud turtles seems stable in Missouri, it is of utmost importance to preserve the natural habitats of this species, especially the remaining cypress swamps, oxbow lakes and sloughs.

Missouri Distribution: The Mississippi mud turtle is restricted to the counties of the Mississippi lowlands of southeastern Missouri. Anderson (1965) showed an isolated population in Jackson County near Kansas City which was probably introduced to the area. No specimens of this species have been reported from that area since his report.

Adult female stinkpot from Stone County.

Stinkpot
Sternotherus odoratus (Latreille)

Description: A very small, dark colored turtle with a domed upper shell and reduced lower shell. Carapace color is dark gray-brown to black. Plastron is much smaller than the carapace and the forward part is movable. It is usually yellow, brown or grayish yellow in color. The fleshy parts are dark gray or black. There are normally two distinct yellow stripes along each side of the head and neck. Small projections of the skin called "barbels" are present on the chin and throat. Adult males can be distinguished from females by longer, thicker tails ending in small, clawlike projections, and by the presence of broad fleshy areas along the center of the plastrons.

Adult stinkpots range in carapace length from 80 to 115 mm (3 1/4 to 4 1/2 inches; Conant, 1975). Largest Missouri specimen recorded is 117 mm (4 9/16 inches; Powell *et al.*, 1982). The record is 137 mm (5 3/8 inches; Conant, 1975).

Habits and Habitat: This species is most often observed in shallow water, but can also be seen basking on logs, rocks or small, horizontal tree trunks. The active season for the stinkpot probably lasts from March to November. This species was studied by Mahmoud (1968) in Oklahoma and found to be most active from 4 to 10:20 a.m. and from 5:40 to 9 p.m.

In Missouri, the stinkpot is most abundant in the rivers and larger streams of the Ozarks, the swamps and sloughs of the Bootheel, and in a few rivers in the northeast. Stinkpots overwinter in mud at the bottom of rivers or sloughs.

The food of this species includes aquatic insects, earthworms, crayfish, fish eggs, minnows, tadpoles, algae and dead animals (Ernst and Barbour, 1972). Fishermen occasionally catch stinkpots on a hook-and-line when using minnows, worms or crayfish for bait.

Adult male stinkpot from Stoddard County (left) *and male plastron* (right).

Breeding: Courtship and mating probably take place from late April through June. Eggs are laid in late June through August. From two to five eggs are laid per female. The eggs are white, small (averaging 27.6 mm long), and elliptical; they have a thick, brittle shell (Ernst and Barbour, 1972). It takes from two to three months for the eggs to hatch. At hatching the young turtles average 23 mm in carapace length (Risley, 1933).

Remarks: The name "stinkpot" refers to the odor given off by this species when captured. Musk glands are located along the sides in the skin just below their carapace (Johnson, 1979a).

Missouri Distribution: This species is found statewide except for the northern and northwestern third of the state.

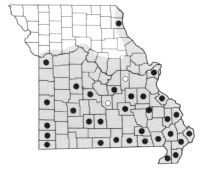

Family Emydidae

Basking, Marsh and Box Turtles

The family Emydidae is the largest living family of turtles in the world. It comprises 26 genera, containing more than 80 species. In general, turtles of this family are small to medium in size, and are adapted to a variety of habitats. This family includes a number of colorful species. Although the majority of species are aquatic, several kinds are either semi-aquatic, or have taken to life on land (i.e., box turtles).

In Missouri, this family is represented by 9 genera with a total of 11 species.

Three-toed Box Turtle

Adult western painted turtle from Clark County.

Western Painted Turtle
Chrysemys picta bellii (Gray)

Description: A small, brightly colored aquatic turtle with a smooth upper shell. General color is olive or olive-brown to nearly black. Carapace usually has irregular yellow lines; marginal scutes may have one or more yellow bars and a red-orange outer edge. Exposed skin is dark brown or black, and strongly patterned with yellow lines. Lines on neck and front legs can be orange or red. Plastron is yellow-orange or bright orange with a prominent pattern of brown markings. Adult male western painted turtles have longer foreclaws and longer, thicker tails than females.

Adult western painted turtles range in carapace length from 125 to 180 mm (5 to 7 inches; Conant, 1975). Largest Missouri specimen recorded is 203 mm (8 inches; Powell *et al.*, 1982). The record length is 251 mm (9 7/8 inches; Conant, 1975).

Habits and Habitat: This species is usually active from late March to October at air temperatures of 68°F or above (Collins, 1982). Painted turtles are active by day, and sleep during the night in pools or ponds. Daytime activity consists of alternately basking on logs and foraging in the water.

In Missouri, the western painted turtle may occur in slow-moving rivers, sloughs, oxbow lakes, ponds or drainage ditches, especially where there is ample mud at the bottom and abundant aquatic vegetation. Partly submerged logs, rocks or other objects on which the turtles can climb to bask are also required.

Western painted turtle plastron (left) *and western painted turtle hatchling from Henry County* (right).

Natural foods of this species include aquatic plants, snails, crayfish, insects and fish. Young painted turtles have been reported to eat more animal matter than adults (Ernst and Barbour, 1972).

Breeding: Courtship and mating take place in shallow water from April to June. Collins (1982) gave a detailed description of the courting ritual of this species: "Courtship starts with a slow pursuit of the female by the male. Upon catching up with her, the male faces her and strokes her head and neck with the backs of the long claws on his front limbs. The female responds by stroking his front limbs with the claws on her front feet. The male periodically swims away as if trying to entice the female to follow. After a period of time, the female sinks to the bottom and the male swims down and mounts on her back. He secures himself on her upper shell with his claws, curls his tail down under hers until their cloacal openings meet, and copulation occurs."

Females laden with eggs will leave the water and search for a suitable place to dig a hole and lay eggs. A south-facing, gentle slope with loose dirt or sand and some low vegetation is an ideal location for nesting. In Missouri, the western painted turtle will produce eggs from mid-May through July. Eggs of this species are elliptical, white and average 30 mm (1 3/16 inches) in length. From 4 to 20 eggs may be laid per female, and hatching normally takes place in 2 to 2 1/4 months (Collins, 1982). Newly hatched young remain underground until spring if the eggs were laid late in the summer (Vogt, 1981). Hatchling painted turtles average 33 mm (1 1/4 inches) in carapace length.

Subspecies: The southern painted turtle (*Chrysemys picta dorsalis* Agassiz) is a smaller geographic race of painted turtle that occurs in southeastern Missouri. The carapace is olive-brown to almost black with a prominent yellow, orange or red longitudinal stripe down the center. Outer edge of carapace is yellow or orange. Plastron is plain yellow; some specimens may have a faint brownish blotch along the center. Adult southern painted turtles have an upper shell length of 10 to 12.5 cm (4 to 5 inches). Record size is 15.6 cm (6 1/8 inches; Conant, 1975).

Southern painted turtle from Stoddard County (left) *and southern painted turtle plastron* (right).

This small, colorful turtle resides in the quiet water of shallow swamps, sloughs, oxbow lakes or drainage ditches. Behavior and natural history are similar to the western painted turtle. Average clutch size is four eggs (Moll, 1973). Anderson (1965) reported finding a freshly laid clutch of eggs on June 12, in New Madrid County. Six eggs were present, and they averaged 29 mm (1 3/16 inches) in length.

The small size of the southern painted turtle is possibly due to competition with a number of sympatric species. The reduced size allows these reptiles to utilize a niche which is usually not occupied by larger semi-aquatic species (Moll, 1973).

Remarks: Ewert (1979) reported finding a population of painted turtles in Washington County with some characteristics of the midland painted turtle (*Chrysemys picta marginata* Agassiz). Field work is needed in the Indian Creek drainage to determine the taxonomic status of this population.

Missouri Distribution: The western painted turtle occurs over most of Missouri; it is replaced by the southern painted turtle in the extreme southeastern corner (hatch lines).

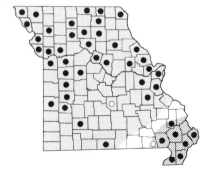

Adult western chicken turtle.

Western Chicken Turtle
Deirochelys reticularia miaria Schwartz

Description: A small to medium-size turtle with an oval shell and extremely long neck. Carapace may be light brown or olive, with faint, broad lines forming a netlike pattern. This species has a rather flattened appearance caused by the low, broad shape of the shell. Plastron is yellow with light brown markings along scute seams. Exposed skin is brown or black with numerous yellow or yellow-green stripes. Forelegs have a wide yellow stripe; rump has distinct vertical yellow stripes. Underside of head and neck of adults is plain yellow. Adult male western chicken turtles are smaller than females and have longer, thicker tails.

Adult western chicken turtles range in carapace length from 100 to 150 mm (4 to 6 inches; Conant, 1975). Largest Missouri specimen recorded is 202 mm (8 1/6 inches; Powell *et al.*, 1982). The record length is 254 mm (10 inches; Conant, 1975).

Habits and Habitat: The western chicken turtle is semi-aquatic; it spends nearly as much time wandering about on land as in the water. In Missouri, its active season is probably mid-March to October. This species will bask in the sun on partially submerged logs, often in association with other kinds of turtles.

Chicken turtles prefer still or slow moving aquatic habitats, including swamps, river sloughs, oxbow lakes and drainage ditches. This species takes shelter in mud at the bottom of pools to overwinter.

Plants and a variety of aquatic animals, including insects and crayfish, are presumably eaten by this species.

Western chicken turtle plastron.

Breeding: Little is known about the reproduction of this species. Courtship and mating presumably take place in water during spring and early summer. Anderson (1965) reported 12 eggs produced by a female collected in Butler County. Ernst and Barbour (1972) stated that from 5 to 15 eggs may be laid per female. They are laid in loose soil approximately 4 inches underground. The white eggs measure from 36.7 to 39.9 mm long (Anderson, 1965). Hatching probably takes place in late summer or early fall; hatchlings are about 29 mm (1 1/8 inches; Conant, 1975).

Remarks: The western chicken turtle was first reported in Missouri by Anderson (1957). Only a few specimens have been located since then; because of the low numbers and reduction of natural habitat in southeast Missouri, this turtle has been listed as rare on the Missouri rare and endangered species list.

Missouri Distribution: Extreme southeastern part of the state.

Adult Blanding's turtle from Clark County.

Blanding's Turtle
Emydoidea blandingii (Holbrook)

Description: Blanding's turtles are medium-size with an oval, moderately high-domed carapace, and a long head and neck. General color of carapace is dark brown or black with many yellow spots or bars. Plastron has a "hinge" across the forward third of the shell; it is brownish yellow with large brown or black blotches on the outer portions of each scute. Exposed skin is brown and yellow. Upper jaw may be covered with black pigment forming a "mustache." Underside of head and neck is bright yellow. Adult male Blanding's turtles can be distinguished from adult females by a longer, thicker tail that has the anal opening extending beyond the edge of the carapace, and by a slightly concaved plastron.

Adult Blanding's turtles range in carapace length from 125 to 190 mm (5 to 7 1/2 inches; Conant, 1975). Largest Missouri specimen recorded is 213 mm (8 5/16 inches; Kofron and Schreiber, 1982). The record is 268 mm (10 9/16 inches; Conant, 1975).

Habits and Habitat: This species is semi-aquatic; it spends a considerable amount of time in shallow water along the edge of marshes or ponds. Blanding's turtles bask on logs or muskrat houses; their yellow throats are visible for a considerable distance. When captured, a specimen will withdraw into its shell and close the forward part of the plastron tightly against the carapace. In Missouri, this species is active from late March to early October. It overwinters in mud at the bottom of marshes or ponds. Habitats used by this species include natural marshes and

Blanding's turtle plastron.

sloughs, ponds and drainage ditches. Abundant aquatic and emergent vegetation and a mud bottom are important habitat components.

A population of this species was studied in extreme northeastern Missouri (Kofron and Schreiber, 1982); some of the information that follows is from that study. This species was found to be more aquatic than reported in other states (Minton, 1972; Conant, 1975; Vogt, 1981). During the active season it feeds in two phases: between early April and mid-July, and again from mid-August through mid-September. The diet of Blanding's turtles in northeastern Missouri consisted of crayfish, aquatic larvae of insects, some terrestrial insects and frogs. A study of Michigan Blanding's turtles showed a similar diet (Lagler, 1943).

Breeding: Courtship and mating take place in April and early June. Vogt (1981) described breeding activity of Blanding's turtles observed in Wisconsin. Once a female is located in the water, a male will position himself behind the female and quickly mount her carapace. The male will stimulate the female by biting at her head and forelegs. During mating the male will expose his bright yellow throat in front of the female's head and wave it back and forth. The pair may remain together for several hours.

Females will move overland to select a nesting site with sandy, well drained soil and good exposure to the sun. The eggs are normally laid during June. A female produces from 6 to 15 cream colored, pliable eggs which average 24 by 38 mm (1 by 1 1/2 inches; Vogt, 1981). Hatching takes place in September; the newly emerged young average 31 mm in carapace length (1 1/4 inches). The tail of hatchlings is nearly as long as the length of the carapace.

Remarks: Anderson (1965) was the first to discover this species in Missouri. The Blanding's turtle is listed as endangered in Missouri due to a low population and reduced natural habitat.

Missouri Distribution: Extreme northeast and northwest corners of the state.

Adult female map turtle from Stone County.

Map Turtle

Graptemys geographica (Le Sueur)

Description: A medium-size aquatic turtle with a low ridge or dorsal keel, and marginal scales strongly serrated at the rear. Carapace may be brown or olive-brown with a netlike pattern of fine yellow lines, giving the shell the appearance of a road map. Plastron is light yellow; seams between scutes are dark brown. Exposed skin is brown with thin yellow stripes. A small yellow spot behind the eye may have one or two prongs that point toward the back, or may form a horizontal "V." Adult female map turtles are larger than males and have broad heads. Males have a longer, thicker tail than females.

Adult map turtles range in carapace length from 180 to 273 mm (7 to 10 3/4 inches; Conant, 1975). Largest Missouri specimen recorded is 227 mm (8 7/8 inches; Powell *et al.*, 1982).

Habits and Habitat: The active season of the map turtle normally begins in late March and lasts until October. This species is fond of basking in the sun on logs or other objects sticking out of the water. The slightest disturbance will cause it to dash into the water. Foraging for food takes place in early morning and late evening. Several authors have reported that map turtles remain active in winter, and have been seen swimming under the ice in rivers (Ernst and Barbour, 1972; Collins, 1982).

Rivers, sloughs and oxbow lakes are preferred habitats for map turtles, provided there is an abundance of basking sites, a mud bottom and adequate aquatic vegetation.

Map turtle plastron (left) *and map turtle nest with 12 eggs from Pulaski County* (right).

Map turtles eat molluscs, snails, crayfish and some insects. The jaws of females are adapted for cracking the shells of molluscs and snails.

Breeding: Courtship and mating take place in the water, probably from late March through May. This species has been observed breeding in autumn in other states (Ernst and Barbour, 1972). Female map turtles will leave the water and may move a considerable distance before locating a suitable site to lay their eggs. Nests may be dug along the edge of plowed fields, in patches of sand or in clay banks. In Missouri this species produces eggs from late May through early July. A freshly laid nest observed in Pulaski County on June 12 contained 12 eggs. From 10 to 16 eggs may be laid per female (Ernst and Barbour, 1972). The eggs are white, elliptical and are from 32 to 35 mm long. Hatching normally takes place in late summer or early autumn, or the young turtles may not hatch until the following spring. Hatchlings average 32 mm (1 1/4 inches) in carapace length.

Remarks: This river species has been declining in Missouri, possibly due to water pollution, siltation and unlawful shooting.

Missouri Distribution: Map turtles occur statewide except for extreme northern Missouri.

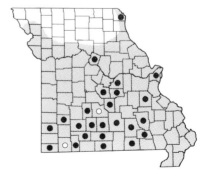

Adult female Mississippi map turtle.

Mississippi Map Turtle
Graptemys kohnii (Baur)

Description: Mississippi map turtles are medium in size, have a low keel along the center of the carapace, and the marginal scales along the rear of the carapace are strongly serrated. Carapace is brown or olive, with several narrow, light, connected circles on each large scale (vertebrals and pleurals). Plastron is greenish yellow with a pattern consisting of two or more light brown lines which follow each scute seam. This pattern may fade as the turtles grow older. Exposed skin is brown or greenish gray, with numerous yellow lines bordered by dark brown or black. The yellow marking behind each eye is crescent-shaped and runs from the bottom to the back of the eye to the top of the head. This marking prevents any of the thin yellow stripes on the side of the neck from reaching the eye. A close examination of the eyes of Mississippi map turtles will reveal a bright yellow ring with a round black pupil, giving the turtle a "wide-eyed" appearance. Adult females are larger than adult males, but males have longer foreclaws and a longer, thicker tail.

Adult female Mississippi map turtles range in carapace length from 150 to 254 mm (6 to 10 inches), and males from 90 to 127 mm (3 1/2 to 5 inches; Conant, 1975). Largest Missouri specimen recorded is 157 mm (6 3/16 inches; Powell *et al.*, 1982).

Habits and Habitat: In Missouri, the Mississippi map turtle is probably active from late March to mid-October. Very little is known about the life history of this species because of its shy nature. It will often bask

173

Head (left) *and plastron* (right) *of Mississippi map turtle.*

on logs or rocks, but will quickly drop off into the water at the slightest sign of danger. This aquatic species lives primarily in rivers, river sloughs and oxbow lakes; it prefers an abundance of basking sites and aquatic vegetation.

Both plant and animal matter are eaten by this species, including various aquatic plants, snails, aquatic insects, crayfish and possibly dead fish.

Breeding: Nothing is known about the reproductive biology of the Mississippi map turtle in this state. It is presumed that courtship and mating take place in the water, and that males use their long foreclaws to stimulate females. Eggs are laid on land. The number of eggs which are produced is not known.

Remarks: As with all our species of *Graptemys*, this turtle is on the decline, probably due to water pollution, river channelization, reduction of suitable nesting sites, siltation, and unlawful shooting. This species is known to hybridize with the false map turtle, causing a combination of characteristics and confusion when trying to identify them. Vogt (1981) decided to reclassify *Graptemys kohnii* as a subspecies of the false map turtle, *G. pseudogeographica*. I prefer to retain full species status for the Mississippi map turtle until a revision of this group is published.

Missouri Distribution: Presumed to be statewide in occurrence.

Adult male false map turtle.

False Map Turtle
Graptemys pseudogeographica pseudogeographica (Gray)

Description: This is a medium-size aquatic turtle with a prominent keel on the upper shell and yellow lines on the head, neck and legs. Carapace is brown or olive, with round or oval light markings and small dark blotches on each pleural scute. The dorsal keel is usually high and forms a low spine at the rear edge of each vertebral scute. Rear of carapace is strongly serrated. Plastron is plain yellow but may show dark lines along scute seams on young turtles. Exposed skin is brown or olive with numerous thin yellow lines. Yellow marking behind the eye extends upwards then backward, forming a backward "L." This marking allows up to three yellow neck stripes to reach the eye. Adult males are smaller than females and have a longer, thicker tail and long foreclaws.

Adult female false map turtles range in carapace length from 125 to 273 mm (5 to 10 3/4 inches) and males from 90 to 146 mm (3 1/2 to 5 3/4 inches; Conant, 1975). Largest Missouri specimen recorded is 123 mm (4 7/8 inches).

Habits and Habitat: The false map turtle may be active from late March to early October. Much time is devoted to basking in the sun during the day on logs projecting from the water. Feeding takes place in early morning. This species normally takes shelter in mud at the bottom of sloughs or lakes to overwinter, but may remain semi-active during mild winters in the southern third of the state.

This species occurs in slow moving rivers, river sloughs and oxbow lakes, lakes and reservoirs. An abundance of aquatic vegetation and basking sites is required by false map turtles.

False map turtle plastron.

Natural food includes insects, worms, crayfish, snails, dead fish and some aquatic plants (Ernst and Barbour, 1972).

Breeding: Courtship and breeding take place in the water, usually in the spring. The males use their long foreclaws to stimulate a female by stroking her head while swimming in front of her. As soon as the female sinks to the bottom the male will follow and mount her. Egg-laying begins in June and lasts through July, with from 6 to 13 eggs being produced per female. The white, elliptical, leathery eggs average 38.5 mm (1 1/2 inches) in length (Ernst and Barbour, 1972). Hatching takes place in late summer or early autumn; the young turtles average 33 mm (1 1/4 inches) in carapace length.

Ouachita map turtle plastron (left) *and head of Ouachita map turtle* (right).

Subspecies: This turtle has two geographic races or subspecies: the nominate race, the false map turtle, *Graptemys pseudogeographica pseudogeographica* (Gray), described above; and the Ouachita map turtle,

176

Adult female Ouachita map turtle from Stone County.

Graptemys pseudogeographica ouachitensis Cagle. A large area of inter-gradation exists between the two in northern Missouri so accurate identification is difficult. The major difference between the two subspecies is the shape of the yellow mark behind each eye. The false map turtle has a backward "L" mark; the Ouachita map turtle has a large rectangular or square mark as well as yellow spots under the eye and on the chin. Adult size is somewhat smaller than in the false map turtle. The natural history of the Ouachita map turtle is similar to that of the nominate race. Vogt (1981) elevated *G. p. ouachitensis* as a full species. I have retained the subspecies status until there is a published revision of the midwestern species of map turtles.

Remarks: The two races of *Graptemys pseudogeographica* are known to hybridize with the Mississippi map turtle.

Missouri Distribution: Statewide. Lack of sufficient specimens prevents delineation of the distribution of the two races in Missouri.

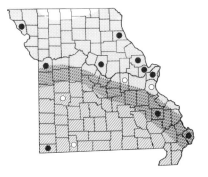

177

Adult Missouri River cooter from Stone County.

Missouri River Cooter
Pseudemys concinna metteri Ward

Description: The cooter is a medium-size aquatic turtle with a broad shell and numerous stripes on the head. The carapace is olive-brown, brown or nearly black, with numerous yellow lines or markings. The plastron is normally yellow; it may either be devoid of markings or have gray-brown markings along the scute seams—especially anteriorly. Exposed skin may be olive-brown or black with many yellow lines. Adult males can be told from adult females by their long foreclaws and large tails.

Adult cooters range in carapace length from 200 to 330 mm (9 to 13 inches). Largest Missouri specimen recorded is 300 mm (11 11/16 inches; Powell *et al.*, 1982). Record size is 324 mm (12 3/4 inches; Conant, 1975).

Habits and Habitat: This species spends a considerable amount of time basking on logs, and will quickly slide into the water at the slightest disturbance. Cooters actively forage during early morning or late afternoon.

This species is found in rivers and sloughs, but has also taken up residence in several of Missouri's large reservoirs.

Cooters are predominantly vegetarian. A wide variety of aquatic plants are consumed; several authors have reported that molluscs, crayfish and insects are also eaten (Ernst and Barbour, 1972).

Breeding: Courtship and mating take place in the water. The male will swim above the female and occasionally titillate the head of the female

Missouri River cooter plastron.

with rapid vibrations of his long foreclaws. If copulation ensues, the pair will sink to the bottom and remain there until completion. Egg-laying is presumed to take place in late May through June. Freshly laid eggs are elongated with a soft, pale pink, leathery shell. The eggs average about 39 mm (1 9/16 inches) in length. Up to 20 eggs are laid per female. Hatching normally takes place in late August or September (Ernst and Barbour, 1972).

Remarks: Ward (1984) re-evaluated the morphological features used to classify chrysemyd turtles (painted turtles, cooters and sliders) and proposed a new subspecies of *Pseudemys concinna*, the Missouri River cooter (*P. c. metteri*). I concur with his proposal, and until there is published evidence to the contrary, the name is herein applied to the Missouri population of the cooter.

Missouri Distribution: Presumed to occur throughout southern Missouri. The population in the southeastern corner is in an area of known intergradation between several subspecies of *Pseudemys concinna* (Ward, 1984); study is needed to determine taxonomic status.

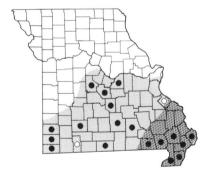

Adult male three-toed box turtle from St. Louis County.

Three-toed Box Turtle
Terrapene carolina triunguis (Agassiz)

Description: A small, terrestrial turtle with a high domed shell and normally three toes on each hind foot. There is usually a ridge along the center of the carapace. Color of carapace may be olive, or olive-brown with faint yellow or orange lines radiating from the center of each large scute. Plastron has a distinct single hinge across the forward third of the shell; it allows the turtle to tightly close the lower shell against the inside edge of the upper shell. Color of plastron is plain yellow, or yellow with brown smudges or lines which sometimes follow the scute seams. Exposed skin is dark brown or black; scales on the head and forelimbs may be yellow or orange. The entire head and portions of forelimbs of males are often bright orange. Although most specimens have three toes on each hind foot, some individuals may have four toes per hind foot. Most adult males can be distinguished from females by the greater amount of orange on the head and neck, thicker tail, slightly concaved plastron and red eyes. Adult females have a very small tail and most have yellow-brown eyes.

Adult three-toed box turtles range in carapace length from 115 to 145 mm (4 1/2 to 6 inches). Largest Missouri specimen recorded is 142 mm (5 5/8 inches; Powell *et al.*, 1982). Record length is 165 mm (6 1/2 inches; Conant, 1975).

Habits and Habitat: The three-toed box turtle was extensively studied by Schwartz and Schwartz (1974, 1984) in central Missouri; most of the following information is based on their work. In central Missouri, this

Three-toed box turtle plastron.

species generally becomes active soon after the last killing frost, between late March and late April. The turtles generally enter overwintering retreats shortly after the first killing frost of autumn, usually between mid-September and early November.

Daily activity begins with a period of feeding followed by basking in the sun in an open area. In warm weather, box turtles will crawl into a clump of dense grass or dead leaves and rest. Early evening activity usually consists of searching for a suitable site to retreat for the night.

The central Missouri population studied by Schwartz and Schwartz showed a habitat preference for mature, oak-hickory forests with numerous openings and edge areas along brushy fields. Home range of adults varied from 1.8 to 4.9 acres (5 adults studied). Reagan (1974) studied a population in Arkansas, and noticed a seasonal shift in habitat use from grasslands in late spring and early autumn to wooded areas in the summer, early spring and late autumn. The use of grasslands by the box turtles coincided with mild temperatures and high moisture conditions. The turtles' inability to dig deep enough into leaf litter and soil during cold weather may cause a high incidence of winter mortality. Although very young turtles probably make up a sizable portion of a population, their secretiveness causes them to seem scarce.

Food habits of the three-toed box turtle change as the turtle matures. Young turtles eat mostly insects and earthworms, but older turtles eat a proportionately larger amount of plant matter, including berries, mushrooms and young shoots of various plants and grasses. Adults will occasionally consume earthworms and insects.

Breeding: Courtship and mating of the three-toed box turtle last from late April until late June or early July, but may be observed in late summer. According to Ernst and Barbour (1972), a male courts a female by standing a few inches away from her, holding his head high and pulsating his orange colored throat. When the female moves closer to him, he begins to stimulate her by mounting her shell while he scratches with all four legs. He may nip at the forward part of her shell, then move backward and rest his carapace on the ground, at which time breeding takes place.

In Missouri most egg-laying probably takes place from mid-May to early July. A female will select an elevated, open patch of loose soil or sand and dig a 3 to 4 inch hole with her hind legs. This usually begins at dusk and the eggs are laid at night. From three to eight elongated white eggs may be laid by a female; the eggs are from 29 to 40 mm (1 3/16 to 1 9/16 inches) in length (Ernst and Barbour, 1972). The baby turtles hatch in about three months, but eggs laid late in the summer will not hatch until the following spring. A hatchling will have a carapace length of from 30 to 33 mm (1 3/16 to 1 1/4 inches). Hatchling three-toed box turtles have a flatter carapace compared to adults and a distinct dorsal ridge The carapace is brownish gray and there is a yellow spot on each large scute. Young box turtles are unable to close their plastron to protect themselves.

Female box turtles have the ability to store viable sperm and produce fertilized eggs up to four years after mating.

Remarks: Box turtle eggs and young are eaten by skunks, raccoons and badgers. The primary causes of death in adults are extreme cold and man. Thousands of these reptiles are killed annually while crossing roads and highways.

Many box turtles are captured by people on weekend outings and taken home to be kept in a basement to "control bugs." Such captive conditions are in direct conflict with the biological needs of these turtles; they may slowly starve to death or grow abnormal shells, claws and beaks. These reptiles are an interesting part of outdoor Missouri and should not be kept in captivity.

Missouri Distribution: Statewide except for extreme northern and northwestern sections of the state.

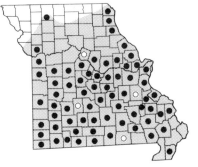

Adult male ornate box turtle from Pettis County.

Ornate Box Turtle
Terrapene ornata ornata (Agassiz)

Description: A small terrestrial turtle with a domed carapace and hinged plastron which allows it to close its shell. The carapace has a flattened appearance along the dorsal surface, and normally has no ridge. The upper shell is brown with numerous yellow lines radiating from the center of each scute. A mid-dorsal yellow stripe is often present. The plastron is brown with distinct yellow radiating lines. Exposed skin is gray-brown with faint yellow spots or blotches; the chin and upper jaw are yellow. There are normally four toes on each hind leg. Adult male ornate box turtles are smaller than females and have a concave plastron, enlarged and inward-facing first toe of the hind legs, and red eyes. The eye of a female is yellowish brown.

Adult ornate box turtles range in carapace length from 100 to 125 mm (4 to 5 inches). Largest Missouri specimen recorded is 124 mm (4 15/16 inches; Powell *et al.*, 1982). The record length is 146 mm (5 3/4 inches; Conant, 1975).

Habits and Habitat: In Missouri the ornate box turtle is active between late March and mid-October. In Kansas, the onset of warm, rainy weather will bring this species out of overwintering retreats (Legler, 1960). Daily activity consists of basking for a short period soon after sunrise, followed by a period of foraging for food, a rest period during the heat of the day, and a short feeding session before entering a shallow burrow or "form" for the night. During the hot, dry days of mid- to late summer, these turtles are generally inactive, but will appear in

Ornate box turtle plastron.

numbers after a heavy rain. Ornate box turtles will take shelter in clumps of grass, bury themselves in loose soil or sand, or enter the burrows made by other animals. They will escape the cold temperatures of winter by burrowing down below the frost line which may be 18 inches or more; those which take shelter in a wooded area may not burrow as deeply.

This species is primarily an inhabitant of prairies and open brushy areas; it may be found in pastures, open woods and on cedar glades. Legler (1960) found that an individual turtle may have a home range comprising about five acres. His study area had a population density of at least one turtle per acre. Rose (1978) found a density of two adult turtles per acre in east central Kansas.

This species is primarily insectivorous, with grasshoppers, beetles and caterpillars comprising nearly 90 percent of their diet. Berries—especially mulberries—are also eaten, as well as other plant material (Ernst and Barbour, 1974).

Breeding: In his study of this species in Kansas, Legler (1960) noted that males are mature at a plastron length of 100 to 109 mm (4 to 4 1/4 inches) at an age of eight to nine years. Females were found to be mature at a plastron length of 110 to 119 mm (4 3/8 to 4 15/16 inches) at an age of 10 to 11 years. Blair (1976) studied this species in Texas and found that males mature at age seven and females at eight years. The oldest specimen Blair found was 32 years old and he discovered that the population had an almost complete turnover every 32 years. Blair concluded that it is improbable that the ornate box turtle could normally live to 100 years of age.

Courtship and mating are most common in the spring. Breeding activity tapers off during the summer, but may be observed during early autumn. A courting male will nip at the edge of the upper shell of a female for a short time, then mount her from behind and clasp onto her carapace with his forelegs. The male's hind legs grasp the female's plastron, her hind legs wrap around his, and breeding commences. The pair may remain in this position for up to two hours.

A female ready to lay her clutch of eggs locates an exposed area with loose soil or sand, digs a shallow hole with her hind legs and deposits her eggs. From two to eight elongated, white eggs may be laid per female. The eggs are carefully covered with dirt and left to incubate. Usually, only one clutch is produced per female, but up to a third of the females in a population may lay a second clutch (Collins, 1982). Eggs of the ornate box turtle average 36.06 mm in length (Legler, 1960). The eggs normally hatch in two or three months. The hatchlings average 30 mm in carapace length.

Remarks: See the Remarks section of the three-toed box turtle account.

Missouri Distribution: Statewide except for the southeast corner. This species is more common in the northern and western parts of the state.

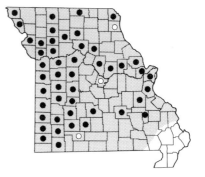

Young red-eared slider from Clark County.

Red-eared Slider
Trachemys scripta elegans (Wied)

Description: The red-eared slider is a medium-size aquatic turtle with a patch of red on each side of the head. Carapace is olive-brown with numerous black and yellow lines. Plastron is yellow, with each scute normally having a large dark brown or black blotch. Exposed skin is dark green with narrow black and yellow lines. A wide red or orange stripe is present on each side of the head behind the eye. Old specimens sometimes have an excess of black pigment which obscures most of the yellow stripes on skin and shell, including the red stripe behind the eye. This condition is known as "melanism" and is associated with old males. Adult male red-eared sliders have longer, thicker tails, longer foreclaws and smaller shells than females.

Adult red-eared sliders range in carapace length from 125 to 200 mm (5 to 8 inches). Largest Missouri specimen recorded is 251 mm (10 inches; Powell *et al.*, 1982). Record length is 279 mm (11 inches; Conant, 1975).

Habits and Habitat: This turtle becomes active in March, when the air temperature reaches 50° F or higher, and remains active until mid-October. Foraging takes place in early morning and late afternoon. On sunny days, basking in the sun on logs or other objects projecting from the water begins in mid-morning and generally lasts until mid-afternoon. At night, red-eared sliders will sleep while resting on the bottom, or floating on the surface. Both aquatic plants and animals are eaten.

This species may be found in a wide variety of aquatic habitats, but prefers a mud bottom, plenty of aquatic plants and abundant basking

Melanistic male red-eared slider from Stone County.

sites. Both natural waters (rivers, sloughs, oxbow lakes) and man-made waters (ponds and reservoirs) are utilized by this turtle.

Breeding: Courtship and mating take place between mid-March and mid-June. Several authors have stated that this species breeds in autumn (Cagle, 1950; Anderson, 1965; Collins, 1974). The courtship ritual is similar to that of the painted turtle. Females ready to lay their eggs leave the water and search for a suitable egg-laying site. A clutch of 4 to 20 eggs are laid per female between April and mid-July. Some females may lay more than one clutch during a season (Anderson, 1965). The eggs are oval with a white, granular shell; they average from 23.5 to 44.2 mm in length.

Hatching usually takes place in late summer or early autumn, but young turtles may occasionally overwinter in the egg and hatch the following spring. Newly hatched young average between 20 and 35 mm in length (Cagle, 1950).

Red-eared slider plastron (left) *and hatchling red-eared slider from Washington County* (right).

187

Remarks: For many years red-eared sliders were placed in the genus *Pseudemys*. Ward (1984) studied numerous morphological characteristics of painted turtles, cooters and sliders and proposed a revision of their classification. He concluded that the red-eared turtle was distinct and belonged in a separate genus; he resurrected the generic name *Trachemys*. I have followed Ward's proposed use of *Trachemys* for the red-eared slider.

Prior to 1970, millions of baby red-eared sliders were sold as pets, most of them dying due to lack of proper care. The sale of these turtles was curtailed because of possible *Salmonella* contamination which could be transmitted to children by handling the turtles or the water in which they were kept.

Missouri Distribution: Statewide except for a few counties in the extreme northern and northwestern sections.

Family Trionychidae
Softshells

Softshells occur in Asia, Africa and North America. The family has 22 species in seven genera. Only one genus, with three species, occurs in the U.S. External characteristics which separate turtles in this family from others include: a round, flat appearance; carapace and plastron covered with skin; lack of any scutes; a long, tubular snout; and extensive webbing on both front and hind limbs.

Missouri has two species of softshells. These turtles live primarily in rivers, but are also known to occur in large reservoirs. The lack of protection caused by the soft shell and the absence of scutes is compensated by strong jaws and a fast striking ability. Softshells also use their strong, sharp claws to defend themselves when picked up. Live softshells should be handled very carefully to avoid injury.

These turtles are classified as game species in Missouri. The Missouri Department of Conservation regulates a season and bag limit on them. The meat of softshells is delicious—these reptiles are economically valuable as a human food source.

Young Western Spiny Softshell

Adult male midland smooth softshell from Kansas. Photo by Joseph T. Collins.

Midland Smooth Softshell
Trionyx muticus muticus Le Sueur

Description: This is a rather plain-looking member of the softshell group. The front of the carapace lacks any small bumps or spines, and the overall shell is quite smooth. The carapace may be olive-gray or brown; males and young may have faint markings in the form of dots and dashes. Adult females have a mottled carapace with blotches of gray, olive or brown. Plastron is cream colored and lacks any markings but the underlying bones are usually visible. Upper surfaces of neck and limbs are olive or gray; underside is light gray or cream. A light line bordered by black extends backward from each eye along sides of head. Adult males are smaller, have a longer, thicker tail and longer foreclaws than females. Females have longer hindclaws.

Adult female midland smooth softshells range in carapace length from 180 to 356 mm (7 to 14 inches); males 125 to 178 mm (5 to 7 inches; Conant, 1975). Largest Missouri specimen recorded is 197 mm (8 inches; Powell *et al.*, 1982).

Habits and Habitats: The midland smooth softshell is active from early April to mid-October. It is more aquatic than other softshells and does not bask in the sun as often as other turtles. If a smooth softshell emerges to bask, it will usually do so on a sandbar or mud flat. The slightest disturbance will cause it to dash into the water for protection. Softshells actively search for food during the morning and late evening. When resting they will bury themselves in mud or sand in shallow water with only the head and neck exposed. Air is taken in by protruding the

190

Head of smooth softshell. Photo by Joseph T. Collins.

tip of the snorkel-like snout out of the water. In this manner the turtles are inconspicuous. These turtles can also remain submerged and carry on gaseous exchange from the water by pumping water in and out of the mouth and the cloaca.

Softshells protect themselves from freezing weather by burying themselves in the mud at the bottom of river pools.

This species is primarily carnivorous; it feeds on fish, crayfish, salamanders, tadpoles, frogs, snails and aquatic insects (Ernst and Barbour, 1972). Plummer and Farrar (1981) reported on a study of the food habits of smooth softshells in eastern Kansas. Male and female turtles were found to differ significantly in types of food eaten. Up to 71 percent (by volume) of prey eaten by females consisted of aquatic insect larvae captured in deep water. Male turtles consumed terrestrial insects (67 percent by volume) located in shallow water near shore.

Breeding: Smooth softshells breed in April and May. Autumn breeding has also been reported in this species. Females are sexually mature at a carapace length of from 170 to 220 mm at the age of six to seven years. The smaller males mature at a carapace length of 110 to 126 mm (Ernst and Barbour, 1972). During the breeding season a male will rapidly swim after a female with his neck extended. He will occasionally probe the underside of her shell on either side with his head. If the female is receptive, she will become quiet and the male will mount her from above (Collins, 1982).

Egg-laying takes place from late May through June. The number of eggs produced depends on the size of the female. From 4 to 33 eggs have been reported, with an average clutch of 18 to 22 eggs. A female will select a sandbank, sandbar or river island on which to dig her nest—always in direct sunlight (Ernst and Barbour, 1972). The eggs may take up to 2 1/2 months to hatch. Hatchlings average about 3.2 to 4.4 cm (1 1/4 to 1 3/4 inches) in carapace length (Conant, 1975). Young of this species are olive with distinct dots and short lines covering the carapace.

Remarks: A comparative study of the forage habits of smooth and spiny softshells was undertaken in Iowa (Williams and Christiansen, 1981). It was found that spiny softshells are less specialized in their habitat requirements than smooth softshells. Spiny softshells searched for food on the bottom, while smooth softshells located food in the water column.

Softshells are considered a game species in Missouri; they have a season and daily bag limit. In recent years, softshells have been on the decline in a number of midwestern states. A survey is needed to determine population status in Missouri. Channelization of rivers, siltation and water pollution contribute to a declining population of these fast-swimming, river-dwelling reptiles.

Although nearly any species of fish may be preyed upon by soft-shells, there is no evidence to show they harm a fish population in natural waters. Smooth softshells seldom attempt to bite when captured.

Missouri Distribution: The midland smooth softshell is presumed to occur statewide.

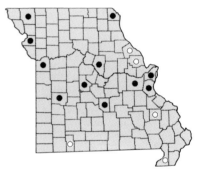

192

Adult eastern spiny softshell from Stoddard County.

Eastern Spiny Softshell
Trionyx spinifer spinifer Le Sueur

Description: The eastern spiny softshell is a medium to large turtle with dark spots on front and hind limbs, a small ridge on each side of the snorkel-like snout, and small bumps or spines on the front of the carapace. Color of the carapace varies with sex and age. Young females and males of any age have an olive or grayish-tan carapace with a black line along the margin and distinct small black dots and circles. The circular markings (known as *ocelli*) may have a dark center. Adult females have a dark olive or tan carapace with brown and gray blotches. Spiny softshells have a plain, cream colored plastron; underlying bones can be seen through the skin. Upper surface of the head, neck and limbs are tan or olive with small brown or black markings. A yellowish stripe, bordered by dark brown, extends from the snout through each eye, and along the sides of the head. Another light stripe runs from the angle of the jaw onto the neck.

Adult males are smaller than females; they also have dark spots and small bumps on the carapace and a large, thick tail with the anal opening well beyond the edge of the shell.

Adult female spiny softshells range in carapace length from 180 to 432 mm (7 to 17 inches); males from 125 to 235 mm (5 to 9 1/4 inches; Conant, 1975). Largest Missouri specimen recorded is 219 mm (8 15/16 inches; Powell *et al.*, 1982).

Habits and Habitat: The eastern spiny softshell is active between March and October. Daily activity includes foraging for food in early morning,

Head of eastern spiny softshell (left) and spiny softshell egg from Cole County (right).

basking in the sun on logs or along the bank, and resting in shallow water with the shell covered by mud or sand. There is a short period of feeding during the evening which may extend into the night. Spiny softshells have a habit of floating near the surface in deep water, but will quickly dive to safety with the slightest disturbance.

To escape the cold temperatures of winter, this species will dig two to four inches into the mud at the bottom of a river or lake (Ernst and Barbour, 1972).

The eastern spiny softshell resides in large rivers and streams as well as lakes and large ponds. A muddy or sandy bottom is preferred.

This species eats a variety of aquatic animal life including crayfish, insects, snails, fish, tadpoles and salamanders.

Breeding: Male spiny softshells become sexually mature at a carapace length of from 9 to 10 cm (3 5/8 to 4 inches); females are probably mature when their carapace reaches from 18 to 20 cm (7 1/8 to 7 7/8 inches; Webb, 1962). Courtship and mating occur in April and May. The courtship behavior is probably similar to that of the smooth softshell (Collins, 1982).

Eggs are laid from late May to July. A gravid female will select a sand or gravel bar, or a sandy opening near water to nest. From 4 to 32 round, white eggs may be laid, depending on the size of the female (Ernst and Barbour, 1972). Anderson (1965) reported 19 eggs taken from a female spiny softshell which was caught by fishermen on July 2. Eggs of this species average about 28 mm in diameter (Ernst and Barbour, 1972). Hatching occurs from late August to October. The young turtles are from 30 to 40 mm in carapace length at hatching.

Subspecies: Two subspecies of *Trionyx spinifer* occur in Missouri: the nominate race, the eastern spiny softshell (*Trionyx spinifer spinifer* Le Sueur) described above, and the western spiny softshell (*Trionyx spinifer hartwegi* Conant & Goin). The western spiny softshell has small *ocelli* along the center of the carapace. The eastern spiny softshell has *ocelli* which are much larger along the center of the carapace. The natural history of the western subspecies is similar to that of the eastern spiny softshell.

Remarks: See Remarks section in the account of the smooth softshell. Spiny softshells are ill-tempered and will try to bite when captured.

Missouri Distribution: The eastern spiny softshell is found in eastern Missouri; it is replaced by the western spiny softshell in the western half of the state. There is a broad area of intergradation between the two subspecies through the center of the state.

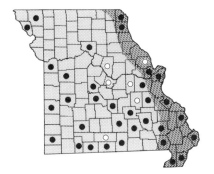

Lizards and Snakes

(Order Squamata)

Lizards

(Suborder Sauria)

Because lizards and snakes have a number of similar characteristics, the two types of reptiles are grouped into one order (Squamata), and placed in separate suborders (Sauria. lizards; Serpentes: snakes) Nearly 95 percent of the reptile species residing on earth today are lizards and snakes.

Scientists today recognize a total of 3,307 species of lizards. There are lizards on every continent, except Antarctica. Today's lizards are grouped into 17 families which have been divided into 363 genera (Duellman, 1979). The general conception of lizards as a group is an animal with four legs, a long tail, eyelids, ear openings, scales and claws, and the capability of quick movement. Although this description may fit the majority of Missouri's lizards, it fails to describe many found elsewhere. Some lizards, for example, have no legs—such as our slender glass lizard (*Ophisaurus attenuatus*). There are many tropical lizards, known as geckos, which have no eyelids—the eyes are instead protected by a clear, nonmovable eye cap. Some lizards, like the horned lizard (*Phrynosoma*) have very short tails.

The lower jaw of both lizards and snakes are attached to the upper jaw by a special bone, known as the quadrate bone, which allows the jaw to open wide when large prey is being swallowed.

Many lizards have also evolved special tail vertebrae which enable the tail to be easily broken off if grabbed by a predator. This is an effective means of self-defense. There are special muscles along the tail which constrict at the break and prevent any blood loss. A new tail will eventually replace the broken section, but will not have the same color or scale pattern as the original tail. The regenerated tail is supported by a fibrous rod rather than vertebrae. Most of Missouri's lizards have the ability to lose their tails to escape a predator. The Texas horned lizard (*Phrynosoma cornutum*) has a very short tail which does not break off when grabbed.

There are only two species of lizards in the world that are venomous. One species, the Gila monster (*Heloderma suspectum*), occurs in the southwestern United States and Sonora, Mexico. The other venomous species, the beaded lizard (*H. horridum*) is found in western Mexico and northern Central America.

Missouri has ten species of lizards. These are classified into four separate families. Missouri's lizards are nonvenomous and beneficial because they eat a variety of insects.

Family Iguanidae

Iguanid Lizards

This is the largest lizard group in the western hemisphere, with 628 species currently recognized. The family is primarily New World, but some iguanid lizards are found in Madagascar and Polynesia. Although the majority of species are small to medium-size, some are large—such as the common green iguana (*Iguana iguana*) of Central and South America, which may grow to over 6 feet (1.82 meters) in total length. This large lizard is used as human food in many tropical American countries. The majority of smaller members of the family are insect eaters, but several large species like the green iguana, Galapogos land iguana and marine iguana, are *herbivorous*.

General characteristics of the family Iguanidae include teeth located on the inner surface of the lower jaw, and a form of communication employing head bobbing and body pushups. Males use these gestures to defend small territories or court a female. Lizards in this family defend themselves by biting and scratching.

Missouri has three species of iguanids representing three genera. The most common is the northern fence lizard (*Sceloporus undulatus hyacinthinus*).

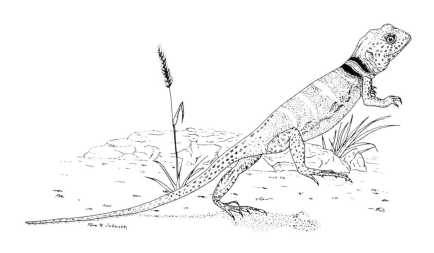

Eastern Collared Lizard

Adult male eastern collared lizard from Taney County.

Eastern Collared Lizard
Crotaphytus collaris collaris (Say)

Description: A colorful, long-tailed lizard with a large head. Color is most conspicuous on males during the breeding season (May and June); general ground color is tan, yellow, green or bluish green. There are usually a number of small light spots scattered over the upper body and legs and dark bands across the dorsum. Both males and females have two dark brown or black irregular lines across the neck producing a "collar." Females are yellowish tan or light brown with faint light spots. Females heavy with eggs have red spots or bars on sides of body and neck (Conant, 1975). Newly hatched young have dark bands and yellowish crossbars (see photo).

Adult eastern collared lizards range in total length from 200 to 356 mm (8 to 14 inches; Conant, 1975). Largest Missouri specimen recorded is 296 mm (11 3/4 inches; Powell *et al.*, 1982).

Habits and Habitat: As with all lizards found in Missouri, the eastern collared lizard is active by day, especially when the weather is sunny and warm. The preferred air temperature for this species is between 73° and 93°F (Collins, 1982). Seasonal activity lasts from April to September, but young lizards may remain active until October (Collins, 1982). A great deal of time is spent basking in the sun on exposed rocks, but these lizards are quick to take shelter under large rocks or in rock crevices when approached. If caught in an open area, a collared lizard can run very fast to escape; it will often run on its hind legs with the forward part of the body held upright. Each lizard defends a home

Adult female eastern collared lizard (left), *and a hatchling eastern collared lizard* (right), *both from Miller County.*

territory by chasing away other collared lizards when a territory is violated. The bright colors of males are used to ward off other males from invading an individual home range.

Collared lizards overwinter in burrows at depths of 20.3 to 30.5 cm (8 to 12 inches) under large rocks (Collins, 1982).

In Missouri the eastern collared lizard lives among rocks on dry, open, south or southwest-facing cedar glades. Limestone, sandstone and granite glades are used.

Collared lizards eat a variety of insects such as grasshoppers, beetles and moths. They also eat spiders, small snakes and lizards.

Breeding: Courtship and mating of this lizard take place from mid-May to early June. An adult male will court a female by showing off his brightly colored throat and body as he prances around her. This is normally followed by the male walking around and over the female, bobbing his head up and down as he moves. If the female is willing to mate, the male will mount her back, grasp a few folds of her neck skin in his mouth, and move the rear part of his body beneath her tail, at which time copulation takes place. From 2 to 21 creamy-white, leathery eggs are laid by a female. Egg-laying usually takes place within 20 days after breeding; eggs are laid in a burrow beneath a large rock (Fitch, 1956b; Collins, 1982). Hatching takes place within two to three months and the hatchlings average 8.9 cm (3 1/2 inches; Conant, 1975) in total length.

Remarks: A popular common name for this lizard is the "mountain boomer." This name probably originated in the southwestern United States, where settlers may have *seen* the lizard on rocks while *hearing* the barking call of a local frog species. In reality, the collared lizard is voiceless (Johnson, 1978).

This species is preyed upon by snakes, hawks and, in southwestern Missouri, by roadrunners.

Missouri Distribution: The eastern collared lizard is found throughout most of the Missouri Ozarks and on glades of the St. Francois Mountains. Populations in Boone and Callaway counties are probably introduced.

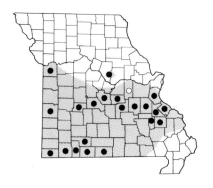

Adult Texas horned lizard.

Texas Horned Lizard
Phrynosoma cornutum (Harlan)

Description: A stocky, short-tailed lizard with several large "horns" protruding from the back of the head. General color is tan, grayish brown or reddish brown. There are two large, dark brown spots behind the head and a series of brown markings on the back. A white or yellowish line extends down the center of the back. Scales on the legs, sides and tail are large and pointed; the head is heavily armored with large scales, some modified to form "horns." The belly is white with several small gray spots.

Adult Texas horned lizards range in total length from 60 to 100 mm (2 1/2 to 4 inches); record length is 181 mm (7 1/8 inches; Conant, 1975).

Habits and Habitat: This species is active by day, as long as the sun is out and the temperature is high. The active season is from April to September. When inactive, the Texas horned lizard seeks shelter just below the surface of the soil. This lizard is best observed during sunny mornings when it basks in open areas.

Horned lizards eat ants primarily, but other insects and spiders may occasionally be eaten. Because of its specialized diet and need for high temperatures, this species is very difficult to keep in captivity.

Texas horned lizards prefer open, dry areas with sandy soil or an abundance of rocks.

Breeding: Very little is known about the courtship and breeding of the Texas horned lizard. Breeding presumably takes place soon after the active season begins, but courtship has not been observed. An average of 22 eggs are laid in loose soil (Collins, 1982). Incubation may take from one to two months. Hatchlings are from 2.9 to 3.2 cm (1 1/8 to 1 1/4 inches; Conant, 1975) in total length.

Remarks: This is the only species of lizard native to Missouri that is not capable of breaking off its tail when grabbed.

The Texas horned lizard has the unusual habit of squirting a few drops of blood from the corners of its eyes when captured. Basking lizards have been observed emitting a small amount of blood from the eyes when the lizard's head becomes warmer than the rest of the body (Collins, 1982).

Missouri Distribution: This lizard is known to occur in southwestern Missouri.

Adult female northern fence lizard from Cole County.

Northern Fence Lizard
Sceloporus undulatus hyacinthinus (Green)

Description: A small, brown, rough-scaled species that resides in wood-lands. General color may be tan, gray, brown or reddish brown. Like collared lizards, male and female northern fence lizards differ in color. Males are either dark gray or brown on the dorsum with little or no pattern. The belly is strongly marked with deep, iridescent blue bordered with black. The throat is also blue. Females have distinct wavy lines crossing the dorsum, some orange or red at the base of the tail and a white belly with faint dark spots. There may be some pale blue color along the sides of the belly.

Adult northern fence lizards range in total length from 100 to 184 mm (4 to 7 1/4 inches). Largest Missouri specimen recorded is 167 mm (6 5/8 inches; Powell *et al.*, 1982).

Habits and Habitat: This species becomes active on sunny days, usually basking in the sun or foraging for insects between 8 a.m. and 1 p.m. It becomes inactive during the heat of the day, then active again during the late afternoon and evening. The seasonal activity of this species is normally from late March to mid-October. Males defend a small territory which may include two or three adult females. When encountered, this lizard will run along a dead, fallen tree, escape into a rock crevice, or quickly climb a tree—always remaining on the opposite side from the intruder.

A wide variety of insects and spiders is eaten by this species.

Male northern fence lizard showing ventral coloration.

In Missouri, northern fence lizards live in open forests or along the edges of woods and fields. Tree stumps, downed trees, rock piles and brushpiles are often a part of this lizard's territory. Rough, split rail fences, firewood piles, old lumber piles and decorative railroad ties are readily utilized by this species.

Northern fence lizard nest containing 15 eggs (left), *and northern fence lizards hatching from eggs* (right), *both from Cole County.*

Breeding: Courtship and mating may take place between April and August, with females producing two egg clutches. A male will approach a female by bobbing its head and performing pushups. Mating occurs when the female allows the male to approach her. From 4 to 17 eggs are produced per female.

The reproductive biology of this species has been studied in eastern Missouri (Marion, 1970). The study showed that females are capable of producing eggs when less than one year old, but only one clutch of eggs is laid the first season. Two-year-old females produce two clutches per season and are the major contributors to the population. There was no indication that any females laid a third clutch of eggs in the eastern Missouri population. The first clutch is laid during late May or early June, and another produced in July. All the eggs hatch during August. A gravid female will locate a suitable nesting site such as a small patch of loose dirt, and dig a flask-shaped hole. On May 26, 1980, I observed a large female digging a hole in an open area in Cole County. The spot was visited the next morning and 15 eggs were discovered in the nest. The eggs were deposited in five layers containing three eggs each, and each layer of eggs was covered with a small amount of dirt. The nest was 8.3 cm (3 1/4 inches) deep. The eggs were between 11.5 and 13 mm in length (average 12.2 mm) and were collected and incubated at an average temperature of 80° F. Hatching took place 52 days later (July 17). Total length of hatchlings was between 4.6 and 4.9 cm (1 9/16 and 1 15/16 inches).

Sexton and Marion (1974) made some valuable observations on egg retention in this species. They reported that when the second clutch of eggs is delayed by being retained in the female, the incubation time is shortened; this allows the young to hatch sooner and have time to grow before the first frost. According to Marion (1970) few fence lizards live longer than three years under natural conditions.

Missouri Distribution: This abundant lizard is found throughout the southern half of the state and into northeastern Missouri among the Mississippi River hills.

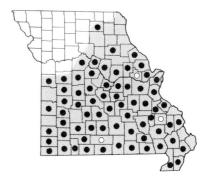

Family Scincidae
Skinks

This is a large group of lizards, with species found on nearly every continent. There are over 1,280 species worldwide, representing about 87 genera. The smallest species may be a mere 3 inches long; the largest (found in Australia) may reach a length of over 2 feet. The majority of species have smooth, overlapping scales, and live either on or under the ground. Three genera, containing a total of 15 species, occur in the United States. Missouri skinks are represented by two genera, with a total of five species. All our skinks have the ability to quickly break off their tails if grasped by a predator. A new tail will be regenerated, but is usually dull gray-brown in color.

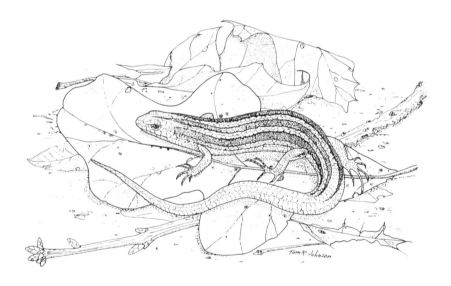

Female Five-lined Skink

Adult southern coal skink from Cole County.

Southern Coal Skink
Eumeces anthracinus pluvialis Cope

Description: The southern coal skink is a small, shiny, brownish lizard with broad, dark lateral stripes. General color is tan, brown or olive-brown. The lateral stripe can be brown or black; it is bordered by a thin light line above and below, and ranges from 2 1/2 to 4 scales wide. There are no light stripes on the head. The chin normally has a single post-mental scale, but some Missouri specimens have two post-mentals (Smith, 1956; Nickerson, pers. comm.).

During the breeding season, adult males can be distinguished from adult females by the presence of dark orange on the sides of the head. Hatchling southern coal skinks are black with faint dorsolateral lines and an overall length of 48 mm (1 7/8 inches; Conant, 1975).

Adult southern coal skinks range in total length from 130 to 178 mm (5 to 7 inches; Conant, 1975). Largest Missouri specimen recorded is 166 mm (6 5/8 inches; Powell *et al.*, 1982).

Habits and Habitat: This shy lizard becomes active mid-morning on sunny days, but will quickly take shelter in dead leaves or under rocks or logs when approached. The active season of coal skinks is from late March to mid-September.

This species occurs in forests near streams, rivers or sloughs, and seems to prefer open, damp, rock-strewn woods where it takes shelter under logs, bark, leaf litter, or rocks. On several occasions I have located coal skinks on dry, rocky, south-facing hillsides (Carter and Cole counties).

A variety of small insects and spiders is eaten by this species.

Breeding: Courtship and mating of the southern coal skink have not been observed in Missouri. It is presumed to be comparable to the breeding of the five-lined skink (*Eumeces fasciatus*). From 8 to 11 eggs are laid in June or early July (Collins, 1982).

Missouri Distribution: The southern coal skink is restricted to the southern half of the state.

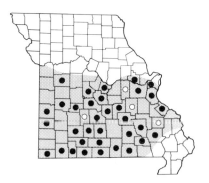

Adult male five-lined skink from Miller County.

Five-lined Skink
Eumeces fasciatus (Linnaeus)

Description: This species has shiny scales and light and dark stripes. Color varies with age and sex. Hatchlings and young adults are black with five yellowish stripes from head to base of tail, and a bright blue tail. Adult females are normally brown with a dark brown lateral stripe, five tan stripes and a blue or blue-gray tail. Adult males are uniform olive or tan with a faded dark lateral stripe and a few light stripes. During the breeding season, males' heads are bright red-orange. Adult males are slightly larger than adult females.

Adult five-lined skinks range in total length from 130 to 205 mm (5 to 8 1/16 inches; Conant, 1975). Largest Missouri specimen recorded is 186 mm (7 3/8 inches; Powell *et al.*, 1982).

Habits and Habitat: Five-lined skinks reside in open woods, near wooded bluffs, and on rocky, south-facing hillsides. Shelters in the form of rocks, downed logs, stumps and standing dead trees are required. This species will occasionally climb trees, especially when searching for insects. Skinks can also be found around farm buildings, rock gardens and patios. This species is active from April to October.

Five-lined skinks eat a variety of insects and spiders.

Breeding: This lizard becomes sexually active a few weeks after leaving its overwintering burrow. During the breeding season, males become aggressive and the orange-red head seems to help in sex recognition. Courtship behavior has not been observed. Male five-lined skinks locate females by smell and sight. During mating the male will grasp the skin behind a female's head.

Female five-lined skink with 13 eggs (left) *from Ste. Genevieve County (photo by Jeffrey W. Lang), and young five-lined skink from Osage County* (right).

In Missouri, egg-laying takes place in late April, May and June. Females nest in leaf litter or under rotten logs, tree stumps or rocks. From 6 to 13 eggs are deposited; the female remains with the eggs until they hatch.

Groves (1982) demonstrated that females do not "guard" their clutch of eggs but brood them. A female can detect an addled (rotted) egg within 24 hours and eat it to remove it from the nest. He observed a female bite a small hole at one end of a bad egg, lick out the contents and eat the shell.

The young five-lined skinks develop and hatch in from one to two months (Collins, 1982). Hatchlings are from 51 to 64 mm in total length (2 to 2 1/2 inches; Conant, 1975).

The bright blue color of juvenile lizards is believed to protect young lizards from attack by aggressive adult males. This intraspecific communication allows juveniles to remain in the territory of an adult male during a time when they are most aggressive (Clark and Hall, 1970).

Remarks: This species and the broadhead skink (*Eumeces laticeps*) can be easily confused; see Description section in the broadhead skink species account.

Missouri Distribution: The five-lined skink is presumed to occur statewide, except for a few counties in extreme northern Missouri.

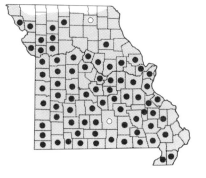

Adult male broadhead skink from Callaway County.

Broadhead Skink
Eumeces laticeps (Schneider)

Description: The broadhead skink is a large, smooth-scaled lizard which lives along the edge of forests. Color varies considerably between sexes and age classes. Adult males are normally olive-brown with little or no stripes along the sides. During the breeding season, males develop an orange-red, swollen head which has given rise to the species' common name. Adult females nearly always show signs of light and dark stripes down the back and sides. The wide, dark stripe down each side is usually the most prominent. Hatchling broadhead skinks are jet black with five thin, yellow lines along the back and sides and have a bright blue tail. Five-lined skinks (*Eumeces fasciatus*) can be distinguished from the broadhead by the presence of two postlabial scales. These scales are absent on broadhead skinks.

Adult broadhead skinks range in total length from 165 to 324 mm (6 1/2 to 12 3/4 inches; Conant, 1975). Largest Missouri specimen recorded is 268 mm (6 11/16 inches; Powell *et al.*, 1982).

Habits and Habitat: As with all Missouri lizards, the broadhead skink is active during the day between April and October. Broadhead skinks spend most of their time in or near trees, stumps, large logs, or dilapidated farm buildings. During field studies in Illinois, Moehn (1980) reported observing this species on the ground or within 1.5 meters of the ground 81 percent of the total number of sightings.

The edges of wood lots and forests seem to be the preferred habitat of this species. Broadhead skinks will often take up residence in a large dead tree, utilizing abandoned woodpecker holes or other cavities.

Female broadhead skink with clutch of 21 eggs from Cole County (left), *and head of male broadhead skink* (right).

Breeding: Courtship and mating presumably take place in late April and throughout May. Breeding activity is probably similar to that of the five-lined skink.

There have been several reports in literature concerning clutch size and the possibility of communal nesting. Anderson (1965) stated that clutches with more than ten eggs may indicate a communal nest. Mount (1975) reported the number of eggs laid by *E. laticeps* to range from 6 to 16 per clutch. Schuette (1980a) published a record of two clutches found in Bollinger County. One clutch contained 14 eggs and the other 17 eggs. I reported on a broadhead skink nest located in Cole County that contained 22 eggs (Johnson, 1979d). Another nest found in Cole County also contained 22 eggs; they were laid July 12 and hatched on August 7. The eggs averaged 12 mm wide and 15 mm in length (7/16 x 9/16 inches). Hatchlings measure from 6.0 to 8.6 cm (2 3/8 to 3 3/8 inches; Conant, 1975).

Remarks: This harmless lizard is commonly called the "scorpion;" many people erroneously believe it to be poisonous.

Missouri Distribution: The broad-head skink occurs in the southern two thirds of the state.

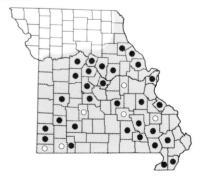

Adult Great Plains skink.

Great Plains Skink
Eumeces obsoletus (Baird and Girard)

Description: A robust ground-dwelling skink, normally found under rocks. This species has light tan to gray ground color, with scales on back and sides edged in brown or black. These dark markings may combine to form irregular stripes. The belly is plain light gray. Body scales on the sides are in oblique rows; this is Missouri's only lizard species with this scale arrangement. There is little difference between the sexes, but adult males have a slightly swollen head during the breeding season. This is the largest species of skink in the United States.

Adult Great Plains skinks range in total length from 165 to 349 mm (6 1/2 to 13 3/4 inches; Conant, 1975). Largest Missouri specimen recorded is 248 mm (9 7/8 inches; Powell *et al.*, 1982). Record length is 350 mm (13 3/4 inches; Collins, 1982).

Habits and Habitat: Although a lot of time is spent under rocks, the Great Plains skink is active on the surface searching for insects between 10 a.m. and 4 p.m., as long as air temperatures are above 70° F. This species is active in Kansas from March to early October (Collins, 1982).

This is a grassland animal and requires rocks sunken in the soil for shelters. Rock-strewn low hills along small streams seem to be the preferred habitat. When captured, a Great Plains skink will inflict a painful bite to defend itself.

A variety of insects and spiders is eaten by this lizard. The food habits of this species were studied in Kansas, and the most common prey eaten were grasshoppers, crickets and beetles (Hall, 1972).

Breeding: Little is known about the natural history of this lizard in Missouri. Fitch (1955) intensively studied the Great Plains skink in eastern Kansas and reported the following data. Courtship and mating take place in May. A male will approach a female and touch her with flicks of his tongue. This is followed by the male grasping the loose skin of the female's shoulder in his jaws, after which copulation occurs. Fitch (*ibid.*) stated that females may not breed every year. Eggs are normally laid in a burrow beneath a large rock. An average of 11 eggs are produced per female. Females remain with their clutch until the eggs hatch (from one to two months). The young are about 64 mm (2 1/2 inches; Conant, 1975) at hatching.

Remarks: The Great Plains skink has probably never been abundant in Missouri. This species is listed as rare by the Missouri Department of Conservation.

Missouri Distribution: Anderson (1965) reported several locations in western Missouri where the Great Plains skinks were found, but no additional specimens have been discovered in this state. Collins (1982) showed this lizard to be found in every Kansas county bordering western Missouri. Watkins and Hinesley (1970) reported a specimen collected near the Missouri River in Atchison County and stated that several more were observed, but not collected. Robison and Douglas
(1978) reported two juvenile *Eumeces obsoletus* taken in northwestern Arkansas, in Benton and Scott counties. From these reports it can be presumed that the Great Plains skink occurs in extreme western Missouri.

Adult ground skink from Cole County.

Ground Skink
Scincella lateralis (Say)

Description: This is Missouri's smallest species of lizard. The ground skink has a brown or grayish-brown ground color with a wide, dark brown or black dorsolateral stripe. This stripe extends from the snout to the middle of the tail. A number of small dark flecks are usually present on the back and sides. The belly is light gray. The ground skink is the only species of lizard in Missouri that has a clear scale on the lower eyelid, enabling it to see when the eyelids are closed. Adult females are larger than adult males.

Adult ground skinks range in total length from 80 to 130 mm (3 to 5 1/8 inches; Conant, 1975). Largest Missouri specimen recorded is 121 mm (4 3/4 inches; Powell *et al.*, 1982). The record length is 145 mm (5 3/4 inches; Collins, 1982).

Habits and Habitat: This species is normally active from April to October. Ground skinks can be seen on warm, sunny days as they move through leaf litter on the forest floor. Ground skinks escape enemies by a rapid, lateral, snakelike movement. They are also known to enter the shallow water of a stream or puddle if no other shelter is handy. This lizard does not normally climb trees or rocks. On cool days during the active season, this species can be found under flat rocks or logs.

This species eats a variety of small insects, spiders and earthworms (Collins, 1982).

The ground skink is a woodland species, seldom venturing into open areas unless there is an abundance of natural shelter.

Ground skink eggs (left) *and a hatchling ground skink* (right), *both from Taney County.*

Breeding: Very little information is available on the reproductive biology of this secretive skink. Courtship and mating is presumed to occur in the spring or early summer. Fitch (1965, 1970) reported that females normally produce two clutches of eggs each season, with from two to seven eggs per clutch. The eggs are often retained inside the female for a considerable period; the embryos are well developed when the eggs are laid. This shortens the incubation period, which may subsequently last only 22 days. Eggs are laid in rotten logs, stumps, under leaf litter or rocks. Anderson (1965) reported a female from Greene County which layed four eggs on May 31 and a second clutch on June 22. The eggs were from 8.1 to 9.2 mm (10/32 to 12/32 inch). The hatchlings were from 43 to 48 mm (1 11/16 to 1 14/16 inches) in total length.

Remarks: The type locality for *Scincella lateralis* is the "banks of the Mississippi River below Cape Girardeau, Cape Girardeau County, Missouri" (Smith, 1961).

Missouri Distribution: The ground skink is known to occur in the southern half of Missouri and is presumed to range into the northeastern part of the state along the Mississippi River.

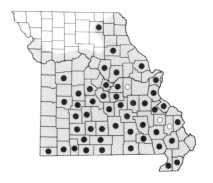

Family Teiidae

Racerunners and Whiptails

This is a large family of lizards containing about 200 species. The family is restricted to the Western Hemisphere and includes species in a surprising variety of sizes and forms. The smallest species is 76 to 102 mm (3 to 4 inches) long; the largest—the caiman lizard of South America—can reach 1,220 mm (4 feet) in length. Several West Indian teiids have been introduced into Florida.

The family Teiidae consists of 40 genera, with the majority of species ranging throughout central and the northern half of South America. Only one genus, *Cnemidophorus*, is native to the United States; it contains species commonly called racerunners and whiptails. These are medium-size lizards with strong hind legs and long, thin tails. Scales on the legs and body are small granules; belly scales are large, quadrangular in shape and placed in uniform, transverse rows. Scales on the head are large symmetrical plates.

There are about a dozen species of *Cnemidophorus* lizards native to the United States; the majority reside in the west. Missouri has one species with one subspecies.

Six-lined Racerunner

Adult female prairie-lined racerunner, a common subspecies of the six-lined racerunner, from Taney County.

Six-lined Racerunner
Cnemidophorus sexlineatus (Linnaeus)

Description: The six-lined racerunner is a long, slender, fast-moving lizard which lives in open areas. The ground color is dark brown or black. There are normally six longitudinal stripes extending from the head along the back and sides onto the tail. The light stripes are yellow, white, gray or pale blue. The tail is gray or brown and rough to the touch. The head and forward part of the body are tinged with blue or green, particularly in males. The belly is gray or bluish gray in males, and salmon-pink to creamy white in females. Adult male six-lined racerunners have a broader head than females, and females have a heavier body.

Adult six-lined racerunners range in total length from 150 to 241 mm (6 to 9 1/2 inches; Conant, 1975). Largest Missouri specimen recorded is 250 mm (9 7/8 inches; Powell *et al.*, 1982).

Habits and Habitat: This fast, alert lizard is normally active on warm, sunny days, between 8 a.m. and 3 p.m. (Fitch, 1958). Its active season may last from May to mid-September. On cool or cloudy days racerunners take shelter in burrows they have dug, or in the burrows of other animals. They also burrow under objects such as flat rocks or boards. Extreme heat causes this species to seek shade or cooler temperatures underground. Racerunners are ground dwellers and are not known to climb trees or bushes. Ayres (1973), however, observed a six-lined racerunner climb a bush while in pursuit of an insect.

Adult male prairie-lined racerunner from Miller County. Prairie-lined racerunners have seven stripes instead of six.

These lizards burrow into loose soil on south or southwest-facing slopes to escape the harsh weather of winter. Juvenile racerunners enter overwintering burrows after adults, and emerge earlier in the spring than adults (Trauth, pers. comm.).

Insects, spiders, scorpions and other invertebrates are eaten by this species.

The six-lined racerunner prefers open areas with loose soil or sand and sparse vegetation. They can be observed on rocky, south-facing hillsides such as cedar glades or in open, sandy areas along river floodplains.

Breeding: Courtship and mating take place between late April and July. A male will court a female by displaying his colorful throat and chest. If the female is receptive the male will grasp the loose skin on the back of her neck, mount her and mate. When copulation has ended the male may follow the female with his tail elevated and his cloaca dragging the ground (Collins, 1982).

From one to six eggs are laid by a female. Females that are over two years old normally lay two clutches per season. Trauth (pers. comm.) found an average of 3.11 eggs per clutch in nests observed in Missouri. Racerunner eggs average 16 mm by 9.1 mm (Anderson, 1965). The female does not remain with the eggs as is the case with Missouri's skinks. Eggs are laid in a burrow about 10 cm (3 7/8 inches) deep in sand or loose dirt. Hatching normally takes place within two months. The hatchlings have an average snout–vent length of 30 mm (1 1/8 inches), a pale blue tail and vivid yellow body stripes.

Subspecies: The prairie-lined racerunner (*Cnemidophorus sexlineatus viridis* Lowe) is a subspecies of the six-lined racerunner. It can be distinguished from the nominate race by having seven light stripes instead of six. The prairie-lined racerunner has a wash of bright green over the head and forward part of the body. The natural history of this subspecies is similar to that of the six-lined racerunner, but it seems to prefer a habitat of open grasslands or river floodplains.

Remarks: Racerunners are sometimes called "fieldstreaks" or "sandlappers" (Conant, 1975). In warm weather this reptile is extremely difficult to capture by hand.

Missouri Distribution: The six-lined racerunner (stippling) is found in eastern and central Missouri; it intergrades with and is subsequently replaced by the prairie-lined racerunner (hatch lines) in southeastern, south central and western sections of the state (Trauth, 1980).

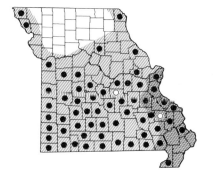

Family Anguidae

Glass Lizards and Their Relatives

This is a small but wide-ranging family of lizards with a great diversity of forms. A number of species are long, slender and legless, causing them to be easily confused with snakes. There are species that have a reduced number of toes, or only two legs; there are also some forms that are more "typical" lizards with four normal limbs.

The Anguidae contains over 70 species representing ten genera. Members of this family occur in North and South America, Europe, Asia and northern Africa. Two genera, with a total of eight species, occur in the United States: *Gerrhonotus*, the alligator lizards, with five species; and *Ophisaurus*, the glass lizards, with three species.

Members of the family Anguidae are distinguished by the presence of bony plates (*osteoderms*) in each scale, and by a prominent, deep groove located along each side of the body. The plates reinforce the scales but reduce flexibility. It is thought that the groove provides flexibility of the body for movement, breathing and swallowing prey, and also for egg development in females. The groove is lined with small, granular scales.

Missouri has one species of glass lizard (genus *Ophisaurus*) native to the state. Glass lizards (also called "glass snakes") have very long, fragile tails which break off easily if grasped by a predator or struck with an object. Glass lizards will try to avoid a predator by a speedy retreat through grass. If captured they will try to escape by biting, and will break off the tail as a last resort.

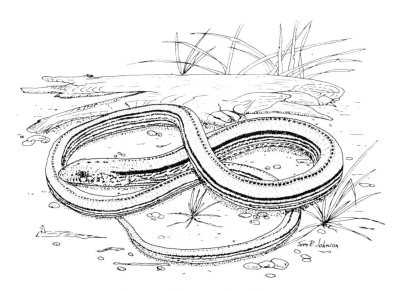

Western Slender Glass Lizard

221

Adult western slender glass lizard from Pettis County.

Western Slender Glass Lizard
Ophisaurus attenuatus attenuatus Cope

Description: A snakelike lizard that is long, slender and legless. Ground color is normally gray, tan or brown with black stripes on the back and sides. Thin, dark stripes located below the lateral groove are prominent on juveniles and subadults, but become faded once adulthood is reached. The dorsal stripe normally changes into a series of dark spots or dark crossbands as the lizards mature. The belly is white and the underside of the tail normally has dark stripes. Although glass lizards strongly resemble snakes, they do have some notable differences. The eyes are protected by movable eyelids, there is an ear opening on either side of the head and there is a lateral groove which runs down the entire length of the body. None of these characteristics are found on snakes. This species has a long tail that is normally two thirds of the total length of the reptile (unless the tail has been broken off and is being regenerated). Missouri specimens have no visible differences between males and females.

Adult western slender glass lizards range in total length from 560 to 1,067 mm (22 to 42 inches; Conant, 1975). Largest Missouri specimen recorded is 658 mm (26 1/8 inches; Powell *et al.*, 1982).

Habits and Habitat: Slender glass lizards are active during the day, as long as air temperatures range from 50° to 90°F. This species has an active season from April to October.

In Missouri, the western slender glass lizard occurs on prairies, pastures, in open woods or on dry, rocky hillsides. Although this lizard

Head of western slender glass lizard.

often takes shelter in clumps of grass or small mammal burrows, it will also burrow into loose soil. Anderson (1965) reports specimens being plowed up by farmers working in grain fields.

A glass lizard sighted in tall grass can quickly escape because its coloration blends so well with the vegetation. If captured, a glass lizard will frantically thrash about and the tail will quickly detach from the body.

Glass lizards consume a variety of insects, including grasshoppers and crickets; they also eat spiders, snails, other lizards and the eggs of ground-nesting birds.

Breeding: This species mates in May; a female will produce from 6 to 17 eggs during June or July. Each female will produce one clutch of eggs per season. It is believed that females will attend the eggs, which may be laid in a rotten log or under a rock, and remain with them until they hatch. Hatchlings average 185 mm (7 1/4 inches). Young take three to four years to reach adulthood (Collins, 1982).

Remarks: Local names for this lizard include "glass snake" and "joint snake." There is no truth to the belief that this or any other lizard can rejoin itself once its tail is detached.

Missouri Distribution: The western slender glass lizard is presumed to occur statewide.

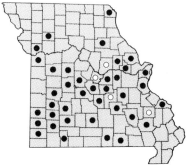

Snakes

(Suborder Serpentes)

Snakes are long, slender reptiles which are covered by scales; they are limbless and lack ear openings and eyelids. The eyes of snakes are protected by a clear, nonmovable scale. Although snakes are legless, they are able to move about with ease. They have an extremely flexible backbone composed of from 200 to 400 vertebrae. The body vertebrae each have a pair of ribs which are attached to muscles. Snakes move forward by a side-to-side movement, or in a straight line by literally walking on their ribs. The internal organs of snakes are elongated so they fit into the tubular body cavity. Most snakes have an elongated right lung and no left lung. A snake's heart is normally located about one third of the distance from the head.

Snakes shed their outer layer of skin periodically as they grow. During the active season young snakes usually shed once every four or five weeks; adults may shed once every six to eight weeks. In the case of rattlesnakes, a new segment is added at the base of the rattle at each shedding. In Missouri, rattlesnakes may shed from two to four times per year. As the rattle becomes longer, the old segments weaken and may break off, so it is not possible to determine the age of a rattlesnake by counting the number of segments.

The snake's long, forked, extendable tongue is often thought to be dangerous; in fact, it is completely harmless. Snakes use their tongue to pick up odors from their environment, which are transferred to special sense organs in the roof of the mouth. Snakes use their tongue to locate a mate during the breeding season, or to find and identify prey.

The food habits of Missouri's snakes are as varied as the types of snakes. Some, like the rough green snake, eat insects, insect larvae and spiders. Others, like the water snakes, eat fish, frogs, tadpoles or crayfish. The black rat snake and bullsnake eat rodents, small birds and bird eggs. Kingsnakes also eat rodents and are important predators of lizards and other snakes, including venomous species. Snakes must swallow their food whole; some can engulf animals three times the diameter of the snake's head.

The lower jaws of snakes are loosely joined to the skull and the upper jaws are movable. A snake grasps its prey (whether fish, frog or mouse) by the head and engulfs it by advancing first one side of the jaw and then the other. The snake's teeth also help it swallow. The teeth are sharp and curve toward the rear of the mouth. They hold the prey and prevent its escape. Some snakes, such as water snakes and garter snakes, eat their prey alive, while venomous snakes usually inject venom into the animal and swallow it after it is dead. Several Missouri snakes, such as rat snakes, kingsnakes, milk snakes and bullsnakes, kill by constriction. The snake grasps the prey in its mouth and immediately wraps several tight coils around it. Thus prevented from breathing, it dies from a lack of oxygen. The prey is then swallowed.

In Missouri, snakes normally breed in the spring, soon after they emerge from winter dormancy. A few species, however, breed in autumn. About half of Missouri's snake species lay eggs; the rest give birth to fully developed young. Some egg-laying species are the black rat snake, bullsnake, kingsnakes, racers, worm snake, ringnecks and green snakes. The size of the egg depends on the species; the number of eggs produced depends on the size of the female. In general, the larger the female, the more eggs she can produce. Snake eggs are elongated and have a tough, leathery shell. Females select rotten logs, stumps or leaf litter in which to deposit their eggs. As a young snake develops within the egg, a small "egg tooth" grows on the tip of the snout; the snake uses this "tooth" to slit the shell when hatching. Afterwards, this "egg tooth" is shed. Snakes usually hatch in late summer or early autumn.

Snakes which retain their young until they are completely developed are water snakes, garter snakes, brown snakes, copperheads, cottonmouths and rattlesnakes. This form of reproduction is slightly advanced over egg-laying, from an evolutionary perspective. Each young snake is protected inside the female in a thin, saclike membrane. The membrane also contains yolk for nourishment. Some of the young snakes break through the membrane while inside the female and emerge from her in a tight coil; others break through after being born. Snakes that develop inside the female are normally born in mid- to late summer.

Herpetologists currently recognize approximately 2,700 species of snakes throughout the world. Missouri, with its wide variety of wildlife habitats—prairies, Ozark hills and valleys, swamps and marshes—has a total of 50 species and subspecies of snakes. Most of our snake species (88 percent) are non-venomous. Although many may bite in self-defense, their bite usually produces nothing more than shallow scratches. There are five species of venomous snakes in Missouri.

The smallest snake native to Missouri is the flathead snake (*Tantilla gracilis*) which averages about 20 cm (8 inches) in total length. The largest is the bullsnake (*Pituophis melanoleucus sayi*) which averages about 152 cm (60 inches) in total length.

Myths

Although the majority of people in the United States have had some biology courses during their school years, it is amazing how many myths about snakes persist. Because snakes are so different from us there has been a tendency for people to believe fantastic stories about these reptiles. The following snake myths are still prevalent in Missouri. There is no biological evidence to support any of these beliefs, but when it comes to snakes, people have a difficult time separating truth from fiction.

1. Snakes are slimy. Like all reptiles, snakes have tough, dry skin which protects them from the harsh life as a land dwelling animal. Salamanders and frogs have moist or slimy skin—not snakes.

2. A snake will swallow young snakes to protect them. No species of snake has this ability. Any snake swallowed by another will quickly die inside the stomach due to a lack of oxygen and strong digestive juices.

3. Snakes move in pairs. All snakes are predators and compete for food. Snakes may be seen together in the general vicinity of prime habitats, but this is due to convenience, not because they live in pairs.

4. Hoop snakes. People may claim to have seen a snake grab its tail in its mouth and roll along the ground like a hoop, but this has never been documented—nor is it possible for any snake to do such a thing.

5. Snakes cannot bite while underwater. Snakes can and do bite underwater—that's how they capture their prey (fish, tadpoles, or salamanders). Water snakes or the venomous cottonmouth are able to defend themselves while underwater.

6. Snakes can steal milk from cows. This falsehood probably originated in areas where kingsnakes and rat snakes enter barns and farm sheds to search for mice. Seeing a snake in a milking shed at about the time a milking cow begins to slow down in production could have caused a farmer to blame the snake for taking milk. Milk from a cow is not a natural food of any reptile. It is likely that snakes do not have the proper enzymes to digest milk.

7. Black snakes breed with copperheads or rattlesnakes. Under no circumstance will a black snake mate with a venomous species. This would be like expecting a chicken to breed with a hawk.

The biology and natural history of Missouri snakes are both interesting and enjoyable to learn. The myths and misunderstandings make interesting stories, but should not be confused with scientific facts.

Family Colubridae
Non-venomous

This snake family contains more species than any other family worldwide. Most of the species in this family are small to medium in length. Members of the family Colubridae usually have large scales on the top of the head, and the scales along the back are either smooth (e.g., on kingsnakes, racers or ringneck snakes), or have a ridge or "keel" which makes them appear rough (e.g., on water snakes, garter snakes and hognose snakes).

None of the members of this family which occur in Missouri are dangerous to man. Our smallest species, known as the flathead snake (*Tantilla gracilis*), has special teeth at the rear of the mouth which allow the snake to administer a toxic saliva into its prey as the animal is held in the mouth. The flathead snake is so small, and the saliva so weak in toxicity that under no circumstances could this species be considered dangerous to man.

There are 31 species of snakes native to Missouri which are members of the family Colubridae; they are grouped into 19 different genera.

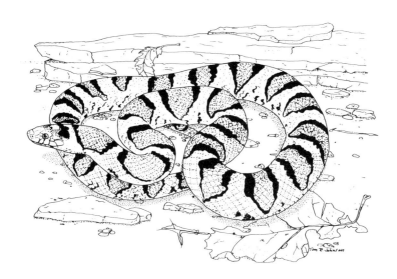

Red Milk Snake

Adult western worm snake from Andrew County.

Western Worm Snake
Carphophis amoenus vermis (Kennicott)

Description: A small two-toned snake which lives in wooded areas or rocky hillsides. Dorsal color is purplish brown to black; ventral area is salmon-pink with color extending up the sides. The head is pointed to aid in burrowing. The tail terminates in a harmless spike which also aids in maneuvering through soil. The western worm snake has smooth scales and a divided anal plate. Males have longer tails than females; they normally possess keels or ridges on the belly scales forward of the anal plate (Collins; 1982).

Adult western worm snakes range in length from 190 to 280 mm (7 1/2 to 11 inches; Conant, 1975). Largest Missouri specimen recorded is 317 mm (12 5/8 inches; Powell, 1982). A report of a specimen collected in Clay County with a length of 391 mm (15 1/2 inches) was sent to me by David Moore (pers. comm.).

Habits and Habitat: This species spends most of its time in burrows under rocks or logs or in damp soil. Worm snakes are secretive, and are seldom, if ever, seen on the surface of the ground. This small snake is usually active between March and October, but may estivate deep in the soil during the hot, dry period of late July and August. Earthworms and some soft-bodied insects are consumed by this species.

Western worm snakes live on rocky, wooded or open hillsides, or along the edge of forest where flat rocks or logs provide suitable shelters. I have found this snake in deep leaf litter which has accumulated in shaded steep-sided ravines. Drda (1968) found a few western worm snakes overwintering in a cave in Jefferson County.

Western worm snake eggs from Taney County (left), *and a western worm snake hatching* (right).

Breeding: This species breeds in the spring, but may also breed in the fall (Collins, 1982). Aldridge and Metter (1973) reported on a study of the reproductive cycle of western worm snakes collected in central Missouri. Adult males store sperm in the *vasa deferentia* throughout the year, but sperm are most prevalent in the autumn. The ovarian cycle in females begins soon after egg-laying, but eggs do not show rapid growth until the following spring. Eggs are laid under rocks or underground during June and early July. A female produces from one to six eggs (Anderson, 1965). The elongated eggs probably hatch in mid- to late August.

Remarks: This common, harmless snake has never been known to bite. When handled, a specimen may attempt to escape by trying to work its head through one's fingers; it will also push the sharp but harmless tail tip against the skin.

Missouri Distribution: Presumed to be statewide in occurrence.

Young northern scarlet snake from Camden County.

Northern Scarlet Snake
Cemophora coccinea copei Jan

Description: A small to medium-size, multi-colored snake. Color consists of wide orange or red bands bordered by narrow black bands and separated by white or yellowish bands. There may be some black pigment present in the red bands on large specimens. The snout is generally red or orange. An important characteristic of this species is a spotless cream colored belly. Dorsal scales are smooth and the anal plate is not divided. Male scarlet snakes have a longer tail and more dorsal bands than females.

Adult northern scarlet snakes range in length from 360 to 510 mm (14 to 20 inches; Conant, 1975). Largest Missouri specimen recorded is 364 mm (14 1/2 inches; Powell *et al.*, 1982).

This uncommon species can be confused with the more common red milk snake (*Lampropeltis triangulum syspila*). A careful reading of the descriptions for both species will facilitate proper identification of a specimen.

Habits and Habitat: The scarlet snake is a secretive species which is seldom seen above ground, except on warm nights or after heavy summer rains. It can be found under flat rocks, logs or other objects; it is probably active from late April until October. This species is known to eat lizards, small snakes and mice. The prey is killed by constriction. Scarlet snakes are also known to eat the eggs of lizards and other snakes. The eggs may be swallowed whole, or the egg shell broken by the snake's teeth and the contents swallowed.

230

The scarlet snake is associated with loose or sandy soil because of its burrowing habits. In general this snake is known to occur in forested regions. The few specimens taken in Missouri were found on wooded, rocky hillsides.

Breeding: Very little is known about the reproductive biology of this species. Mating is presumed to occur in the spring, and the eggs are probably laid during June. From three to eight eggs are produced per female (Anderson, 1965).

Remarks: Because so few specimens of the northern scarlet snake have been reported in Missouri, it is difficult to determine the status of the species. Nelson and Gibbons (1972) found that scarlet snakes are more common than previously reported because of the species' secretive nature and concluded it is an "infrequently encountered species." The Missouri Department of Conservation has listed this secretive snake as "status undetermined" in *The Rare and Endangered Species of Missouri.*

Missouri Distribution: Anderson (1965) reported a specimen from Phelps County, but I was informed that the specimen was actually collected crossing Highway 63 just north of the county line in Maries County (Philip D. Evans, pers. comm.). Nickerson (1967) reported specimens from Miller and Camden counties and I also photographed a specimen from Camden County (Johnson, 1979b). This species is presumed to occur in south central Missouri.

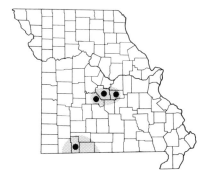

231

Adult eastern yellowbelly racer from Andrew County.

Eastern Yellowbelly Racer
Coluber constrictor flaviventris Say

Description: This is a medium to large, smooth-scaled snake with uniform but variable dorsal color. Adult eastern yellowbelly racers (three years of age or older) can be tan, brown, olive, blue, gray or nearly black. The belly is yellow, ivory or light blue-gray. Racers have a slender body, proportionately long tail, smooth body scales and a divided anal scale. Hatchlings and young racers are strongly patterned with closely spaced gray or brown mid-dorsal blotches and smaller, alternating spots on the sides over a tan ground color. The belly of young racers is normally cream colored with some dark gray speckling. The juvenile pattern fades with age, and by the third season most or all dorsal spots disappear.

Adult eastern yellowbelly racers range in length from 760 to 1,270 mm (30 to 50 inches; Conant, 1975). Largest Missouri specimen recorded is 1,330 mm (52 3/8 inches; Powell *et al.*, 1982). Record length is 1,778 mm (70 inches; Conant, 1975).

Habits and Habitat: The eastern yellowbelly racer has an active season from March to November. Fitch (1963a) conducted an extensive study of this species in eastern Kansas, and reported that racers are active at air temperatures between 60° to 90°F, but seem to prefer a temperature range of 78° to 80°F. Racers are diurnal, and can be observed searching for food or basking on sunny days. This fast moving snake depends on speed and agility to escape an enemy or overtake prey. When alarmed, racers will vibrate their tails. Racers usually struggle violently, bite

232

viciously, and discharge musk and waste matter from their vents when captured.

Eastern yellowbelly racers live in native prairies, grasslands, pastures, brushy areas and along the edges of forests. During spring and fall, racers are found on rocky, wooded, south-facing hillsides. This species will overwinter in such habitat, or will select mammal burrows in open habitat as a winter retreat. Racers (along with black rat snakes) were reported to use a small sandstone cave as a hibernaculum. They were observed using a thermal gradient inside the cave to select optimum overwintering conditions (Sexton and Hunt, 1980). Drda (1968) found a few racers overwintering in a cave in Jefferson County. Although not territorial, racers have been found to have a home range which averages about 25 acres in size (Fitch, 1963).

A variety of animals are eaten by eastern yellowbelly racers, including small rodents, lizards, small snakes, frogs, birds and insects (Fitch, 1963a). Racers collected in Holt County had eaten grasshoppers, rodents and small snakes (Seigel, pers. comm.). Prey is consumed whole and alive.

Eastern yellowbelly racer eggs (left), *and a hatchling eastern yellowbelly racer* (right), *both from Cole County.*

Breeding: Courtship and mating occur soon after racers emerge from overwintering retreats, usually during early April. Adult males locate females by scent. Once a receptive female is found, the male will court her by moving alongside and on top of her, while his body ripples spasmodically. If the female moves the male follows, remaining in contact and continuing the courtship. Once the female remains passive the male moves his tail under hers and copulation occurs.

Egg-laying takes place from mid-June to late July. From 8 to 21 eggs are laid per female; the number depends on the size of the female. The eggs may be laid under logs, in rotten stumps, or in abandoned mammal burrows. Racer eggs are cream colored with a rough texture; they average 29.7 by 17.2 mm (1 1/8 by 11/16 inches; Fitch, 1963). Racer eggs hatch in from two to three months. Hatchling eastern yellowbelly racers average 273.8 mm (10 3/4 inches; Fitch, 1963) in total length.

Subspecies: The southern black racer (*Coluber constrictor priapus* Dunn and Wood) replaces the eastern yellowbelly racer in southeastern Missouri. Adult southern black racers are normally uniform dark gray to bluish black. The belly is light blue or gray; chin color is white.

Little is known about the natural history of the southern black racer. The preferred habitat includes swamps near limestone bluffs (Anderson, 1965). This subspecies is known to eat frogs and rodents.

Remarks: The local name for racers in Missouri is "blue racer."

Missouri Distribution: The eastern yellowbelly racer is found nearly statewide; it is replaced by the southern black racer in southeast Missouri.

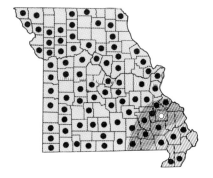

Adult prairie ringneck snake from Cole County.

Prairie Ringneck Snake

Diadophis punctatus arnyi Kennicott

Description: This is a small dark snake with a yellow or orange ring around the neck and a yellow or orange belly. The dorsal color is normally shiny dark gray, but may be gray-brown. The top of the head is usually darker than the body; there is a narrow yellow or light orange neck ring (one or two scale rows wide) which may have a posterior edge of black. The belly is yellow with numerous irregularly placed black spots; the belly changes to bright orange or red along the underside of the tail. Body scales are smooth; anal scale divided. Young ringneck snakes have a darker dorsal color which is often shiny black.

Adult prairie ringneck snakes range in length from 250 to 360 mm (10 to 14 inches). Largest Missouri specimen recorded is 419 mm (16 5/8 inches; Powell *et al.*, 1982).

Habits and Habitat: This secretive snake takes shelter under rocks, boards, logs, or bark slabs. Ringneck snakes are active between late March and early November. Optimal body temperature is maintained by resting under sun-warmed rocks or other objects instead of basking in the sun. Henderson (1970) studied this species in eastern Kansas and found that an optimum feeding temperature was between 25°C and 35°C (76°F and 92°F). Fitch (1975) reported on this species in Douglas County, Kansas. A small number of individuals in a population may reach 15 or more years of age. Ringneck snakes are the most common species of snake in some locations. This species eats primarily earthworms, but also consumes some insects and small salamanders.

Colorful underbelly of a prairie ringneck snake (left), *and prairie ringneck snake eggs from Taney County* (right).

In Missouri the prairie ringneck can be found in a variety of habitats: native prairies, pastures, open woods, along the edge of woodlands, and on dry, rocky glades. Shelter in the form of rocks or logs is required for the species to populate an area. During the hot, dry months of July and August ringneck snakes locate cooler temperatures and moisture by taking shelter in burrows in the soil. Overwinter retreats include animal burrows or deep crevices in rock outcrops.

Breeding: Breeding takes place soon after emergence from overwintering in late March or early April. Egg-laying normally begins in late June and continues through early July. The number of eggs produced per female is from one to ten, with an average of four. The number of eggs produced depends on the size of the female—the larger the females the greater number of eggs produced. Ringneck snake eggs are white and normally elongated, but vary remarkably in shape. Fitch (1975) described the eggs as being "somewhat curved, and sausage shaped." Eggs are from 23 to 28 mm in length (15/16 to 1 1/8 inches). Fitch (1975) found evidence that this species may nest communally. Eggs are laid in abandoned small mammal burrows or under large flat rocks where there is ample moisture. Hatching takes place during late August and early September. Newly hatched young prairie ringneck snakes average 111 mm (4 3/8 inches) in length.

Subspecies: A geographic race of the ringneck snake known as the Mississippi ringneck snake (*Diadophis punctatus stictogenys* Cope) ranges into extreme southeastern Missouri. This subspecies is slightly smaller than the prairie ringneck snake. Dorsal color is similar, but the neck ring may be narrower, or interrupted dorsally. The Mississippi ringneck has a yellow belly; the small black belly spots are normally arranged into two or three longitudinal rows. The natural history of this subspecies is similar to that of the prairie ringneck snake.

Remarks: Ringneck snakes are not known to bite when captured, but will discharge a pungent, unpleasant musk from glands at the base of their tail, along with fecal matter. This species will also coil the tail and expose the brightly colored underside when alarmed.

Missouri Distribution: The prairie ringneck snake is presumed to occur nearly statewide, but is replaced by the Mississippi ringneck snake in southeastern Missouri.

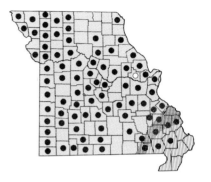

Adult Great Plains rat snake from Taney County.

Great Plains Rat Snake
Elaphe guttata emoryi (Baird and Girard)

Description: A medium-size gray snake with numerous dark brown blotches. Ground color is light gray or brownish gray. There are from 25 to 45 dorsal blotches of dark brown bordered with black (Collins, 1982). A dark brown stripe between the eyes extends through each eye, along the sides of the head, and onto the neck. There is also a "spearpoint" marking on the top of the head. The belly is white with bold, squarish black markings and black or dark gray stripes along the underside of the tail. The body scales are weakly keeled and the anal scale is divided.

Adult Great Plains rat snakes range in length from 610 to 910 mm (24 to 36 inches). Largest Missouri specimen recorded is 1,220 mm (48 inches; Powell *et al.*, 1982). The record length is 1,530 mm (60 1/4 inches; Conant, 1975).

Habits and Habitat: This species is normally nocturnal during the active season (from late March to late September). Daylight hours are spent hiding under rocks, logs, boards, or underground in small mammal burrows. Food consists of rodents, bats and small birds. Rat snakes will often vibrate their tails when alarmed.

In Missouri, the Great Plains rat snake can be found in the vicinity of open woodlands, rocky, wooded hillsides, and possibly near caves where there is a concentration of bats. Drda (1968) found a Great Plains rat snake overwintering in a cave in Jefferson County.

Ventral coloration of a Great Plains rat snake.

Breeding: Little is known about the courtship and mating of this species. It is presumed they breed soon after emerging from their over-wintering retreat. From four to over a dozen eggs are laid usually between late June and early July. Hatching probably takes place in September. Hatchling Great Plains rat snakes are similar in appearance to the young of black rat snakes (*Elaphe obsoleta obsoleta*).

Remarks: Local name "house snake;" may also be called Emory's rat snake by some authors. This species can be confused with the prairie kingsnake (*Lampropeltis calligaster calligaster*). A careful reading of both species' accounts will facilitate proper identification of a specimen. The prairie kingsnake is more commonly encountered than the Great Plains rat snake in Missouri.

Missouri Distribution: In Missouri, the Great Plains rat snake occurs in the southern half of the state.

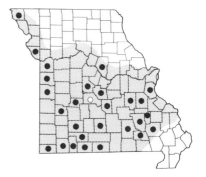

239

Adult black rat snake from Christian County.

Black Rat Snake
Elaphe obsoleta obsoleta (Say)

Description: Commonly known as the "black snake," this is one of Missouri's largest and most familiar species. Color is shiny black, but young adults and specimens in southeastern Missouri may have dark brown blotches. Small patches of red skin may be visible between the scales along the sides of some individuals. The upper lip and chin are usually white. The belly has a black and white checkerboard pattern anteriorly, changing to a mottling of gray, brown and white or yellow posteriorly. Scales along the back are weakly keeled; anal scale is divided. Hatchling black rat snakes differ markedly in color from adults. The ground color is gray; there are distinct black or dark brown blotches along the back and sides. The head of young snakes has a black band that crosses from eye to eye and extends down at an angle toward the mouth. There is a gradual change in the ground color from gray to black as the young snakes mature. The adult color is present after two years of growth.

Adult black rat snakes range in length from 1,070 to 1,830 mm (42 to 72 inches). Largest Missouri specimen recorded is 2,133 mm (84 inches; Anderson, 1965). Record length is 2,565 mm (101 inches; Conant, 1975).

Habits and Habitat: The active season of the black rat snake is from early April to early November. Fitch (1963b) has conducted intensive field studies of this species in eastern Kansas; much of the following information is based on his works. This species is active when air

Black rat snake eating a house mouse.

temperatures are between 15° and 33°C (60° to 88°F). During spring, early summer and autumn, black rat snakes are active during the day; in hot weather they become nocturnal. The population studied by Fitch in eastern Kansas had an average home range of 25 to 30 acres, with a population density of about two or three snakes per acre.

The food of this species consists of a variety of rodents, small rabbits, bats, bird eggs, small birds, and, on occasion, lizards. Cary *et al.* (1981) reported observing a black rat snake constrict and devour an Indiana bat in Texas County. Young rat snakes eat frogs, lizards and insects. Prey is killed by constriction.

The black rat snake is a forest dwelling species; it prefers rocky, wooded hillsides, or sections of woods along streams and rivers (especially in the prairie provinces of Missouri). These snakes take shelter in brushpiles, hollow trees, or even farm buildings where there is often an abundance of mice.

This species overwinters in mammal burrows, rock outcrops, abandoned rock quarries, old stone wells or cisterns and in rotted tree stumps. Winter quarters may be shared with copperheads, rattlesnakes and other species. A small sandstone cave in Johnson County was used by both the black rat snake and eastern yellowbelly racer (Sexton and Hunt, 1980). A few black rat snakes were found overwintering in a cave in Jefferson County (Drda, 1968).

Breeding: Courtship and mating usually occur in spring, but may also take place in summer or autumn. Anderson (1965) observed a breeding pair in April. Females select rotten stumps or logs, sawdust piles, or the moist soil under large rocks as a nest site. From 6 to 30 eggs may be laid, usually in June or early July. Black rat snake eggs adhere to each other when laid, and average 46 by 23.5 mm (1 11/16 by 15/16 inches; Anderson, 1965). Hatching normally takes place during autumn. A clutch of 27 black rat snake eggs was found in St. Louis County on October 20 (Sexton *et al.*, 1976). Two completely formed young hatched from one egg in a clutch of eight eggs laid by a female collected in Lincoln County (Schuette, 1978). Newly hatched young average 328 mm (12 7/8 inches) in length.

Black rat snake hatching from egg (left) *and a newly emerged black rat snake* (right), *both from Cole County.*

Subspecies: A geographic race of the black rat snake, known as the gray rat snake, *Elaphe obsoleta spiloides* (Dumeril, Bibron and Dumeril), has been reported to occur in extreme southeastern Missouri (Anderson, 1965). The gray rat snake is a slightly smaller race; the record size is 2,140 mm (84 1/4 inches; Conant, 1975). It normally retains the gray ground color of juveniles after adulthood is reached. The natural history of the gray rat snake is similar to that of the black rat snake.

Remarks: Rat snakes often vibrate their tail when alarmed. If captured or cornered, they will bite in self-defense. Another form of defense is the release of a pungent, unpleasant musk from glands at the base of the tail.

Black rat snakes help reduce damage to crops and stored grain by mice and rats; they are a valuable, natural rodent control. This service far outweighs the occasional theft of a few hen's eggs or baby chickens.

Hawks are a major predator of adult black rat snakes.

Missouri Distribution: Presumed to be statewide in occurrence. The gray rat snake subspecies has been reported in southeast Missouri (Anderson, 1965). Until more evidence is available, I show the rat snake population of the extreme southeast corner of the state as an intergradation between the two geographic races.

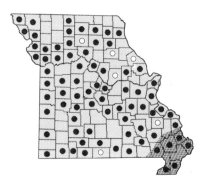

Adult western fox snake from Clark County.

Western Fox Snake
Elaphe vulpina vulpina (Baird and Girard)

Description: The western fox snake is a moderately large snake with distinct brown blotches. Ground color is gray, tan, or yellowish tan. Dorsal blotches are dark brown, edged in black, and range from 35 to 57 in number. There is a series of smaller dark brown blotches along the sides. The head is normally orange or orange-brown, with few distinct markings. The belly is yellowish and boldly checkered with black. Dorsal scales are weakly keeled; anal scale is divided. Young western fox snakes lack the adults' yellowish ground color; they appear gray with bold dark brown or black blotches. The head is boldly marked with a black mask running across the head, through the eyes and slanting back to the angle of the jaw. There are also black markings on the top of the head, and large black spots along the upper lips. All of these dark head markings disappear when adulthood is reached.

Adult western fox snakes range in length from 910 to 1,370 mm (36 to 54 inches). Largest Missouri specimen recorded is 1,155 mm (45 5/8 inches; Powell *et al.*, 1982). Record length is 1,791 mm (70 1/2 inches; Conant, 1975).

Habits and Habitat: Little is known about the habits of this species in Missouri. In other states where this species occurs, fox snakes are found along the edge of wood lots, lowland forests (Vogt, 1981), or fence rows in pastures and farmlands (Smith, 1961). In Missouri, the fox snake is known to occur in association with natural wet prairies or marshes.

Fox snakes are probably active between late April and October.

This species is mostly diurnal; it can be seen sunning or crossing roads in the morning or late afternoon. Fox snakes take shelter under boards, logs, or in mammal burrows.

The name "fox snake" was given to this species because of the musky odor given off by newly captured specimens. Scent glands at the base of the tail produce an odor which resembles the scent of a red fox. Fox snakes defend themselves by vibrating their tail, coiling with head and neck raised, and repeatedly striking at an intruder. Food of this species includes mice, chipmunks, small birds and bird eggs. Their prey is killed by constriction. Young fox snakes eat frogs and insects.

Ventral coloration of a western fox snake (left), *and a hatchling western fox snake from Holt County* (right).

Breeding: Little is known about the reproductive biology of the western fox snake in Missouri. The species is presumed to court and breed in April, soon after emerging from overwintering dens. Gillingham (1974) studied the courtship and mating behavior of the western fox snake in Wisconsin. He observed that a male begins courting a female with a chase that may last from 6 to 40 minutes. Once the female becomes quiet, the male moves along her side, rapidly flicking his tongue, then nudges her at mid-body with his head. Jerking movements follow, and the male then moves his head forward along the female's body. Their tails begin twitching, and the male moves his body over her. Once he has mounted her, their tails intertwine and mating occurs. During copulation the male often grasps the female behind the head with his mouth and continues to do so until intromission is completed (from 10 to 40 minutes). A female lays from 8 to 27 eggs which adhere to each other and average 45 by 28 mm in size (Vogt, 1981). The eggs are laid in rotten stumps or logs, sawdust piles, or leaf litter, probably during June. A female captured in Holt County laid nine eggs, which averaged 22 mm by 45 mm (7/8 by 1 3/4 inches; Seigel, pers. comm.). Hatching takes place in August or September. Newly hatched young resemble those of black rat snakes (*Elaphe obsoleta obsoleta*) and measure up to 31 cm in length.

Remarks: This snake may be mistaken for a copperhead, but the round, dark brown blotches of the fox snake differ from the distinctly hourglass-shaped markings of the copperhead.

Studies are needed to determine the status, distribution and habitat requirements of the western fox snake in Missouri. It is valuable as a controller of destructive rodents. The western fox snake is listed as rare in the Missouri rare and endangered species list.

Missouri Distribution: At one time presumed to occur in the northern one third of Missouri. Presently known to occur in east central, northeastern and northwestern sections of the state.

Adult western mud snake from Stoddard County.

Western Mud Snake
Farancia abacura reinwardtii Schlegel

Description: A medium-size, smooth, glossy black snake with a red and black checkered belly. Dorsal color is black or bluish black, and extends onto the belly to form irregular bands. These bands of black are separated by red or orange. The head and body appear slightly flattened. The dorsal scales are smooth; anal plate is divided. The tip of the tail normally terminates in a sharp, but harmless, spine. Young western mud snakes are the same color as adults.

Adult western mud snakes range in length from 1,020 to 1,370 mm (40 to 54 inches). Largest Missouri specimen recorded is 1,124 mm (48 3/16 inches; Powell *et al.*, 1982). Record length is 2,057 mm (81 inches; Conant, 1975).

Habits and Habitat: This semi-aquatic snake is probably active between April and October. Mud snakes are highly secretive. Taking shelter under logs or in animal burrows, they are seldom seen during the day. They are swamp dwellers, and prefer shallow areas where there are numerous rotten or water-soaked logs.

Mud snakes are not known to bite to defend themselves, but when freshly captured they will attempt to prick one's skin with the tip of the tail. This behavior may be startling, but the tail spine cannot break the skin.

The western mud snake has a specialized food preference, and normally eats the aquatic amphiuma or the lesser siren. Tadpoles and frogs are occasionally eaten.

246

Colorful underbelly of a western mud snake.

Breeding: Little is known about the courtship and mating of this species in Missouri. Western mud snakes presumably breed in the spring—probably April or May. Eggs are laid in animal burrows or in rotten logs. The leathery, creamy white eggs average 36 by 25.4 mm (1 3/4 by 1 inch) in size (Meade, 1937). From 11 to 50 eggs are laid; female western mud snakes are reported to remain with their clutch of eggs until they hatch (Meade, 1940; Cagle, 1942; Riemer, 1957; Mount, 1975). The eggs hatch in August or September, and the young average between 150 and 254 mm (6 to 10 inches) in total length.

Remarks: Two myths associated with this harmless snake have persisted over the years. One myth involves the sharp spine at the end of the tail which is erroneously believed to be a "stinger" that can deliver a deadly "venom." This has given rise to the local name "stinging snake." The second myth claims that this swamp dweller has the ability to grasp its tail in its mouth and roll across the ground with great speed. There is no truth to either of these "folk tales."

Because this species requires a natural swamp habitat it is important that our native cypress swamps be preserved.

Missouri Distribution: The western mud snake occurs in the natural swamps of the Mississippi lowlands of southeastern Missouri.

Adult plains hognose snake.

Plains Hognose Snake
Heterodon nasicus nasicus Baird and Girard

Description: The plains hognose snake is a stout-bodied, small to medium-size grayish-tan snake with rows of dark brown spots, and an upturned snout. The pattern consists of a row of brown, saddle-shaped dorsal spots, and two alternating rows of brown spots on the sides. There is usually a dark brown diagonal line through the eye and to the angle of the jaw, and an elongated dark brown blotch running along the side of the head and onto the neck. The rostral scale is upturned and elongated, appearing shovel-like. The belly has a wide, blue-black stripe which extends from the neck onto the underside of the tail; it is edged in yellow on some individuals (Collins, 1982). Scales on the body are keeled; anal plate is divided.

Adult plains hognose snakes range in length from 410 to 640 mm (16 to 25 inches). Largest Missouri specimen recorded is 521 mm (20 11/16 inches; Powell *et al.*, 1982). Record length is 895 mm (35 1/4 inches; Conant, 1975).

Habits and Habitat: Little is known about the natural history of this species in Missouri. Platt (1969) studied this snake in east central Kansas. The following information is from his report. This species is generally active from late April to mid-October. This snake takes shelter in burrows it digs in sandy or loose soils. Movements of the species may be restricted to a home range, but the size of the area is variable and dependent on the availability of food and shelter.

The plains hognose snake resides in dry, sandy or loose soil prairies.

In Missouri, it has been found in extreme northwest Missouri where the rough, rolling loess hills meet the floodplain of the Missouri River.

When threatened, this harmless species may react in a variety of ways. A specimen may try to escape by crawling toward shelter; it may coil and try to hide its head; or it may hiss loudly, spread its head and neck, and strike at the intruder (with mouth closed). If the intruder is persistent, the snake will writhe about, open its mouth, extend the tongue, regurgitate any freshly eaten food, roll on its back and "play dead." If left alone, the snake will eventually right itself and move away.

The plains hognose snake locates its prey by smell. It uses the upturned snout to dig animals out of their burrows in loose or sandy soils. Food consists primarily of rodents, plus toads, frogs, small lizards and snakes and reptile eggs (Platt, 1969).

Breeding: Mating normally takes place in the spring, but some will mate in autumn. The eggs are laid in a shallow burrow in loose or sandy soil. From 4 to 23 eggs are laid during July, and average 32.5 by 17.9 mm in size (1 1/4 by 11/16 inches). Female plains hognose snakes produce eggs on a biennial cycle (Platt, 1969). The eggs hatch in August or September. Hatchlings are from 140 to 200 mm (5 1/2 to 7 3/4 inches; Conant, 1975) in total length; they are the same color as adults.

Subspecies: The dusty hognose snake (*Heterodon nasicus gloydi* Edgren) is a subspecies of the plains hognose snake that is known to occur in southeastern Missouri. The only characteristic that supposedly separates the two races is the number of dorsal blotches from the head to the base of the tail. *Heterodon n. nasicus* has an average of 35 or more blotches in males and 40 or more in females; *Heterodon nasicus gloydi* has 32 or less in males and 37 or less in females.

The natural history of the dusty hognose snake is similar to that of the nominate race.

Remarks: Due to restricted distribution in Missouri, both subspecies of *Heterodon nasicus* are listed as rare in *Rare and Endangered Species of Missouri.*

Hognose snakes have a pair of enlarged teeth at the rear of the mouth on the upper jaw; it is presumed the teeth help them swallow large prey. There are no venom glands and the teeth are solid, not hollow.

Missouri Distribution: Both subspecies of *Heterodon nasicus* have a restricted distribution in Missouri. The plains hognose snake is only known from the extreme northwestern part of the state; the dusty hognose snake is known from two counties in southeastern Missouri (Anderson, 1965).

Adult eastern hognose snake in a defensive posture, from Cole County.

Eastern Hognose Snake
Heterodon platyrhinos Latreille

Description: Known locally as the "spreadhead," "puff adder," or "hissing viper," this harmless snake is medium-size with a heavy body and pronounced upturned snout. Its color is highly variable. Ground color is gray, tan, yellow, brown, or olive; specimens can either have a series of brown dorsal blotches (from 20 to 30), or can be dull colored and lack dorsal markings. The belly is gray, yellow or pinkish, mottled with gray or greenish gray. The underside of the tail is normally lighter than the belly. Even on specimens with no dorsal markings there is always a pair of large dark brown or black blotches behind the head. Dorsal scales are keeled; anal plate divided. Newly hatched eastern hognose snakes are more colorful than adults.

Adult eastern hognose snakes range in length from 510 to 840 mm (20 to 33 inches). Largest Missouri specimen recorded is 842 mm (33 1/16 inches; Powell *et al.*, 1982). Record length is 1,156 mm (45 1/2 inches; Conant, 1975).

Habits and Habitat: Eastern hognose snakes are active by day. The active season is from mid-April to October. The eastern hognose snake does not seem to have a definite home range. It will either burrow into loose soil or sand or enter the burrow of small mammals. This species occasionally takes shelter under objects such as rocks or boards.

The eastern hognose snake utilizes a variety of habitats, but seems to prefer areas that have sandy or loose soil. It occurs on the sandy floodplains of rivers, in old fields, open woods, or on rocky wooded

An eastern hognose snake "playing dead" (left), *and eating an American toad* (right).

hillsides. Hognose snakes may spend their winter dormancy in abandoned small mammal burrows.

Food of this species consists of toads, frogs and occasionally salamanders. A pair of enlarged teeth are present on the upper jaw at the back of the mouth and are presumed to assist in swallowing large prey.

The local names "spreadhead" and "puff adder" have been given to the eastern hognose snake because of the way it defends itself. When approached it flattens its head and neck, hisses loudly and even strikes—but the mouth is closed. If this fierce act fails to drive away an intruder and if further provoked, the hognose will go into convulsions, open its mouth, let the tongue hang out, writhe about, release feces from its cloaca, roll over on its back and "play dead." If left unmolested, the snake will eventually roll over very slowly, look about to make sure it is safe, and retreat to a nearby shelter. Munyer (1967) saw an eastern hognose snake feign death while in the water; it appeared bloated and dead with belly up and the mouth closed. Sexton (1979) remarked on the importance of the hognose snake turning its head toward the body while exposing the coiled tail as a means of protecting the head.

Hatchling eastern hognose snake from Cole County (left), *and an unusual amelanistic hatchling from Macon County* (right).

251

Breeding: The eastern hognose snake mates in April and May. The courtship of this species has not been investigated. Platt (1969) studied this species in east central Kansas, and his data is included in this account. From 4 to 61 eggs are laid per female, usually in a shallow burrow in sand or loose soil. A captive female from Cole County laid 24 eggs on June 28 while in my care. The white eggs averaged 35 by 23 mm (1 3/8 by 7/8 inches) in size. Hatching takes place in August or September. The brightly colored young of the eastern hognose have an average total length of 234 mm (9 1/4 inches) at hatching.

Missouri Distribution: The eastern hognose snake is presumed to occur statewide.

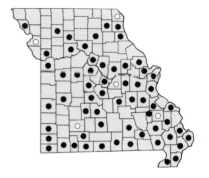

Adult prairie kingsnake from Audrain County.

Prairie Kingsnake
Lampropeltis calligaster calligaster (Harlan)

Description: A medium-size tan or gray snake with numerous brown blotches. Up to 60 brown or reddish-brown, black-edged blotches occur along the back, with two rows of smaller blotches along the sides. Older specimens often are darker overall due to a darkened ground color; this is more often observed on specimens from the southern half of Missouri. The top of the head usually has a backward pointing arrowhead-shaped marking. The belly is yellow with rectangular brown markings. The dorsal scales are smooth and the anal plate is single.

Adult prairie kingsnakes range in length from 760 to 1,070 mm (30 to 42 inches). Largest Missouri specimen recorded is 1,306 mm (51 7/16 inches; Powell *et al.*, 1982). Record length is 1,324 mm (52 1/8 inches; Conant, 1975).

Habits and Habitat: The active season of this species is normally from April to October. During spring and autumn prairie kingsnakes are active in the morning and early evening, but they become nocturnal during the summer. As with most kingsnakes, this species is rather secretive; it takes shelter under objects such as logs, rocks and boards, or utilizes small mammal burrows.

The name "prairie" kingsnake is somewhat misleading, for this common harmless snake not only can be found in native prairie habitats, but also along the edge of crop fields, hayfields or wood lots, on rocky, wooded hillsides and near farm buildings.

When alarmed a prairie kingsnake will vibrate its tail; if captured, it may try to bite to defend itself.

A young prairie kingsnake from Audrain County (left), *and hatchlings emerging from eggs* (right) *from Cole County.*

Food consists of mice, lizards and occasionally small snakes. Prey is killed by constriction.

Breeding: This species mates in early spring soon after emerging from winter dormancy. Males locate females by following their scent. Prairie kingsnakes lay their eggs during June and early July. A female may lay from 6 to 13 eggs (Anderson, 1965). The eggs, laid under rocks, logs or in old sawdust piles, adhere to each other. A female collected in Audrain County laid eight eggs on June 30. The eggs had an average measurement of 43.1 by 21.5 mm (1 11/16 by 14/16 inches). These were incubated at 28°C (82°F), and hatched on August 16. The hatchlings ranged from 285 to 294 mm (11 1/4 to 11 1/2 inches) in length.

Remarks: The prairie kingsnake is often misidentified as a copperhead and needlessly killed. The dorsal markings of this species are round; those of the copperhead are hourglass-shaped. Because the prairie kingsnake consumes many destructive rodents, it should be protected.

The prairie kingsnake was described as a species from specimens collected "in the vicinity of St. Louis, Missouri" in 1827 (Schmidt, 1953).

Missouri Distribution: This species is presumed to occur statewide.

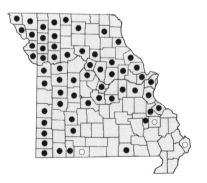

254

Adult speckled kingsnake from Cole County.

Speckled Kingsnake
Lampropeltis getulus holbrooki Stejneger

Description: A medium to large, shiny black snake covered with small yellow spots; known locally as the "salt-and-pepper snake." Ground color dark brown or black. Each dorsal scale normally has one white or yellowish spot which causes the snake to appear speckled. Occasionally the light spots form crossbars along the back. This condition is apparent on young speckled kingsnakes, but changes to an overall speckled appearance with age. The belly is yellow with a series of large black rectangular markings. The dorsal scales are smooth; the anal plate is single.

Adult speckled kingsnakes range in length from 910 to 1,220 mm (36 to 46 inches). Largest Missouri specimen recorded is 1,522 mm (60 inches; Anderson, 1965). The record length is 1,892 mm (72 inches; Conant, 1975).

Habits and Habitat: This species is active between April and October. During spring, early summer and autumn, speckled kingsnakes are active during daylight. They become active at night during the summer to avoid hot temperatures. This species is rather secretive; it takes shelter under rocks, logs, rotted stumps, boards, and in small mammal burrows.

This handsome snake occurs in a wide variety of habitats—prairies, brushy areas, forest edge, rocky, wooded hillsides and along the edges of swamps or marshes.

The speckled kingsnake kills its prey by constriction, and consumes rodents, small birds, lizards and small snakes. This snake is immune to the venom of the various pit vipers native to Missouri.

Light colored underbelly of a speckled kingsnake (left), *and a hatchling speckled kingsnake from Cole County* (right).

Speckled kingsnakes probably spend their winter dormancy underground in small mammal burrows. A speckled kingsnake was found overwintering in a cave in Jefferson County (Drda, 1968).

Breeding: Courtship and mating occur in late April or May. Six to 14 eggs are laid during the summer (Anderson, 1965). Hatching takes place in late summer.

Remarks: As with many species of harmless snakes, speckled kingsnakes vibrate their tails when alarmed. Freshly collected specimens may try to bite, but they quickly calm down and can be easily handled.

Missouri Distribution: The speckled kingsnake is presumed to occur statewide.

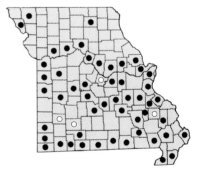

Adult red milk snake from Taney County.

Red Milk Snake
Lampropeltis triangulum syspila (Cope)

Description: A brightly colored, medium-size snake with smooth scales. This is Missouri's most colorful snake. The ground color is white or yellowish; there is a series of 20 to 30 red or orange-red dorsal blotches, bordered in black. There is also a row of smaller, black blotches along the sides. The top of the head is red or orange and the belly is boldly marked with black and white. The dorsal scales are smooth; anal plate single.

Adult red milk snakes range in length from 530 to 710 mm (21 to 28 inches). Largest Missouri specimen recorded is 835 mm (33 inches; Powell *et al.*, 1982). The record length is 1,067 mm (42 inches; Conant, 1975).

Habits and Habitat: Red milk snakes are active from April until late October. This species is secretive and seldom seen in the open; it takes shelter under rocks and logs or in rodent burrows. During hot weather this snake moves underground into animal burrows or under large rocks.

Red milk snakes feed on lizards, small snakes and mice; prey is killed by constriction.

In Missouri this species resides under rocks on rocky, south-facing wooded hillsides—especially on cedar glades. It may also be found along the edge of forests where there are some rocks and logs. Winter dormancy is spent in rodent burrows or in dens along rocky hillsides.

Breeding: Courtship and mating occur in the spring. Eggs may be laid under large rocks, in leaf litter, or in a rotten stump. The following

Ventral coloration of a red milk snake (left), *and a hatchling red milk snake from Cole County* (right).

information on the reproduction of red milk snakes was provided by Robert Krager (pers. comm.) who has studied this species in Missouri for a number of years. Data was collected on 17 clutches of eggs, all of which were produced during June and July. Each clutch contained from 1 to 13 eggs, with an average of 5. Eggs hatch from mid-August to early September. Hatchling red milk snakes averaged 221 mm (8 1/4 inches) in total length. Newly hatched red milk snakes have vivid red blotches.

Remarks: The red milk snake is often mistaken for a coral snake, a venomous species which does not occur in Missouri.

At one time this snake and various subspecies were thought to have the ability to suck milk from cows. Most people now realize the improbability of this behavior and recognize it as a myth.

Missouri Distribution: The red milk snake is presumed to occur statewide.

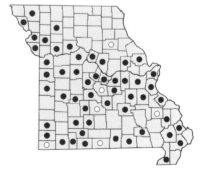

Adult eastern coachwhip from Maries County.

Eastern Coachwhip
Masticophis flagellum flagellum (Shaw)

Description: A large, slender, fast moving snake with dark color anteriorly and light color posteriorly. Color varies, but generally the anterior two thirds is dark brown or black; the posterior one third of the body is tan or reddish brown. The belly color corresponds to that of the back. Specimens from southwest Missouri are often completely black or dark brown. Juvenile eastern coachwhips are marked with numerous dark brown crossbands over a tan ground color anteriorly which fades to an overall tan color on the posterior. The dark markings disappear with age. Dorsal scales are smooth; the anal plate is divided.

Adult eastern coachwhip snakes range in length from 1,070 to 1,520 mm (42 to 60 inches). Largest Missouri specimen recorded is 1,880 mm (74 inches; Resetarits, pers. comm.). The record length is 2,590 mm (102 inches; Conant, 1975).

Habits and Habitat: This species is active during sunny days from April until October. When approached, a coachwhip will normally escape with an explosive burst of speed. If an individual is cornered, it will maneuver into a defensive coil, vibrate its tail, fight savagely and bite to defend itself.

This species eats mice, small birds, lizards and small snakes. The coachwhip is not a constrictor. Young coachwhips consume insects and small lizards.

In Missouri the eastern coachwhip can be found on dry, rocky, brushy or wooded hillsides—especially cedar glades. It also occurs along

Eastern coachwhip underbelly (left), *and a hatchling eastern coachwhip from Maries County* (right).

the edge of prairies where there is ample brush and other shelter. On cool days coachwhip snakes hide under flat rocks or in small mammal burrows. This species overwinters in rock crevices or burrows.

Breeding: Little is known about the courtship and mating of this species. Mating is likely to occur in April or May. From 8 to 24 eggs are laid per female. The eggs are white, have a granular texture, and have an average measurement of 48 by 26 mm (1 7/8 by 1 inches; Anderson, 1965). Eggs are laid during late June through July in loose soil or leaf litter, and hatch in late August or September. Newly hatched eastern coachwhip snakes average 330 mm (13 inches) in length.

Remarks: The eastern coachwhip is considered Missouri's fastest snake, but in reality it cannot move as fast as a man can run.

Missouri Distribution: This species is restricted to the Missouri Ozarks and the Ozark border areas.

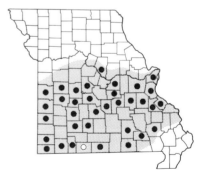

Adult green water snake.

Green Water Snake
Nerodia cyclopion cyclopion (Dumeril, Bibron and Dumeril)

Description: A medium-size dark colored, semi-aquatic snake which may have once been common in southeastern Missouri, but is now classified as endangered. This harmless, heavy-bodied snake has a ground color of greenish brown with numerous small, obscure olive-brown or dark brown markings. Close examination of the head will reveal a short row of scales (*suboculars*) between the eye and the upper lip scales. No other water snake native to Missouri has this characteristic. The belly is dark gray with numerous yellow markings—most of them in the form of half-moons. Dorsal markings are more distinct on young specimens. Dorsal scales are keeled; anal plate is divided.

Adult green water snakes range in length from 760 to 1,140 mm (30 to 45 inches). Largest Missouri specimen recorded is 911 mm (36 inches; Powell *et al.*, 1982). Record length is 1,270 mm (50 inches; Conant, 1975).

Habits and Habitat: Very little is known about the natural history of this species in Missouri. It is probably active between late March and October. This water snake is normally active on warm days, and can be observed sunning on branches overhanging water (Hebrard and Mushinsky, 1978). Green water snakes search for food during early evening, or at night when the weather is hot. This species will bite and smear a foul-smelling musk onto its captor.

Food of the green water snake consists of fish, salamanders, frogs, and possibly crayfish. Kofron (1978) reported that Louisiana specimens

Head of a green water snake (left), *and ventral coloration* (right).

ate mostly small fish (94 percent frequency). Garton, *et al.* (1970) found western lesser sirens in three green water snakes collected in southern Illinois.

This is primarily a swamp dwelling snake. Preferred habitats in Missouri are the cypress swamps and river sloughs of the Mississippi lowlands.

Breeding: The reproductive biology of the green water snake has not been studied in Missouri. In general, courtship and mating are presumed to occur in the spring, probably in April or May. Eggs are retained and the young develop within the females (a reproductive method known as *ovoviviparous*). The young are born during August and early September. In general, the number of young produced per female has a direct relation to the size of the female: the larger the female the greater the number of young that can be produced. Kofron (1979) reported female green water snakes in Louisiana had an average litter size of 18. Barbour (1971) stated that a litter may average between 10 and 20, and that average length of the newborn young of this species is between 228 and 254 mm (9 to 10 inches).

Remarks: The green water snake has been designated endangered in Missouri due to the very low number of biologists' reports of this species in southeast Missouri and the drastic reduction in native cypress swamps. Commenting on the low population of this snake in both extreme southern Illinois and southeastern Missouri, Garton, *et al.* (1970) stated: "Large fluctuations in population density are not unexpected in peripheral populations where ecological conditions presumably are marginal."

Missouri Distribution: Presumed to occur in the natural cypress swamps of extreme southeastern Missouri.

Adult yellowbelly water snake from Dunklin County.

Yellowbelly Water Snake
Nerodia erythrogaster flavigaster (Conant)

Description: A medium-size, heavy-bodied, dark colored, semi-aquatic snake with a plain yellow belly. Adults are gray, greenish gray, or brownish black, with little or no pattern along the dorsum. The belly is plain yellow with some orange showing on occasional individuals. Young yellowbelly water snakes are strongly patterned with brown dorsal and lateral blotches which may be joined to form transverse bars. These markings fade with age. Dorsal scales keeled; anal plate divided.

Adult yellowbelly water snakes range in length from 760 to 1,220 mm (30 to 48 inches). Largest Missouri specimen recorded is 1,235 mm (48 5/8 inches; Powell *et al.*, 1982). Record length is 1,349 mm (53 1/8 inches; Conant, 1975).

Habits and Habitat: This species is apparently active from late March through October. Specimens can be observed basking on logs in shallow water, on branches above the water, or along the shore. As with most of our water snakes, this species is pugnacious and will strike or bite viciously when captured. A foul-smelling musk is also excreted from glands in the base of the tail; it is often mixed with feces and smeared on the captor.

This water snake preys on fish, toads and frogs, tadpoles, salamanders and crayfish.

The yellowbelly water snake prefers quiet bodies of water such as swamps, sloughs, oxbow lakes and ponds.

Ventral coloration of a yellowbelly water snake (left), *and a juvenile yellowbelly water snake from Butler County* (right).

Breeding: Courtship and mating take place during April and early May. As with most live-bearing species, the number of young increases with the size of females. From 10 to as many as 30 young may be produced, with an average length of 228 to 305 mm (9 to 12 inches). A female collected in east central Kansas produced 28 young (Donald Smith, pers. comm.). The young are born during August and early September.

Adult blotched water snake.

Subspecies: A geographic race of the yellowbelly water snake, known as the blotched water snake, *Nerodia erythrogaster transversa* (Hallowell), occurs in southwestern and western Missouri. The blotched water snake is gray or greenish brown with numerous brown blotches along the back and sides. Unlike the yellowbelly, the blotched water snakes do not fade with age. The belly is plain yellow with a wash of orange—especially along the underside of the tail. Record length of this subspecies is 1,473 mm (58 inches; Conant, 1975).

The blotched water snake occurs in ponds, swamps, sloughs, or near slow moving streams. Specimens may be encountered during the summer on land, well removed from any body of water. Food habits and breeding are similar to the yellowbelly water snake discussed above.

Missouri Distribution: The yellow-belly water snake occurs in south-eastern Missouri and may range northward in suitable habitat along the Mississippi River floodplain to St. Charles County. A young adult *Nerodia erythrogaster flavigaster* was collected in eastern St. Charles County (Bader, pers. comm.). The blotched water snake (hatch lines) occurs throughout western and west central Missouri.

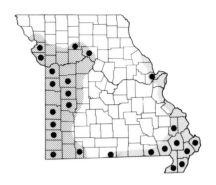

Adult broad-banded water snake from Dunklin County.

Broad-banded Water Snake
Nerodia fasciata confluens (Blanchard)

Description: The broad-banded water snake is a medium-size, semi-aquatic snake with broad, dark blotches or bands. The bands may be brown, red-brown or black, separated by yellow or yellowish gray. There are normally 11 to 17 bands; although irregular in shape, they are broadest on the back. Some of the bands may be connected. There is often a faint dark line which runs diagonally from the eye past the corner of the mouth. The belly is yellowish and boldly marked with black. The dorsal scales are keeled; anal plate is divided. Young broad-banded water snakes are more brightly colored than adults.

Adult broad-banded water snakes range in length from 590 to 910 mm (22 to 36 inches). Largest Missouri specimen recorded is 1,014 mm (36 5/16 inches; Powell *et al.*, 1982). Record length is 1,143 mm (45 inches; Conant, 1975).

Habits and Habitat: This species is normally active between late March and October. Although the broad-banded water snake may be observed basking on logs or branches overhanging the water, it is more active at night, especially during hot weather. If a specimen is encountered and not allowed to escape, it will vigorously try to defend itself. Once captured it will bite viciously and smear its captor with a foul-smelling musk excreted from glands at the base of the tail.

Food of this species includes fish, frogs and toads, and tadpoles.

The broad-banded water snake resides in and along the edge of cypress swamps, river sloughs and oxbow lakes.

Ventral coloration of a broad-banded water snake.

Breeding: Courtship and mating occur during April and early May. The young are born alive during late July, August or early September; a litter may consist of 7 to 40 young. They range in length from 180 to 240 mm (7 to 9 1/2 inches; Conant, 1975).

Remarks: The type locality of this subspecies was designated as Butler County, Missouri by Blanchard (1923).

This species of water snake is often misidentified as the venomous western cottonmouth, *Agkistrodon piscivorus leucostoma*. The true cottonmouth is more heavy-bodied, darker in color, and has a light line from each eye to the corner of the mouth.

Missouri Distribution: This species occurs in the Mississippi lowlands of southeastern Missouri.

267

Adult diamondback water snake.

Diamondback Water Snake
Nerodia rhombifer rhombifer (Hallowell)

Description: A large, heavy-bodied snake with numerous diamond-shaped light markings along the back. This is Missouri's largest species of water snake. The ground color may be gray, light brown, or dull yellow. There are 30 to 65 dark brown bands along the back which are normally connected to form a chainlike pattern. The belly is yellow with several irregular rows of dark brown spots or half-moons. The dorsal scales are strongly keeled; anal plate divided.

Adult diamondback water snakes range in length from 760 to 1,220 mm (30 to 48 inches). Largest Missouri specimen recorded is 1,272 mm (50 1/16 inches; Powell *et al.*, 1982). Record length is 1,600 mm (63 inches; Conant, 1975).

Habits and Habitat: This species is active from late March through October. During spring, early summer and autumn, diamondback water snakes can be observed basking on branches or logs. This species becomes distinctly nocturnal during the hot summer months. Diamondback water snakes bite viciously to defend themselves and also secrete a strong-smelling musk from glands at the base of the tail.

Fish, especially slow moving or dead fish, frogs, toads and salamanders are eaten by this species. Kofron and Dixon (1980) described a diamondback water snake forming an enclosure with its body to catch small fish.

This large water snake occurs in a variety of aquatic habitats, but is most abundant in swamps, sloughs, oxbow lakes and marshes.

*Female diamondback water snake giving birth, from
Pemiscot County.*

Breeding: Courtship and mating take place in the spring, probably during April or early May. Male diamondback water snakes have a cluster of tiny raised bumps on their chin which are likely used during courtship—the male rubs his chin along a receptive female's back to stimulate her. Young diamondback water snakes are born during late August through early October. A female I collected in Pemiscot County gave birth to 35 young on September 22; they averaged 294 mm (11 5/8 inches) in length. From 14 to 62 young can be produced (Collins, 1982). The young measure from 230 to 330 mm (9 to 13 1/8 inches; Conant, 1975) in length and often have some orange coloration on their bellies.

Remarks: This semi-aquatic species may be misidentified as the venomous western cottonmouth. The cottonmouth does not have the chainlike dark pattern on the back. Cottonmouths have a distinct triangular head, a sensory pit between the eye and nostril on either side of the head, and a light line from each eye to the corner of the mouth.

Missouri Distribution: The diamondback water snake occurs in the southeast and over most of the northern, western and southwestern parts of the state. Suitable habitat for this species (swamps and marshes) is lacking in the Ozarks.

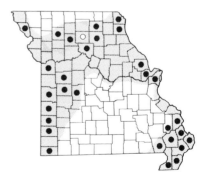

Adult northern water snake from Pulaski County.

Northern Water Snake
Nerodia sipedon sipedon (Linnaeus)

Description: Known locally as the "banded water snake" or "common water snake," this is a gray to brown snake with numerous dark brown bands or blotches. Dorsal crossbands are reddish brown, dark brown or nearly black. Color of the belly varies, but generally it is a combination of yellow ground color and irregularly spaced half-moons or spots of orange or red, bordered by gray or black. Dorsal scales are keeled; anal plate is divided. Male northern water snakes are smaller and have longer tails than females.

Adult northern water snakes range in length from 610 to 1,070 mm (24 to 42 inches). Largest Missouri specimen recorded is 1,133 mm (44 3/4 inches; Powell *et al.*, 1982). The record length is 1,346 mm (53 inches; Conant, 1975).

Habits and Habitat: This is the most common species of water snake in Missouri. Northern water snakes are usually active from early April until October. Individuals bask on branches overhanging the water or on logs along the water's edge during spring and early summer. This species becomes mostly nocturnal during hot weather; it is known to take shelter under rocks or other objects along the edge of rivers or ponds.

Like other members of the genus *Nerodia*, this species is pugnacious when captured, and will flatten the head and neck and bite to defend itself. A strong-smelling musk is discharged from glands at the base of the tail and is used as a means of defense.

Underside of a northern water snake (left), *and a juvenile northern water snake from Linn County.*

Small fish (mostly nongame species) make up to 95 percent of the diet of northern water snakes, but frogs, toads and tadpoles are also eaten.

Northern water snakes live in a wide variety of aquatic habitats: creeks, rivers, sloughs, ponds, lakes and swamps.

Breeding: Courtship and mating of this species occur during the spring; males locate females by sensing a particular odor they release. Courtship involves a male rubbing his chin along the back of the female and at the same time jerking spasmodically in order to stimulate her to copulate. More than one male may try to court and mate with a receptive female. Gestation may last from three to four months. The young are born during August and September. A litter contains from 8 to 46 young, with an average litter size of 26. Young range in length from about 203 to 254 mm (8 to 10 inches). Young northern water snakes are light gray or tan contrasting with dark brown or black crossbands.

Subspecies: Throughout much of the southern third of Missouri the northern water snake intergrades with—or is replaced by—a geographic race or subspecies known as the midland water snake, *Nerodia sipedon pleuralis (*Cope). The midland water snake has a tan or reddish-brown ground color with brown or reddish-brown crossbands and blotches. Some specimens are almost orange with brown markings. The belly is usually yellow with irregularly spaced orange, red, or brown markings in the form of spots or half-moons.

Anderson (1965) stated that the midland water snake primarily lives in and near the clear, cool, gravel-bed creeks and rivers which are typical of the southern Missouri Ozarks. Other natural history and reproductive biology information of this subspecies are similar to that of the nominate race described above.

Remarks: Missouri fishermen (and women) have persecuted water snakes for years because of the mistaken belief that these reptiles eat game fish and are detrimental to their sport. In reality, just the opposite

271

Adult midland water snake from Ozark County.

is the case. Game fish are too agile for water snakes to catch—unless a fish is injured or diseased. Numerous studies (Pope, 1944; Lagler and Salyer, 1947; Raney and Roecker, 1947; and Trembley, 1948) have shown that water snakes in association with natural bodies of water improve fishing by preventing the spread of fish diseases, by reducing fish over-population, and by providing food for game species (large game fish eat young water snakes). They are a natural part of our outdoor heritage and a valuable component of the waters of our state.

Nickerson and Krager (1975) reported the collection of two aberrant specimens from Miller County that lacked the dorsal blotches and crossbands.

Missouri Distribution: The northern water snake occurs throughout the northern two thirds of Missouri, and intergrades with or is replaced by the midland water snake in the southern third of Missouri (hatch lines).

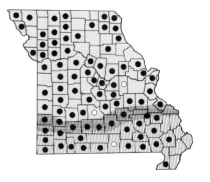

Adult rough green snake from Taney County.

Rough Green Snake
Opheodrys aestivus (Linnaeus)

Description: A slender, light green, arboreal snake. The dorsal color is plain light green; the belly is yellow or cream colored and devoid of any markings. Scales along the sides and back are weakly keeled; the anal plate is divided. This species has a slender tail of medium length that may account for an average of 38 percent of the total length (Anderson, 1965).

Adult rough green snakes range in length from 460 to 660 mm (18 to 26 inches). Largest Missouri specimen recorded is 735 mm (29 inches; Powell *et al.*, 1982).

Habits and Habitat: The active season of this species lasts from April through September. Rough green snakes are diurnal and spend most of their time among the branches of low trees and bushes. At night these snakes coil among the leaves near the end of branches (Plummer, 1981).

This inoffensive snake seldom tries to bite when captured. It remains motionless among the leaves and branches and relies on its coloration to remain undetected. If a slight wind moves the branches, the green snake will bend and wave in unison.

The diet of this species is restricted to insects and spiders. Plummer (1981) listed caterpillars, spiders, grasshoppers, crickets, dragonflies and damselflies as comprising 85 percent of the diet of rough green snakes studied in Arkansas.

This arboreal species resides in the dense vegetation along creeks, rivers and the edge of ponds. Plummer (*ibid.*) found that rough green

273

A rough green snake eating a grasshopper (left), and a hatchling rough green snake from Cole County (right).

snakes select resting places among branches from 1 to 4 meters (3 to 13 feet) above the ground. Anderson (1965) stated that this species can occur in buckbrush, bittersweet vines, wild blackberry vines, and willow trees with branches overhanging water. Plummer (*ibid.*) noted that willow and ironwood were used only slightly more than other species of vegetation, and concluded that this species did not seem to prefer any particular species of plant. Specimens may be found on rocky, forested hillsides and river bluffs.

Breeding: Mating takes place in the spring and during autumn. Gravid females move out of their arboreal haunts to select a nesting spot: leaf litter, brushpiles or rotten stumps. The white, elongated eggs are laid during late June and July. From 3 to 12 eggs are produced per female (Collins, 1982). A female I collected in Miller County laid 7 eggs on July 13. The eggs averaged 24 by 11 mm (1 by 7/16 inches) in size. The eggs hatched on August 23, after 42 days of incubation. The newly hatched rough green snakes averaged 184 mm (7 1/4 inches) in total length and were brownish green dorsally and white ventrally. In nature the eggs can take up to two months to hatch.

Remarks: Grobman (1984) suggested that two subspecies of rough green snakes occur in Missouri: the western rough green snake, *Opheodrys aestivus majalis* (Baird and Gerard) which has a medium-length tail with from 110 to 142 caudal scales; and the eastern rough green snake, *Opheodrys aestivus aestivus* (Linneaus), which has a long tail with from 119 to 155 caudal scales. More research is needed on this issue before I can be comfortable in recognizing the proposed subspecies for the Missouri population.

Missouri Distribution: The rough green snake occurs throughout the southern two thirds of the state and among the Mississippi River hills in northern Missouri.

Adult western smooth green snake.

Western Smooth Green Snake
Opheodrys vernalis blanchardi Grobman

Description: The western smooth green snake is a small, gentle, secretive species. The dorsal color is light green without any markings; the belly is plain white or with some yellow color along the sides. In Illinois, Michigan and Wisconsin this species may also be a uniform light tan color, but this color morph has not been reported in Missouri. The dorsal scales are smooth; the anal plate is divided.

Adult western smooth green snakes range in length from 360 to 510 mm (14 to 20 inches). Largest Missouri specimen recorded is 462 mm (14 3/8 inches; Powell *et al.*, 1982). Record length is 660 mm (26 inches; Conant, 1975).

Habits and Habitat: The active season of this species lasts from April through September. Smooth green snakes search for food or move about among grasses and shrubbery during the day, and hide under rocks, boards, or mats of dead grass at night. When captured, a specimen may struggle to escape, but seldom attempts to bite.

This species feeds on slugs and a variety of insects and spiders. I was able to induce Wisconsin specimens to eat smooth caterpillars, small crickets and grasshoppers.

The western smooth green snake lives in grassy meadows along the edge of forests, marshes, and moist prairies. Anderson (1965) collected several specimens in a bluegrass pasture in Audrain County.

This species probably overwinters in the ground using abandoned small mammal burrows. It has been reported to spend the winter inside abandoned ant mounds in northern Minnesota (Lang, 1969).

Breeding: Nothing is known about the reproductive biology of this species in Missouri. In other states, this species mates in the spring, but may also breed in early autumn. The eggs are laid in rotten logs or in mounds of decaying vegetation or leaf litter. More than one female may deposit eggs in the same nest site. There may be from 5 to 15 eggs per clutch. The average clutch size for Illinois and Wisconsin populations is six (Smith, 1961; Vogt, 1981). The eggs are white, elongated, and have average measurements of 23 by 13 mm (15/16 by 1/2 inch). Gravid females seem to retain the eggs for a period of time during early summer, and the eggs consequently hatch sooner after being laid than those of most other North American species. Eggs laid in June usually hatch in July. Vogt (1981) stated that the incubation period for the Wisconsin population is 30 days. Hatchling smooth green snakes are olive-tan in color and from 120 to 150 mm (4 3/4 to 5 7/16 inches) in length.

Remarks: The western smooth green snake can be distinguished from the rough green snake (*Opheodrys aestivus*) by its smaller size, shorter tail, and the smooth (unkeeled) dorsal scales.

This species is considered endangered in Missouri. The destruction of its habitat and the use of agricultural insecticides are primarily responsible for the decline of this species in northern Missouri. If isolated colonies of the western smooth green snake are located in Missouri, special measures will be needed to ensure their survival, including protecting and improving the habitat, eliminating pesticide use, monitoring reproduction and population changes, and discouraging collecting.

Missouri Distribution: Anderson (1965) showed the range of this species as including the northern half of the state. Due to a lack of recent records and the decline of available habitat, I have restricted the distribution map to include the locations of western smooth green snake reports.

Adult bullsnake from Dade County.

Bullsnake
Pituophis melanoleucus sayi (Schlegel)

Description: This is the largest snake species native to Missouri. The bullsnake is a medium to large, tan, yellowish or white snake with 38 to 53 dark brown or black blotches along the back. Markings along the back and sides are generally black on the neck and tail, brownish at mid-body. There is usually a black line from the eye to the angle of the jaw, and black bars along the upper lip. The head is large and the snout terminates with an enlarged, projecting rostral scale. The belly is yellow and strongly checkered with square or rectangular black markings. The scales along the back are keeled; the anal plate is single.

Adult bullsnakes range in length from 1,270 to 1,830 mm (50 to 72 inches). Largest Missouri specimen recorded is 1,782 mm (70 5/16 inches; Powell *et al.*, 1982). Record length is 2,540 mm (100 inches; Conant, 1975).

Habits and Habitat: In Missouri, bullsnakes may be active from April until early November. This species basks in the sun or searches for food by day; at night it takes shelter in mammal burrows, clumps of vegetation, within rock piles, or under objects.

If approached or cornered, a bullsnake will coil, vibrate its tail, and hiss loudly with the mouth partly open. The loud hiss is made by air being forced from the lungs and out the windpipe, which has a special flap of skin that vibrates as air passes over it. Once captured a bullsnake will bite to defend itself, but normally calms down quickly and can be handled with ease in a short time.

A two-headed bullsnake mutation from Holt County.

Food of the bullsnake includes mice, rats, ground squirrels, pocket gophers, small rabbits, birds and bird eggs. This snake is a powerful constrictor.

In Missouri, bullsnakes occur on native prairies, pastures, old fields, savannahs and along some river bluffs.

This species overwinters in small mammal burrows, beneath rock piles, or in rock crevices on rocky hillsides.

Breeding: Courtship and mating take place during April and early May. Adult males probably locate females by smell. Once a female is located, the male will court her by following her, moving alongside her, and producing jerking body movements. Once the female becomes passive, the male moves alongside and drapes his body over hers. Their cloacas meet when the male moves his tail under that of the female, and mating occurs. During this time the male grasps the female by the neck with his mouth.

Eggs are laid during June or early July; from 5 to 19 eggs are laid per clutch (Collins, 1982). The eggs average 50 by 40 mm (2 by 1 9/16 inches) in size (Vogt, 1981) and stick to each other after being laid. Female bullsnakes normally lay their eggs in sandy or loose soil, in abandoned small mammal burrows, or under large stumps or logs. The eggs hatch during late August through September. Newly hatched bullsnakes average 365 mm (14 3/8 inches) in total length. Their color is similar to that of adult bullsnakes, except that their blotches are somewhat lighter.

Remarks: This large, non-venomous species is a valuable neighbor to farmers because of the large number of crop-destroying rodents it eats. Consequently, the bullsnake is the most economically beneficial snake in Missouri, and rural Missourians should make every effort to protect this species.

Missouri Distribution: Bullsnakes occur over most of Missouri excluding the eastern Ozarks and the southeastern corner of the state.

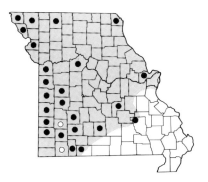

Adult Graham's crayfish snake from Linn County.

Graham's Crayfish Snake
Regina grahamii Baird and Girard

Description: This is a medium-size, dull colored, semi-aquatic snake known from prairie streams, marshes and ponds. The ground color is brown or yellowish brown above, with a yellow stripe along the lower sides which may be bordered by a thin, dark brown line. Some individuals may have a faint tan dorsal stripe. The belly is yellow with a central row of gray or brownish dots. Scales along the back and sides are keeled; the anal plate is divided.

Adult Graham's crayfish snakes range in length from 460 to 710 mm (18 to 28 inches). Largest Missouri specimen recorded is 855 mm (33 3/8 inches; Powell *et al.*, 1982). Record length is 1194 mm (47 inches; Conant, 1975).

Habits and Habitat: This harmless species is generally active from April through October. Graham's crayfish snakes can be observed basking among branches overhanging water during spring and early summer. This species often takes shelter under rocks or logs along the water's edge or in crayfish burrows. During hot weather this snake becomes nocturnal.

This is a shy, secretive species that is difficult to approach when observed sunning on branches or in the open. Once captured, they generally do not bite, but usually release a foul-smelling musk mixed with feces.

Graham's crayfish snakes feed primarily on soft-bodied crayfish (those which have recently shed their exoskeleton). Other foods include tadpoles and frogs.

Ventral coloration of a Graham's crayfish snake.

The habitat of this species is slow moving prairie streams, sloughs, marshes and ponds.

During winter this species takes shelter in crayfish burrows.

Breeding: This live-bearing species mates during April and May. Anderson (1965), on two occasions, found groups of male Graham's crayfish snakes competing to mate with a single female. The young are born from late July through September. A litter may contain from 9 to 39 young, with an average of 17 or 18 (Collins, 1982). The young range in length from 200 to 250 mm (8 to 10 inches); color is similar to that of adults.

Remarks: Because of the specialized diet (soft-bodied crayfish) of this species, it is difficult to maintain in captivity.

A population of Graham's crayfish snakes still persists in Forest Park in St. Louis, although completely surrounded by an urban environment.

Missouri Distribution: This species may be found throughout much of Missouri, excluding the Ozarks.

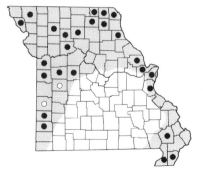

Adult ground snake from Taney County.

Ground Snake
Sonora semiannulata Baird and Girard

Description: The ground snake is a small species with smooth shiny scales, and a highly variable color. The ground color of this gentle, secretive species can be gray, light brown, or reddish brown. Individuals may have dark brown or black bands along their entire length, a few bands or blotches along the forward part of the body, or be totally patternless. Missouri specimens often have an orange or reddish tinge between crossbands. The belly is white or cream colored. The underside of the tail has numerous transverse, dark gray bars. Scales along the back are smooth; the anal plate is divided.

Adult ground snakes range in length from 230 to 300 mm (9 to 12 inches). Largest Missouri specimen recorded is 343 mm (13 3/4 inches; Powell *et al.*, 1982). Record length is 384 mm (15 1/8 inches; Conant, 1975).

Habits and Habitat: Ground snakes are generally active from April until early November. This species is not normally seen above ground during the day when it usually remains under rocks, but specimens may become active on the surface at night. During hot weather, ground snakes burrow underground to find cooler temperatures and higher humidity.

Food of this small snake includes scorpions, centipedes, spiders and soft-bodied insects.

In Missouri this species resides on rocky, wooded hillsides which face south or southwest. Cedar glades are a favored habitat and ground

Ventral coloration of a ground snake.

snakes can be found in association with the flathead snake (*Tantilla gracilis;* Anderson, 1965).

Breeding: Courtship and mating normally take place during April or May, but autumn mating has been reported (Anderson, 1965). Courtship involves the male rubbing his chin along the back of a female and occasionally biting her on the neck. Mating occurs when the tail of the male curls beneath that of the female. The eggs are laid in the loose, damp soil under rocks, during June and July; each female lays from four to six eggs. Hatching takes approximately two months after the eggs are laid; the young are from 98 to 109 mm (3 7/8 to 4 5/16 inches) in length.

Remarks: Missouri's population of ground snakes depends on the availability of natural cedar glades. As long as this type of habitat is protected, the species should continue to survive.

This burrowing species has been reported to have special nasal valves which, when closed, prevent sand or soil particles from entering the nostrils during burrowing activities.

Missouri Distribution: In Missouri, the ground snake is restricted to the cedar glades of the southwestern corner of the state.

Adult midland brown snake in a tan color phase, from Cole County.

Midland Brown Snake
Storeria dekayi wrightorum Trapido

Description: The midland brown snake is a small, secretive species which prefers a moist environment. The color may vary from gray to brown to reddish brown. There is usually a tan dorsal stripe which is bordered by two rows of small brown spots. These small spots are normally connected by a thin brown line. A dark spot is usually present under each eye and on each side of the neck. The belly is cream colored, yellowish or pinkish. The scales along the back are keeled; the anal plate is divided.

Adult midland brown snakes range in length from 230 to 330 mm (9 to 13 inches). Largest Missouri specimen recorded is 342 mm (13 1/2 inches; Powell *et al.*, 1982). Record length is 492 mm (19 3/8 inches; Conant, 1975).

Habits and Habitat: In Missouri, brown snakes are active from April to early November. This species takes shelter under logs, rocks, boards or other objects. Although an individual may move from one hiding place to another during the day, they are generally secretive and seldom seen out in the open. During hot weather, brown snakes may be active at night. I found a specimen crossing a Gasconade County blacktop road during a rainy night in September.

This species is not known to bite, but when captured will release a musky secretion from glands at the base of the tail.

Brown snakes feed primarily on earthworms, slugs and soft-bodied insects. While studying snakes in northwest Missouri, Seigel (pers.

Adult Texas brown snake in a reddish-brown color phase (left), *and a juvenile midland brown snake from Cole County* (right).

comm.) found this species' diet to be 75 percent slugs and 25 percent earthworms.

This snake prefers a moist environment, and can occur along the edges of marshes, swamps, or in river floodplains and forests.

Breeding: Brown snakes generally mate in the spring soon after emerging from their overwintering retreats, but autumn mating can also occur. This species is ovoviviparous; from 3 to 27 young are born between late July and September (Collins, 1982). The largest litter size reported is 41 young from a female captured in east central Illinois (Morris, 1974). Newly born brown snakes average 88 mm (3 1/4 inches) in length.

Subspecies: Missouri brown snakes are separated into two subspecies with a broad area of intergradation—the midland brown snake (*Storeria dekayi wrightorum,* described above), and the Texas brown snake (*Storeria dekayi texana* Trapido). Color of the Texas brown snake differs from that of the midland brown snake in two ways: the short bars between the small dark spots along the back are thinner and less obvious, and the dark spot on either side of the neck is larger.

Brown snakes were found to be an important food of young massasauga rattlesnakes in a northwestern Missouri marsh (Seigel, pers. comm.).

Missouri Distribution: The midland brown snake occurs in the eastern half of the state, and intergrades with the Texas brown snake in western Missouri.

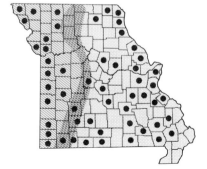

Adult northern redbelly snake from Barry County.

Northern Redbelly Snake
Storeria occipitomaculata occipitomaculata (Storer)

Description: A small, woodland snake that is either gray or reddish brown, with normally four narrow, dark stripes, a faint light mid-dorsal stripe, or a combination of these stripes present. The head is usually darker than the body, and the nape of the neck has three light spots, which occasionally fuse to form a tan collar behind the head. The belly is yellow, orange, red, or occasionally pink. Scales along the back and sides are keeled; the anal plate is divided.

Adult northern redbelly snakes range in length from 200 to 250 mm (8 to 10 inches). Largest Missouri specimen recorded is 303 mm (12 inches; Powell *et al.*, 1982). Record length is 406 mm (16 inches; Conant, 1975).

Habits and Habitat: This secretive species is active from late March through October. A great deal of time is spent hiding beneath rocks, boards, scattered tree bark, logs and other objects; however, specimens have been observed basking in the sun. I saw a northern redbelly snake basking on a log in Pulaski County during mid-May.

This small snake is not known to bite, and is completely inoffensive and gentle to handle. A freshly captured specimen will secrete a musky odor from glands at the base of the tail. Jordan (1970) reported on an Alabama specimen he observed which, when provoked, went into convulsions, rolled over several times, opened its mouth and remained motionless on its back—true death-feigning behavior.

Ventral coloration of a northern redbelly snake.

Northern redbelly snakes eat forest slugs, earthworms and occasionally soft-bodied insects.

This is a forest species, and occurs in moist woodlands where there is ample shelter such as rocks, logs and leaf litter.

Breeding: Courtship and mating take place in the spring, summer or autumn. The young are born during late summer or early autumn. Litter size has been reported to range from 1 to 21 young. At birth the young snakes are from 70 to 100 mm (2 3/4 to 4 inches; Conant, 1975) in length.

Remarks: This small, inoffensive snake is often mistaken for a young copperhead and needlessly killed.

Missouri Distribution: The northern redbelly snake is nearly statewide in occurrence, but is absent from northwestern Missouri.

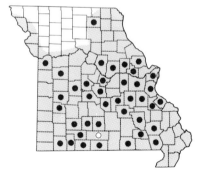

Adult flathead snake from Maries County.

Flathead Snake
Tantilla gracilis Baird and Girard

Description: This is Missouri's smallest species of snake. Dorsal color is gray, tan, brown, or slightly reddish brown. The head is normally darker in color than the body. The belly of this species is salmon-pink. Scales along the back and sides are smooth; the anal plate is divided.

Adult flathead snakes range in length from 180 to 200 mm (7 to 8 inches). Largest Missouri specimen recorded is 249 mm (9 7/8 inches; Powell *et al.*, 1982), which may be the record length for the species.

Habits and Habitat: This burrowing species is normally active from April through October. It spends a great deal of time in slightly moist soil under rocks, or in underground burrows.

Flathead snakes prefer rocky hillsides, and are most often encountered where sandy soil is in association with limestone.

This species is not known to bite when captured.

The food of this snake includes scorpions, spiders, centipedes and a variety of insects.

During hot weather as well as during the winter, flathead snakes burrow into the ground to escape the extreme temperatures.

Breeding: Courtship and mating take place during late April and May. The eggs are deposited in moist soil under rocks during June with from one to four eggs laid per female. Hatching takes place during August and September; the newly hatched young average about 76 mm (3 inches in length; Anderson, 1965).

Ventral coloration of a flathead snake.

Missouri Distribution: The flathead snake occurs throughout the Missouri Ozarks.

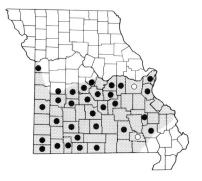

Adult western ribbon snake from Osage County.

Western Ribbon Snake
Thamnophis proximus proximus (Say)

Description: The western ribbon snake is a long, slender, colorful member of the garter snake group. There are normally two wide, black stripes along the back and a narrow black stripe on each side. The mid-dorsal stripe is orange or yellow. A narrow yellow stripe is present along each side. The head is black and usually has an orange or yellow spot on the top. The belly is cream or light green and unmarked. Scales along the back and sides are keeled; the anal plate is single.

Adult western ribbon snakes range in length from 510 to 760 mm (20 to 30 inches). Largest Missouri specimen recorded is 801 mm (31 5/8 inches, Powell *et al.*, 1982). Record length is 956 mm (37 5/8 inches; Conant, 1975).

Habits and Habitat: In Missouri, this slender snake is active from April through October. When temperatures are mild, it is active during the day, but may become nocturnal during hot weather.

When encountered, western ribbon snakes are quick and agile, and once startled may be difficult to capture. This species will not hesitate to enter water.

This slender species of garter snake is seldom found far from water. It lives near swamps, marshes, sloughs, streams and rivers. I observed several western ribbon snakes in a Linn County marsh during June feeding on tadpoles and young frogs.

Small frogs, toads, salamanders and minnows are the major prey of this species. Seigel (pers. comm.) found earthworms in the stomachs of western ribbon snakes taken in Holt County.

Breeding: Mating takes place during April and early May. The young are born from late June to September. A litter may contain from 4 to 27 young with an average of 12 or 13 (Collins, 1982). Anderson (1965) reported that a St. Clair County female gave birth to nine young on July 21. Seigel (pers. comm.) gathered data from ten gravid females from Holt County, and the mean number per litter was ten young. At birth, young western ribbon snakes are from 230 to 250 mm (9 to 10 inches) in length.

Missouri Distribution: The western ribbon snake is statewide in occurrence.

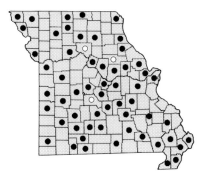

Adult western plains garter snake, a subspecies of the eastern plains garter snake. The two subspecies differ very little in appearance.

Eastern Plains Garter Snake
Thamnophis radix radix (Baird and Girard)

Description: This is a medium-size snake of wet meadows and marshes. Ground color is greenish gray, olive or brown. The narrow dorsal stripe is only one scale wide and is orange or orange-yellow. The light stripe on each side is on scale rows three and four; it may be yellow, greenish, or bluish. The area between light stripes usually has an alternating double row of black spots. The light green upper lip has black bars along the edges of the scales. The belly is gray or greenish gray with a row of black spots along each side. The scales along the back and sides are keeled; the anal plate is single.

Adult eastern plains garter snakes range in length from 510 to 710 mm (20 to 28 inches). Largest Missouri specimen recorded is 787 mm (31 1/8 inches; Powell *et al.*, 1982). Record length is 1,016 mm (40 inches; Conant, 1975).

Habits and Habitat: This attractive garter snake is normally active from late March to late October. Plains garter snakes spend warm, sunny days basking in the sun or searching for food. They take shelter under logs, boards, rocks or other objects. Winter is spent in burrows, probably abandoned rodent tunnels.

As with all garter snakes, the eastern plains garter snake will smear a musky secretion from glands at the base of the tail when captured or molested. Most of the specimens I have encountered have not tried to bite when captured.

Food of this species includes earthworms, frogs, toads, salamanders, minnows and occasionally small rodents.

In Missouri, this species can be found in or near meadows, wet prairies, marshes, lakes and ponds.

Breeding: Courtship and mating occur in the spring, although autumn mating has been reported (Collins, 1982). Young are born from late July through early September. From 5 to over 60 young can be produced in a litter. A mean of 9 young per female was found in a total of 45 females taken in Holt County (Seigel, pers. comm.). Newly born eastern plains garter snakes average about 190 mm (7 1/2 inches; Conant, 1975) in length.

Subspecies: The western plains garter snake, *Thamnophis radix haydenii* (Kennicott), is a subspecies of the eastern plains garter snake. It can be distinguished from the nominate race by the following: *Thamnophis radix radix* normally has 154 or fewer ventral scales, and 19 scale rows on the neck. *Thamnophis radix haydenii* normally has 155 or more ventral scales, and 21 scale rows on the neck. The western subspecies also has smaller black spots along the sides than the eastern subspecies. The natural history of these two subspecies is similar.

Missouri Distribution: The eastern plains garter snake occurs in eastern Missouri north of St. Louis, intergrading with and replaced by the western plains garter snake in the north central and northwestern parts of the state.

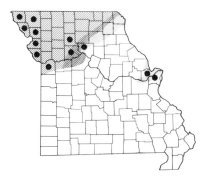

Adult eastern garter snake from Cole County.

Eastern Garter Snake
Thamnophis sirtalis sirtalis (Linnaeus)

Description: This is one of the most common and widely distributed species of snakes in North America. The general color is quite variable. The ground color may be black, brown or olive. There are usually three distinct light stripes which are yellow, brownish, greenish or bluish. One stripe runs along the back, and there is a stripe on either side which involves scale rows two and three. The area between the stripes on each side usually has a double row of alternating dark spots. The belly is greenish with two rows of faint black spots that are somewhat hidden by the overlapping scales. Scales along the back are keeled; the anal plate is single.

Adult eastern garter snakes range in length from 460 to 660 mm (18 to 26 inches). Largest Missouri specimen recorded is 980 mm (41 5/8 inches; Powell *et al.*, 1982). Record length is 1,238 mm (48 3/4 inches; Conant, 1975).

Habits and Habitat: This common species is normally active from March through early November, but may be observed in any month during a mild winter. Eastern garter snakes move about during the day searching for food. When approached by a predator, a specimen quickly moves to a hiding place such as an animal burrow, a pile of rocks or boards, or thick brush. If a body of water is near, this species will not hesitate to enter the water to escape.

When cornered, an eastern garter snake often flattens its head and body and strikes at the intruder. Once captured it will try to bite and

An eastern garter snake eating a southern leopard frog (left), *and an albino eastern garter snake from Boone County* (right).

smear a foul-smelling musk from glands at the base of the tail onto its captor.

The food of the eastern garter snake includes frogs, tadpoles, toads, salamanders and earthworms. Minnows, small mice and small snakes of other species are occasionally eaten.

Eastern garter snakes live in a variety of habitats, but favor areas near water, such as near ponds or marshes, swamps, and in damp woods or forested areas along creeks and rivers. Empty lots and old abandoned farms are also places where this species may occur.

During the winter, eastern garter snakes take shelter in animal burrows or congregate in deep cracks in south facing limestone bluffs or rocky hillsides.

Breeding: Courtship and mating normally occur in the spring, soon after emergence from the overwintering retreat; this species may occasionally mate in the autumn. Males locate females by their scent, and a number of males may try to court and mate with one female. There is much writhing as the males try to rub their bodies along the sides and top of the female. Mating occurs when a male curls his tail beneath that of the female so that their cloacas meet.

The young are born during late summer and early fall. A litter may contain from 7 to 80 young (Collins, 1982). Seventeen females captured in Holt County had a mean litter size of 12 young (Seigel, pers. comm.). A female eastern garter snake captured in southern Illinois gave birth to 103 young (Dyrkacz, 1975). Young garter snakes average 130 to 230 mm (5 to 9 inches; Conant, 1975) in length at birth.

Subspecies: Two subspecies of *Thamnophis sirtalis* occur in Missouri: the nominate subspecies, the eastern garter snake, *Thamnophis sirtalis sirtalis* (Linnaeus), described above, and the red-sided garter snake, *Thamnophis sirtalis parietalis* (Say). The major difference between the two subspecies is the presence of red or orange-red skin between the scales along the sides of the red-sided garter. The natural history of both races is similar.

Adult red-sided garter snake.

Missouri Distribution: Statewide. The eastern garter snake (stippling) occurs in the eastern half of the state, intergrading with and replaced by the red-sided garter snake (hatching lines) in central and western Missouri.

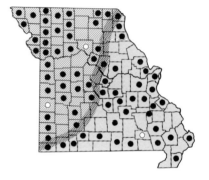

Adult central lined snake from Miller County.

Central Lined Snake
Tropidoclonion lineatum annectens Ramsey

Description: A small, secretive snake similar in appearance to garter snakes. The dark stripes are grayish brown, dark gray, or olive-gray. There are three light stripes, one along the back and one on each side which involves scale rows two and three. The light stripes are light gray, white, or yellowish. The belly is white with two distinct rows of dark gray spots or half-moons along the midline. Scales along the back are keeled; the anal plate is single.

Adult central lined snakes range in length from 220 to 380 mm (8 3/4 to 15 inches). Largest Missouri specimen recorded is 392 mm (15 1/2 inches; Powell *et al.,* 1982). Record length is 533 mm (21 inches; Conant, 1975).

Habits and Habitat: This species is normally active from April through October. During the day it hides under rocks, logs and other debris, becoming active at night. Lined snakes retain a uniform body temperature by selecting shelters of varying colors and thicknesses. A thin, dark colored shelter like tarpaper can heat up quickly and increase the temperature of a snake hiding underneath. A snake hiding under a light colored, flat rock will be heated more gradually (Krohmer, pers. comm.).

When captured, lined snakes release an unpleasant-smelling musk from glands at the base of the tail. This species seldom tries to bite when handled.

Earthworms are the principle food of this species.

Central lined snakes occur in a variety of habitats in Missouri—prairies, cedar glades, empty lots in towns and suburbs, near old trash

297

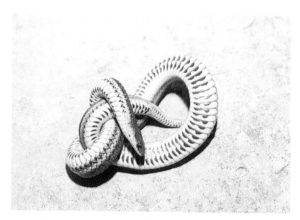

Ventral coloration of a central lined snake.

dumps, along highways where there is abundant debris for shelter and open, rocky woodlands.

Breeding: The reproductive biology of a population of the central lined snake was studied in St. Louis County (Krohmer and Aldridge, 1985 a and b), and the following information is derived from that work. Lined snakes mate in the autumn. Females become sexually mature during mid-summer of their second year at a mean minimum snout–vent length of 221 mm (8 11/16 inches). Each female produces from 2 to 12 young, and only one litter is produced per season. Males have sperm stored in their *vasa deferentia* at a snout–vent length of 200 mm (7 7/8 inches) during the first year. One-year-old males are thus capable of breeding with females during the late summer and early autumn breeding period. Young lined snakes are born during August; average length is 100 to 120 mm (4 to 4 3/4 inches).

Subspecies: The central lined snake (*Tropidoclonion lineatum annectens* Ramsey) is the dominant subspecies of the Missouri population; it can be distinguished by having 143 or more ventral scales. The population of lined snakes in the Kansas City area is an intergradation with the northern lined snake, *Tropidoclonion lineatum lineatum* (Hallowell), which normally has 143, or fewer, ventral scales.

Remarks: A number of new populations of lined snakes have been reported in Missouri in recent years. This is because more people with an interest in herpetology are searching for amphibians and reptiles in areas where little previous collecting has occurred.

Missouri Distribution: The central lined snake (stippling) is known from isolated populations in eastern, central, western and southwestern parts of the state. The population in the Kansas City area is an intergradation with the northern lined snake (hatch lines).

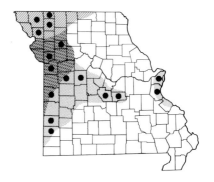

Adult rough earth snake from Miller County.

Rough Earth Snake
Virginia striatula (Linnaeus)

Description: A small, plain-looking, secretive snake of open, rocky woodlands. Color is uniform gray, brown, or reddish brown. Specimens must be examined closely to verify identification. Characteristics to look for include five scales along the upper lip, a horizontal scale (loreal scale) anterior to each eye, and a single scale (internasal scale) between the rostral scales on the snout. The belly is cream colored or light gray, and unmarked. Scales along the back are keeled; anal plate is normally divided, but occasionally single.

Adult rough earth snakes range in length from 180 to 250 mm (7 to 10 inches). Largest Missouri specimen recorded is 286 mm (11 3/8 inches; Powell *et al.*, 1982). Record length is 324 mm (12 3/4 inches; Conant, 1975).

Habits and Habitat: Rough earth snakes are active from April through October. This highly secretive species is seldom seen above ground, remaining hidden under logs, rocks, boards, or in leaf litter. Individuals may become active at night during warm, damp weather. This species is often encountered under flat rocks after rain showers.

This species is not known to bite, but when captured will release a foul-smelling musk from glands at the base of the tail.

Earthworms are the principle food of this species, although slugs, snails, small frogs and insects are occasionally eaten.

In Missouri this species is most abundant on rocky, open, wooded hillsides, along the edge of woodlands, and in open areas where there is abundant cover in the form of rocks, boards, or other ground debris.

Breeding: Mating takes place during April and May. Females give birth to their young from July to September; a litter will contain from two to eight young (Collins, 1982). At birth the young measure from 80 to 120 mm (3 to 4 3/4 inches; Conant, 1975).

Missouri Distribution: The rough earth snake occurs throughout the Missouri Ozarks.

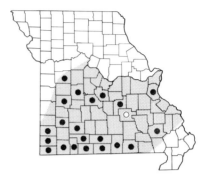

Adult western earth snake from Cole County.

Western Earth Snake
Virginia valeriae elegans Kennicott

Description: The western earth snake is a small, slightly stout, plain colored snake. It is often confused with the rough earth snake. This species is gray, brown, or reddish brown, with a faint, narrow, light stripe down the back that is usually bordered with small black dots. The belly is cream or light yellow and unmarked. For positive identification the following characteristics must be determined: the presence of six scales along the upper lip; a horizontal scale (loreal scale) in front of each eye; and two scales (internasal scales) between the nostrils on the snout. Scales along the back are smooth; the anal plate is divided.

Adult western earth snakes range in length from 180 to 250 mm (7 to 10 inches). Largest Missouri specimen recorded is 393 mm (15 5/8 inches; Laposha and Powell, 1982), which may be the record length for the species.

Habits and Habitat: This species is normally active from April through October. Western earth snakes are most often encountered under rocks, in leaf litter or under other objects. The western earth snake is likely to be active at night during warm, humid weather.

Food includes earthworms, slugs and some soft-bodied insects.

This small, secretive snake can be found under rocks on rocky, wooded hillsides and in moist woods.

Breeding: Mating takes place during May and June, and possibly in the autumn. The young are born in August through September. Litter

Ventral coloration of a western earth snake.

size ranges from 2 to 12 (Collins, 1982). Newborn young are from 80 to 110 mm (3 1/8 to 4 1/2 inches; Conant, 1975) in length.

Missouri Distribution: The western earth snake is presumed to occur throughout Missouri except for the northwest corner of the state.

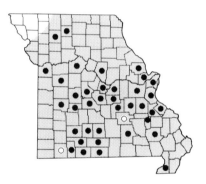

Family Viperidae: Vipers and Pit Vipers

Subfamily Crotalinae: Pit Vipers
Copperheads, Cottonmouths, Rattlesnakes

VENOMOUS

The viper family occurs worldwide, and contains approximately 290 species. The subfamily Crotalinae ranges from southeastern Europe through central and southern Asia to Malaysia, and from Canada through the United States, Mexico and Central America to northern Argentina.

Characteristics of pit vipers include a stout body, broad head, a pair of hollow fangs located at the front of the upper jaw, a heat-sensitive pit found between the nostril and eye on each side of the head, eyes with a vertical pupil, and a single row of scales along the underside of the tail.

The heat-sensitive pits of these snakes are used to detect warm-blooded prey. Even in total darkness, pit vipers can sense the location of a mouse or rat within a 1 1/2 to 2 foot radius and can strike with great accuracy. Rattlesnakes (genera *Crotalus* and *Sistrurus*) are considered the most evolutionarily advanced group of snakes. These reptiles have evolved a distinct rattle on the tip of the tail that consists of hollow segments (specialized scales) which are loosely connected and hit against each other when the tail is rapidly vibrated, causing a buzzing sound.

The five species of venomous snakes native to Missouri are pit vipers. They are represented by three genera: *Agkistrodon* (copperheads and the cottonmouth); *Crotalus* (rattlesnakes) and *Sistrurus* (pygmy and massasauga rattlesnakes). These venomous species are dangerous to man, and should be avoided. Even freshly killed specimens can inflict a dangerous bite due to reflex action. Your local American Red Cross office can furnish up-to-date information on venomous snakebite first-aid. In the event of a snakebite caused by a venomous species, the victim should be transferred to a hospital emergency room as soon as possible. Most bites occur when people are trying to kill or handle venomous snakes. Learning to distinguish venomous from non-venomous species by their color and pattern is recommended.

Accidental bites can be avoided by staying away from areas where there may be a concentration of venomous snakes. Wear protective footwear in habitats where dangerous snakes may occur. Never place your hands under rocks or logs; do not step over rocks or logs. Step on them first, then over. When walking in a forest, step lively. Look the ground over, particularly around large rocks or logs, when you stop to stand or sit. Pit vipers are most active in late evening and at night; be extra careful during these times. Wear rubber boots when fishing in streams or swampy areas that may harbor the venomous cottonmouth. One more word of caution: avoid any snake you cannot identify. Most species of venomous snakes are shy and normally avoid people. When encountered in the wild they usually try to escape detection by remaining motionless. Often, a specimen that is provoked will try to escape rather than defend itself. Once cornered, however, these snakes will do their best to defend themselves.

Western Pygmy Rattlesnake

Adult Osage copperhead from Pettis County.

Osage Copperhead
Agkistrodon contortrix phaeogaster Gloyd

VENOMOUS

Description: A medium-size, stout-bodied snake with a sensory pit between each nostril and eye. Color is gray, tannish, or pinkish tan with hourglass-shaped markings of dark brown. The markings are often edged in white. The top of the head can be gray, tan or reddish and without any markings. The eyes have vertical pupils. The belly is cream colored with large, dark gray or brown blotches along the edges that extend partly up onto the sides of the body. Young Osage copperheads and some adults have a yellowish tail. Scales along the back are weakly keeled; the anal plate is single.

Adult Osage copperheads range in length from 610 to 910 mm (24 to 36 inches). Largest Missouri specimen recorded is 1,100 mm (43 1/4 inches; David Tylka, pers. comm.). Record length is 1,346 mm (53 inches; Conant, 1975).

Habits and Habitat: This species is normally active from April through November. Fitch (1960) studied the Osage copperhead in eastern Kansas, and some of his data is used below. The optimal temperature for this species is 27°C (80°F). On warm, sunny days, copperheads can be seen basking, especially in the morning. During late June, July and August, this species becomes nocturnal. Home ranges for this species vary in size from 8 to 25 acres.

Mice make up the bulk of the prey eaten by copperheads, but

A juvenile Osage copperhead from Cole County (left), *and an adult southern copperhead from Barry County* (right).

frogs, lizards, small birds, insects (especially cicadas) and an occasional small snake are also eaten. Young copperheads use their yellowish tail as a lure to attract small frogs or lizards (Collins, 1982).

Osage copperheads live in a variety of habitats—rocky, wooded hillsides, brushy areas along creeks, near abandoned farm buildings or old sawmills. Populations of this species congregate at favorite over-wintering sites in autumn—usually south-facing, rocky ledges. This is especially true in the northern half of Missouri. Drda (1968) observed several copperheads overwintering in a small cave in Jefferson County.

Copperheads often rely on their camouflage pattern when resting in dead leaves, and will usually remain motionless when encountered. This species is not particularly aggressive, and will seldom strike unless provoked. Data from a study of copperheads in Kansas by Vial, *et al.* (1977), showed an estimated natural longevity of up to 15 years for this species.

Breeding: Courtship and mating take place in the spring. The young are born in August, September and early October. A litter may contain from 1 to 14 young (Collins, 1982). Studies have indicated that female copperheads produce young every other year. Young copperheads are born with functional fangs and venom glands. Anderson (1965) reported the length of newborn copperheads to be from 179 to 204 mm (7 to 8 inches).

Subspecies: Missouri has two subspecies of copperheads—the Osage copperhead (*Agkistrodon contortrix phaeogaster* Gloyd), described above, and the southern copperhead, *Agkistrodon contortrix contortrix* (Linnaeus). The southern copperhead is normally paler than the Osage copperhead, and the hourglass markings are narrower across the back. The southern copperhead has a natural history similar to that of *A. c. phaeogaster* described above, except that it is an inhabitant of more moist or lowland habitats such as the swamps of southeastern Missouri.

Remarks: Copperheads are the most commonly encountered venomous species in Missouri. From 100 to 200 people are bitten by copperheads in Missouri each year, but there has never been a human death caused by this species in the state. With common sense and a knowledge of copperhead habits and habitat, most bites by this species can be avoided.

Missouri Distribution: The Osage copperhead occurs throughout most of Missouri, except for a few counties along the northern border. It intergrades with and is replaced by the southern copperhead along the southern border and in the Bootheel.

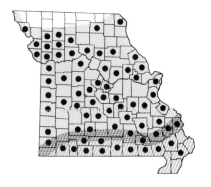

Adult western cottonmouth.

Western Cottonmouth
Agkistrodon piscivorus leucostoma (Troost)

VENOMOUS

Description: A heavy-bodied, dark colored, semi-aquatic snake that is dark olive-brown, to nearly black. Dark crossbands are normally indistinct. The head is noticeably wider than the neck. The top of the head is dark brown or black. A black stripe may be present from the snout through the eye and onto the neck. Most specimens have a white upper lip. There is a large sensory pit located between the nostril and eye on either side of the head. The eyes have a vertical pupil. The belly is cream colored and heavily mottled with dark brown blotches and smudges. Scales along the back and sides are heavily keeled; the anal plate is single. Young western cottonmouths are lighter in color and the 10 to 15 broad crossbands are distinct. Newborn cottonmouths have a yellow tail.

Adult western cottonmouths range in length from 760 to 1,070 mm (30 to 42 inches). Largest Missouri specimen recorded is 1,086 mm (42 5/8 inches; Powell *et al.*, 1982). Record length is 1,410 mm (55 1/2 inches; Conant, 1975).

Habits and Habitat: In Missouri, the western cottonmouth is active from late April through early October. Specimens can be seen basking in the sun during the spring, but for the most part this species is nocturnal.

If encountered near brush or other cover, the western cottonmouth

Underside of a western cottonmouth (left) *and in a defensive posture* (right).

will try to escape. When found in an open area, this snake remains in a loose coil and stands its ground. Cottonmouths often gap their mouth in a defensive posture, showing the white lining which is the origin of the common name "cottonmouth." The tail is vibrated, and a cottonmouth will not hesitate to strike at an intruder. Also, a strong-smelling musk may be released from glands at the base of the tail.

When swimming through the water, a cottonmouth will hold its head above the surface, exposing the back.

This species often overwinters in rock crevices along limestone bluffs. In some areas, cottonmouths are known to migrate from swamp habitats to bluffs in autumn, and return to the swamps in the spring. These denning sites are often shared with racers, black rat snakes, copperheads and timber rattlesnakes (Ditmars, 1931; Smith, 1961; Burkett, 1966; Drda, 1968).

Cottonmouths are known to eat a variety of animals—fish, frogs, other snakes, lizards, rodents and small birds.

In Missouri, the western cottonmouth occurs in two distinct habitats. In southeastern Missouri, this species occurs in the cypress swamps, sloughs and oxbow lakes of the Mississippi lowlands. In the Ozarks, this species occurs in scattered populations in cool, spring-fed, rocky creeks and small rivers. In the latter habitat, cottonmouths are highly nocturnal and secretive.

Missouri is the northwestern limit of the range of the cottonmouth. Low winter temperatures are reported to be an important limiting factor in the distribution of this species (Burkett, 1966).

Breeding: Courtship and mating may occur anytime within the active season, but are most likely in the spring after emergence from overwintering sites. A litter may contain from 1 to 15 young with an average of 6 or 7 (Burkett, 1966). Cottonmouths give birth during August and September. In some areas in Missouri, gravid female cottonmouths move into wooded bluffs or rocky hillsides during the summer to give birth. It is speculated that in Missouri, western cottonmouths give birth every other season (biennial). Newborn of this species are from 150 to 280 mm (6 to 11 inches) in length (Conant, 1975). Young cottonmouths are light colored with distinct markings. The tip of the tail is yellow. The yellow tail has been reported to be used as a moving lure to attract frogs, lizards and other prey (Wharton, 1960).

Remarks: There have been many common names associated with cotton-mouth, causing some confusion among the general public. The names "cottonmouth, water moccasin, lowland moccasin, trapjaw and gapper" have been used for this species. Some Missourians use the common name of "cottonmouth" for this species and "water moccasin" for the various non-venomous water snakes (*Nerodia*).

Throughout the state any dark colored snake found in or near an aquatic habitat is considered a venomous cottonmouth and either killed or greatly feared. The western cottonmouth has a limited range in Missouri; it is likely that most semi-aquatic snakes seen or killed are in fact non-venomous water snakes. It is hoped that this book will help Missourians properly identify both venomous and non-venomous species and refrain from destroying every snake that is encountered.

The bite of the western cottonmouth is dangerous and medical treatment should be sought immediately. Within the known range of the cottonmouth in the United States, about 6.6 percent of the venomous snakebite deaths (12 to 14 per year) can be attributed to this species (Parrish, 1963).

Missouri Distribution: The western cottonmouth occurs in southeastern Missouri and in scattered populations throughout most of the Ozarks. A population of this species was reported in Livingston County by Anderson (1965), but current information indicates that this species no longer occurs in that county or anywhere north of the Missouri River.

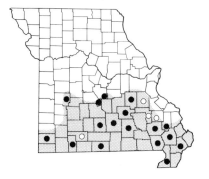

311

Adult timber rattlesnake from Jackson County.

Timber Rattlesnake
Crotalus horridus Linnaeus

VENOMOUS

Description: This is Missouri's largest venomous snake species. Timber rattlesnakes are heavy-bodied and have a prominent rattle at the end of the tail. Color may be yellow, tan, brown, or gray, with dark brown markings. The head normally has a dark brown line from each eye to the angle of the jaw. Dark markings along the body are rounded anteriorly, changing to bands or V-shaped lines along the mid-body to the tail. There is often a rust colored dorsal stripe. The tail is black. The top of the head is light tan or yellowish, and unmarked. There is a large sensory pit located between the nostril and eye on either side of the head. The belly is tan or light gray and sprinkled with small gray or brownish specks. Scales along the back are keeled; the anal plate is single. Most of the scales along the underside of the tail are in one row. The large rattle is straw colored. Young timber rattlesnakes and adults have similar coloring.

Adult timber rattlesnakes range in length from 910 to 1,520 mm (36 to 60 inches), not including the rattle. Largest Missouri specimen recorded is 1,826 mm (72 inches; Anderson, 1965). Record length is 1,892 mm (74 1/2 inches; Conant, 1975).

Habits and Habitat: In Missouri, timber rattlesnakes are active from April through early October. During spring and autumn individuals can be observed basking in the sun on south-facing rock ledges and bluffs.

A juvenile timber rattlesnake from Boone County (left), *and rattles from two mature timber rattlesnakes* (right).

They emerge from overwintering dens during periods of sunny weather and warm air temperatures, 23.8° to 26.6°C (75° to 80°F). During the summer this species becomes mostly nocturnal.

Timber rattlesnakes are shy. If encountered, they may remain motionless to avoid detection, relying on their color to camouflage them among low bushes, branches and dead leaves. Once disturbed, a specimen may quickly move away and try to escape, or coil in a defense posture and rattle.

During the active season, a great deal of time is spent coiled in a secure site. Inactive timber rattlesnakes are either lying-in-wait for a rodent to venture close, or resting while a meal is digested. Gravid female timber rattlesnakes move into rocky, south-facing, wooded habitats during July and early August; they do not eat while awaiting the birth of their young.

Timber rattlesnakes eat a variety of rodents, small rabbits, and occasionally, small birds.

This species prefers a habitat of mature forests and heavily wooded, rocky, south- and southwest-facing hillsides. In general, timber rattlesnakes may be associated with large areas of rugged, hilly, heavily forested terrain with ledges and bluffs. In the northern half of Missouri there are special rock ledges and river bluffs where this species and others (such as copperheads and black rat snakes) congregate in overwintering dens. In the southern half of the state there are so many suitable overwintering sites that denning in large numbers is rare.

Breeding: Courtship and mating usually take place in the spring shortly after emergence from overwintering dens, and occasionally in autumn. A male courting a female will move alongside and on top of a receptive female, rubbing his head and body against hers, and stimulating her with jerking movements. Copulation occurs when the male curls his tail under the female's tail and their cloacal openings meet. Female timber rattlesnakes in Missouri produce a litter of young every other year. Studies have shown that females are able to produce a litter at the age

313

*Head of a timber rattlesnake. The vertical pupil is
indicative of venomous species in Missouri.*

of four or five years (Keenlyne, 1978). The young are born during
August, September and early October; a litter may contain from 5 to 17
young (average litter size is ten; Collins, 1982). Newborn timber rattlesnakes range in length from 250 to 330 mm (10 to 13 inches). They are
born with a single button on their tail and each time the skin is shed a
new segment is added to the base of the rattle. A timber rattlesnake
may shed from three to five times during an active season. As the rattle
becomes longer, the terminal segments tend to become weak and break
off. (I have seen rattles that appeared to have been partly eaten by
insects, which would further weaken the rattle and cause a loss of segments.) Thus, counting the number of segments is not an accurate
method for determining the age of a rattlesnake.

Remarks: A subspecies of the timber rattlesnake, known as the cane-
brake rattlesnake (*Crotalus horridus atricaudatus* Latreille) was recognized
in the southeastern and southern portions of the range of the species,
which included southeastern Missouri. A recent study has shown that
the characteristics which separate the two races tend to be clinal and the
subspecies *atricaudatus*, was considered invalid (Pisani *et al.*, 1973). The
species, *Crotalus horridus*, is considered monotypic.

A number of people in Missouri mistakenly call timber rattlesnakes
"diamondbacks."

The bite of a timber rattlesnake is dangerous and can cause human
death. Due to the rough country where this species normally occurs,
and the fact that it is mostly nocturnal during the summer, few Missourians encounter this species. There are very few cases of people being
bitten by this species in Missouri.

There has been a continuous decline of the timber rattlesnake in
Missouri due to habitat loss and persecution.

Missouri Distribution: At one time statewide. There are now a number of counties where this species has been eliminated.

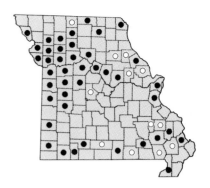

Adult eastern massasauga from Chariton County.

Massasauga Rattlesnake

Sistrurus catenatus (Rafinesque)

VENOMOUS

Description: Massasaugas are medium-size, dark colored rattlesnakes associated with natural marsh habitats of the northern half of Missouri. General color may be light to dark gray or gray-brown with from 29 to 50 dark brown or black dorsal blotches. There are normally three alternating rows of round, dark blotches along the sides. The head is noticeably wider than the neck and has nine large scales on the top. There are two dark stripes along each side of the head, edged in white. A sensory pit is located between the nostril and eye on each side of the head. The tail is light with dark bands. The tail terminates in a distinct rattle. The belly is dark gray to nearly black or gray with dark gray mottling. Scales along the back are keeled; the anal plate is single.

Adult massasauga rattlesnakes range in length from 450 to 660 mm (18 to 26 inches), not including the rattle. Largest Missouri specimen recorded is 764 mm (30 1/8 inches; Powell *et al.*, 1982). Record length is 883 mm (34 3/4 inches; Conant, 1975).

Habits and Habitat: In Missouri, this species is active from April through October. Considerable time is spent basking during sunny, warm spring days. Massasaugas may be seen basking on abandoned ant mounds, grass hummocks, or near the entrance to crayfish burrows. It has been reported that in northwestern Missouri massasaugas move from a moist prairie habitat to drier conditions during spring (Seigel, 1981;

Ventral coloration of an eastern massasauga.

1983). This species is primarily diurnal, but becomes nocturnal during July and August.

When approached, massasaugas may remain motionless to avoid detection, but they will become defensive and sound their rattles when disturbed. This small rattlesnake will not hesitate to defend itself when cornered.

Natural food of this snake consists mainly of mice. In Missouri, voles and deer mice are primary prey species of adult massasaugas (Seigel, 1983). A study in Wisconsin showed similar food preferences: vole 85.7 percent, deer mosue 4.4 percent, eastern garter snake 4.4 percent, jumping mouse 2.2 percent and shrew 1.1. percent (Keenlyne and Beer, 1973). Young garter snakes were eaten by young massasaugas. Seigel (1983) found brown snakes to be important prey of juvenile massasaugas. Young massasaugas have been known to attract frogs by slight movements of their tail (caudal luring).

In Missouri, massasaugas are restricted to marshes or moist prairie habitats located within or in close proximity to large river floodplains. Due to extensive habitat loss, the range of this species has been reduced to a few isolated areas in eastern, north central and northwestern Missouri.

Breeding: Courtship and mating may occur in spring or autumn. Observations by Seigel (1981) suggest that female massasaugas in Missouri produce a litter of young every other year. In Missouri, the number of young per litter is four to ten. The size of the female dictates the size of the litter: the larger the female the greater number of young in her litter. Birth takes place during August and early September; newborn massasaugas range in length from 206 to 275 mm (8 1/8 to 10 7/8 inches). The young have a lighter ground color and darker blotches than adults. The tail of newborn young has a yellow tip and a single "button." Sexual maturity is reached at an age of three to four years (Seigel, 1983).

Subspecies: Anderson (1965) indicated the presence of two subspecies of massasauga rattlesnakes in Missouri: the eastern massasauga, *Sistrurus catenatus catenatus* (Rafinesque), and the western massasauga, *Sistrurus catenatus tergeminus* (Say). Until more data is gathered on the taxonomic characteristics of the Missouri populations of this snake, I will continue to recognize the presence of these two subspecies. Different characteristics of these subspecies are as follows: eastern massasaugas are gray with 29 to 39 dark gray to black dorsal blotches. The belly is dark gray to nearly black. Average length is 635 mm (25 inches). Western massasaugas are tannish gray to brownish gray with 34 to 50 dark brown dorsal blotches. The belly is gray with some dark gray mottling. Average length is 560 mm (22 inches).

Remarks: Although this species has been found to have a highly toxic venom, there are very few records of human deaths caused by this small rattlesnake over its entire range.

There are three small populations of massasauga rattlesnakes currently known in Missouri. Due to their low numbers and greatly reduced natural habitat, the Missouri Department of Conservation has classified the massasauga as endangered. If a specimen is located away from the areas shown on the range map, please contact your county conservation agent.

Missouri Distribution: The eastern massasauga rattlesnake is known to occur in St. Charles County and in several north central Missouri counties (stippling). An intergrade population of the eastern and western massasauga rattlesnake occurs in Holt County (hatch lines).

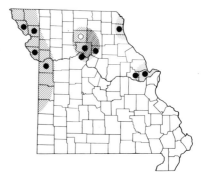

Adult western pygmy rattlesnake from Taney County.

Western Pygmy Rattlesnake
Sistrurus miliarius streckeri Gloyd

VENOMOUS

Description: A small, colorful rattlesnake with a slender tail and tiny rattle. This is one of the smallest species of rattlesnake in North America. General color is brownish gray with small dark brown or black blotches. There are from 20 to 30 dorsal markings; they are round or in the form of short bars. There are one or two alternating rows of round, dark blotches along the sides. A narrow orange-brown dorsal stripe is usually present. The head has a distinct black stripe which angles from the eye to the corner of the mouth, and a sensory pit located between each nostril and eye. The slender tail has six to eight dark bands, and terminates in a small rattle. Belly color is dusky cream with numerous irregularly spaced transverse bars. The scales along the back and sides are keeled; the anal plate is single.

Adult western pygmy rattlesnakes range in length from 380 to 510 mm (15 to 20 inches). Largest Missouri specimen recorded is 550 mm (22 3/8 inches; Powell *et al.*, 1982). Record length is 638 mm (25 1/8 inches; Conant, 1975).

Habits and Habitat: The western pygmy rattlesnake is normally active from mid-April to mid-October. During late spring and early summer this small snake can be observed sunning in rocky, open areas, near brushpiles, or along the side of roads near forests and cedar glades. During July and August this species tends to be nocturnal, and can be observed crossing roads and highways at night.

319

A juvenile western pygmy rattlesnake from Ozark County.

This species takes shelter under rocks during spring, early summer and autumn. Other retreats include abandoned small mammal burrows, logs and brushpiles.

The disposition of this species when encountered varies from specimen to specimen. Some individual pygmy rattlesnakes will try to defend themselves vigorously—coiling, sounding their rattles, and striking at any movement. Other specimens will remain motionless and try to escape only when touched with a stick or snake hook.

The sound made by the rattle of a western pygmy rattlesnake is a faint buzz reminiscent of the sound made by an insect. It can be heard for only about 1 or 2 meters (39.3 to 78.6 inches).

Food of this species includes a variety of lizards, small snakes, mice and occasionally small frogs and insects. A captive collected in Barry County under my care ate northern fence lizards, five-lined skinks, ground skinks and deer mice.

In Missouri, the western pygmy rattlesnake is most often observed in or near cedar glades, in second growth forests near rock ledges, and along the interface between forests and meadows. Preferred habitat is south-facing, rocky and partially wooded hillsides.

Breeding: Very little information is available on the reproductive biology of this species. Courtship and mating are presumed to take place in the spring. The young are born from late August through September. From 6 to 14 young are produced per litter (Anderson, 1965). Newly born western pygmy rattlesnakes are paler in color than adults, have a yellow tail tip, and are from 100 to 190 mm (4 to 7 1/2 inches) in length.

Remarks: The common local name "ground rattler" is given to the western pygmy rattlesnake in extreme southern Missouri.

There are no known human deaths caused by this species. However, this venomous snake should be respected and left alone.

Missouri Distribution: The western pygmy rattlesnake inhabits rocky, wooded hillsides in extreme southern Missouri along the border with Arkansas, and in the eastern Missouri Ozarks and St. Francois Mountains.

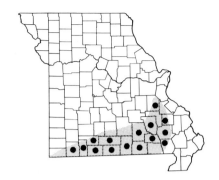

Amphibians and Reptiles of Questionable Occurrence in Missouri

The following species were, at one time, listed as part of the Missouri herpetofauna, or have populations within 25 miles of the state line. Due to their close proximity to Missouri's borders, some may eventually be found in this state.

Amphibians

Spotted Dusky Salamander
Desmognathus fuscus conanti Rossman

This species was reported by Smith (1961) to occur in small colonies in extreme southern Illinois. Conant (1975) showed its occurrence in extreme northeastern Arkansas (Crowley's Ridge area), but his map of the subspecies erroneously shows its distribution as including southeast Missouri (Easterla, pers. comm.).

Northern Two-lined Salamander
Eurycea bislineata bislineata (Green)
Southern Two-lined Salamander
E. b. cirrigera (Green)

Both forms of two-lined salamanders are shown by Conant (1975) to range into southeastern Illinois (*E. b. bislineata*), and into western Kentucky and Tennessee (*E. b. cirrigera*), just across the Mississippi River from southeast Missouri.

Dwarf Salamander
Eurycea quadridigitata (Holbrook)

Since Anderson's (1945) published record of two dwarf salamanders from Barry County, Missouri, no additional specimens have been found in the state. Because the record has not been substantiated by more recent collections and until further evidence indicates otherwise, the dwarf salamander is not considered a part of the Missouri fauna.

Hurter's Spadefoot
Scaphiopus holbrookii hurterii Strecker

This western subspecies of the eastern spadefoot has been shown by both Wasserman (1968) and Conant (1975) to range into extreme southwestern Missouri. Collins (1982) reported that no specimens of this subspecies have been reported from the adjacent areas of southeastern Kansas. To date, the Hurter's spadefoot has not been taken in Missouri.

Bird-voiced Treefrog
Hyla avivoca Viosca

This beautiful little treefrog has been reported in southern Illinois (Smith, 1961 and 1966a), and in northwestern Arkansas (Turnipseed, 1976). Many attempts to locate this species in the remaining swamps of southeastern Missouri have failed. After much field work in that area, Smith doubted this species' occurrence in Missouri. I concur.

Reptiles

Eastern Earless Lizard
Holbrookia maculata perspicua Axtell

Two specimens were reported from a state park in Johnson County, Missouri (Nickerson and Krager, 1972). This is a range extension 115 miles northeast of the nearest natural occurring population in Kansas, and the species was subsequently listed as part of the Missouri herpetofauna (Johnson and Bader, 1974). No additional specimens have been collected in Missouri; this lizard is not considered a member of the Missouri fauna.

Northern Prairie Skink
Eumeces septentrionalis septentrionalis (Baird)

The first Missouri specimen of this skink was taken by the late Paul Anderson in 1949 (Anderson, 1950b, 1965) in Platte County. I am not aware of any additional specimens from this state. Due to a lack of recent records of the northern prairie skink from Missouri, I consider it a species of possible occurrence.

Eastern Glass Lizard
Ophisaurus ventralis (Linnaeus)

Anderson (1965) questioned the validity of three old specimens of this legless lizard from the St. Louis area. Holman (1971b) and Conant (1975) showed these isolated records on the species distribution maps. I concur with Anderson that the eastern glass lizard should not be considered a part of the Missouri herpetofauna.

Kirtland's Snake
Clonophis kirtlandii (Kennicott)

Populations of this small, inoffensive snake have been reported in western Illinois, not far from the Mississippi River (Smith, 1961; Moll, 1962). In May of 1964, a female Kirtland's snake was captured in Marion County, Missouri (Jones, 1967). No additional specimens have been reported from Missouri. This species will not be considered part of Missouri's fauna until additional specimens are reported.

Queen Snake
Regina septemvittata (Say)

Three specimens of this semi-aquatic snake were taken in 1927 in southern Stone County, Missouri (Anderson, 1965). No additional specimens have been taken in the state. However, a small population of queen snakes is still extant in extreme northern Arkansas (Nickerson, *pers. comm.*). This species is currently not recognized as occurring in Missouri.

Eastern Ribbon Snake
Thamnophis sauritus sauritus (Linnaeus)

This species is known from extreme western Kentucky and Tennessee (Conant, 1975). The Mississippi River is probably a natural barrier which has prevented the eastern ribbon snake from occurring in southeastern Missouri.

Southeastern Crowned Snake
Tantilla coronata Baird and Girard

This small snake is known to occur in extreme western Tennessee, not far from the Missouri border (Conant, 1975). The Mississippi River has probably acted as an effective natural barrier in preventing the southeastern crowned snake from occurring in southeastern Missouri.

Western Diamondback Rattlesnake
Crotalus atrox Baird and Girard

People in southern Missouri have believed for years that this species of rattlesnake lives in the southeastern and southwestern corners of the state. The erroneous belief occurred because old reports of this species being taken in northeast Arkansas (Perkins and Lentz, 1934; Ditmars, 1946) were invalid, and because timber rattlesnakes (*Crotalus horridus*) were wrongly identified as diamondbacks. There are no valid records of western diamondback rattlesnakes from Missouri or within 25 miles of the state line (Anderson, 1965; Webb, 1970; Conant, 1975; Collins, 1982).

GUIDE TO SELECTED
TADPOLES OF MISSOURI

This guide is furnished to familiarize the reader with a selected sampling of Missouri tadpoles. Identifying tadpoles is not an easy task. Even professional herpetologists have difficulty separating many species. Some biologists simply avoid working with anuran larvae. But thanks to Gosner (1960) and Altig (1970), a standardized method and key for tadpole identification has been established. I suggest referring to their works for more detailed information.

The descriptions and illustrations which follow depict a developmental age of each tadpole at a point just prior to the growth of hind legs (stage 30; Gosner, 1960). This guide is based on preserved specimens, but some descriptions of live specimens are included when deemed valuable. Preserved tadpoles are necessary if mouthparts are to be examined. Emphasis is placed on mouthparts for the accurate identification of tadpoles in this guide. The number and placement of labial teeth rows on the upper and lower lips are depicted as a numerical fraction; i.e., 2/3 indicates two rows (anterior labial teeth rows) on the upper lip and three rows on the lower lip (posterior labial teeth rows). It is helpful to be familiar with tadpole anatomy before attempting identification. Total length is given for each species only as a general reference. A number of environmental factors may cause tadpoles to develop at different rates— exact measurements are of limited value. It is helpful to know the collecting locations of specimens to be identified. For example, tadpoles of bullfrogs (*Rana catesbeiana*) can be expected in all parts of Missouri, whereas the wood frog (*Rana sylvatica*) has a limited distribution.

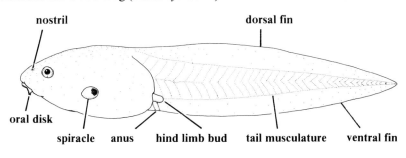

*Anatomy of a tadpole body (*top*) and mouth parts (*bottom*).*

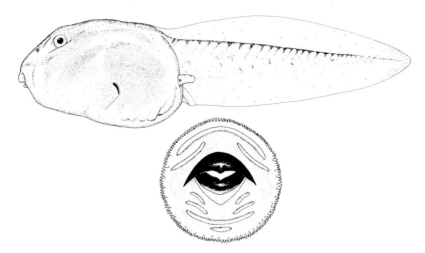

1. **Plains Spadefoot** (*Scaphiopus bombifrons*). A medium-size, deep-bodied tadpole; the body is broadest just behind the eyes. Live specimens are uniformly tan or brown. Eyes are positioned dorsally; the nostrils are small and closely spaced. Tail fins clear and of medium height. Tail musculature delineated with pigment. Oral disk round; marginal papillae small, unpigmented, completely bordering disk. Labial teeth row formula may range from 2/4 to 4/6. Upper jaw cuspate; lower jaw notched. Total length 40 to 48 mm (1 9/16 to 1 7/8 inches). Distribution: See species account.

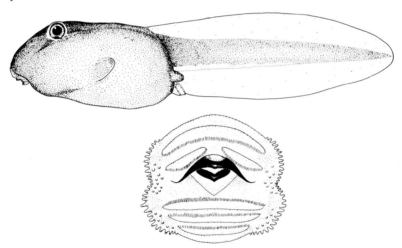

2. **American Toad** (*Bufo americanus*). A very small, dark tadpole. Body somewhat flattened and snout sloping in lateral view. Eyes small, positioned dorsally; nostrils small. Intestinal coil visible. Tail fin low, without pigment, and rounded at tip. Tail musculature without pigment along ventral edge. Oral disk emarginated at jaw edges; without marginal papillae anteriorly and posteriorly. Jaws serrated; upper jaw slightly cuspate, lower jaw notched. Labial teeth row formula 2/3. Total length 18 to 24 mm (11/16 to 15/16 inch). Distribution: Statewide.

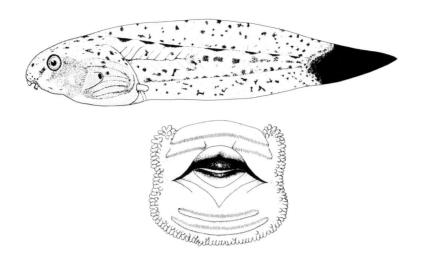

3. **Blanchard's Cricket Frog** (*Acris crepitans blanchardi*). Body depressed dorsoventrally. Eyes positioned dorsolaterally; nostrils large. Up to one half of spiracle tube free from body wall. Intestinal coil visible. Tail fins with faint mottling; dorsum of tail musculature banded. Large section of tail tip black. Oral disk slightly emarginated at jaw edges. Labial teeth row formula 2/2. Total length 27 to 38 mm (1 1/16 to 1 1/2 inches). Distribution: Statewide.

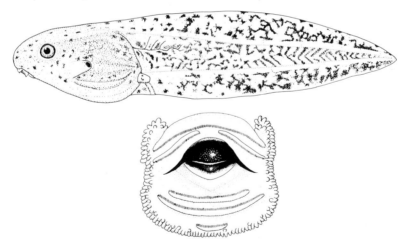

4. **Northern Spring Peeper** (*Hyla crucifer crucifer*). Body length to tail length ratio 1:2. Intestinal coil moderately visible. Tail fins of medium height; dorsal fin slightly higher than ventral fin. Tail fins with large blotches and a clear zone near musculature. Tail musculature mottled. Oral disk slightly emarginated at jaw edges; upper jaw large. Labial teeth row formula 2/3; third posterior teeth row short. Total length 27 to 35 mm (1 1/16 to 1 3/8 inches). Distribution: Statewide except for northwestern corner.

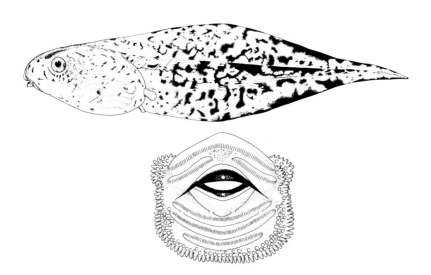

5. **Gray Treefrog** (*Hyla chrysoscelis* and *H. versicolor*). Body length to tail length ratio 1:2. Intestinal coil visible. Tail fins high; tail heavily mottled with black. In life, tail fin often orange or red. Tail usually has a well developed flagellum. Oral disk slightly emarginated at jaw edges. Labial teeth row formula 2/3; third posterior teeth row medium in length. Jaws serrated; lower jaw narrow. Total length 32 to 38 mm (1 1/4 to 1 1/2 inches). Tadpoles develop in fishless ponds and pools. Distribution: Statewide.

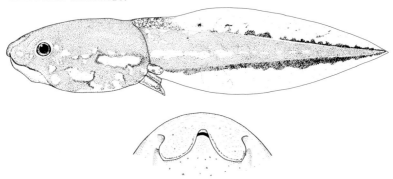

6. **Eastern Narrowmouth Toad** (*Gastrophryne carolinensis*). A small tadpole. Body noticeably flattened. Eyes positioned laterally. Oral disk replaced by labial flaps with a median notch. Nostrils not present until late in development. A single spiracle is present and located immediately ventral to anus. Intestinal coil not visible. Tail fins low, pigmented along dorsal and ventral edges of musculature. Large, light blotches on sides and belly, extending onto tail. Total length 25 to 30 mm (7/8 to 1 3/16 inches). Distribution: Southern half of Missouri including the Bootheel.

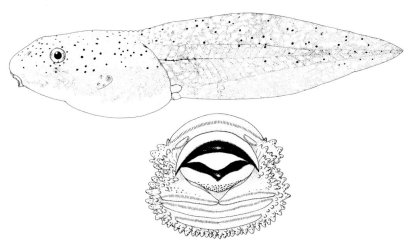

7. **Bullfrog** (*Rana catesbeiana*). A large tadpole. Body length to tail length ratio 1:1.5. Body, tail and tail fins covered with dark mottling. Distinct black spots present on upper body, dorsal tail fin, and along posterior section of tail. Oral disk with large, pigmented papillae; noticeably emarginated at jaw edges. Upper and lower jaws large and serrated. Labial teeth row formula 2/3 or 1/3; second anterior row short. Total length 78 to 121 mm (3 1/16 to 4 3/4 inches). Distribution: Statewide.

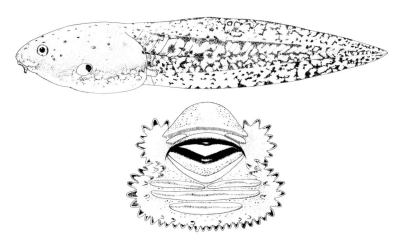

8. **Green Frog** (*Rana clamitans melanota*). Medium to large size. Body length to tail length ratio 1:1.8. Body, tail and tail fins strongly marked with dark mottling. Intestinal coil not visible. A few dark markings present on body, but not as distinct as the black spots found on bullfrogs (*Rana catesbeiana*) tadpoles. Oral disk strongly emarginated; marginal papillae large, somewhat flattened and heavily pigmented. Labial teeth row formula 2/3. Upper jaw slightly cuspate. Total length 74 to 100 mm (2 7/8 to 3 15/16 inches). Distribution: Statewide except for northwestern corner.

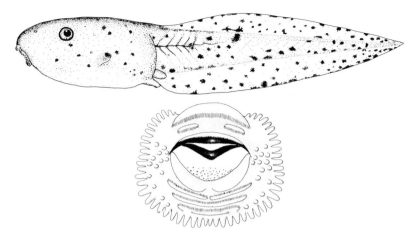

9. **Pickerel Frog** (*Rana palustris*). Medium size. Body length to tail length ratio 1:1.7. A few scattered dark markings present on body. Intestinal coil not visible or only slightly visible. Tail fins low; ventral fin somewhat deeper than height of dorsal fin. Tail heavily marked with dark mottling. Oral disk not emarginated or only slightly emarginated. Marginal papillae large; 10 or fewer papillae below third posterior labial teeth row. Labial teeth row formula 2/3. Lower jaw large. Total length 48 to 55 mm (1 7/8 to 2 1/8 inches). Distribution: Southern and eastern Missouri.

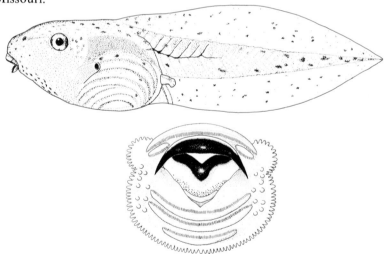

10. **Southern Leopard Frog** (*Rana sphenocephala*). A medium-size tadpole. Body length to tail length ratio 1:1.4. Faint dark markings on body; intestinal coil visible. Tail fins rounded, with a few faint dark markings. Oral disk emarginated. A few submarginal papillae present. Labial teeth row formula 2/3. Lower jaw large. Total length 46 to 52 mm (1 13/16 to 2 1/16 inches). Distribution: Nearly statewide.

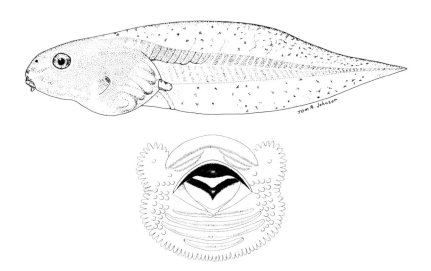

11. **Wood frog** (*Rana sylvatica*). Medium size. Body length to tail length ratio 1:1.8. No distinct markings on body. Intestinal coil partially visible, hidden by subdermal pigmentation. Tail fin rounded dorsally, tapering to a fine point. Faint, small markings on tail fin. Oral disk emarginated; large submarginal papillae present. Labial teeth row formula 3/4. Total length 42 to 48 mm (1 5/8 to 1 15/16 inches). Distribution: Eastern and southwestern Missouri.

GLOSSARY

Amelanism: A color condition of an animal caused by a lack of black pigment.

Amplexus: Sexual embrace of amphibians in which the male grasps the female's body from above with his forelimbs. This allows the eggs to be fertilized externally by the male as they are being laid.

Anal plate: The last belly scale of a snake which covers the anal opening. This scale may be single or divided in two.

Anura: An order of Amphibia comprised of toads and frogs. All have large hind limbs for jumping and swimming. A synonym of Salientia.

Barbels: Fleshy, tubular projections of skin on the chin and throat of some turtles.

Boss: A swollen, rounded area on the middle of the snout. Also called a cranial boss.

Carapace: The upper shell of turtles.

Carnivorous: Consumption and digestion of other animals.

Cirri: Downward projections from the nostrils on males of certain lungless salamanders. The naso-labial groove extends downward to the tip of each cirrus.

Cline: A gradual change of one or more characteristics of an animal from one part of its geographic range to another. This may be observed from north to south or from a lower to a higher elevation.

Cloaca: The common chamber through which the urinary, digestive and reproductive canals discharge their contents. Also called the vent or anus.

Constriction: The act of killing a prey animal by the use of tight coils of a non-venomous snake.

Costal groove: Vertical groove on some salamanders located on the sides of the body between the front and hind limbs.

Cranial crests: Raised ridges on the head located between or behind the eyes on some toads.

Cuspate: Possessing an enlarged point at the middle of the upper jaw (in tadpoles or turtles).

Diploid: Each cell of an animal having the normal two sets of chromosomes.

Diurnal: Active during the day.

Dorsal: The upper surface or back of an animal.

Dorsolateral fold: A line of raised glandular skin along an area between the back and sides.

Dorsum: The entire back of an animal.

Eft: The land dwelling, middle stage of the life cycle of a newt, between the aquatic larva stage and the aquatic adult.

Emarginate: The indentation on either side of the oral disk of some tadpoles.

Facial pit: The deep cavity located between each nostril and eye on the head of pit vipers. Used to detect warm-blooded prey.

Femoral pores: A row of large pores along the underside of the hind limbs on some lizards.

Flagellum: An extension of the tail of some tadpoles which is capable of moving independently of the rest of the tail.

Fossorial: Adapted for living underground.

Hemipenis: One of a pair of copulatory organs of male lizards and snakes which are housed in the base of the tail.

Herbivorous: Consumption and digestion of plants.

Hinge: A joint between the anterior and posterior halves of the plastron of some turtles allowing the closure of the plastron against the carapace.

Herpetology: The branch of science dealing with the study of amphibians and reptiles.

Hind limb bud: A projection at the base of the tail of a tadpole indicating early development of hind legs.

Intraspecific: Characteristics or behavior occurring within a species of animal or pertaining to one species.

Intergradation: When two or more subspecies vary in form or color in a consecutive manner producing intermediate specimens in a given population.

Keeled scales: Body scales along the sides and back of some snakes and lizards having small, raised ridges.

Labial teeth: Tiny, horny projections on the lips of tadpoles which are arranged in rows like the teeth on a comb.

Larva: The aquatic, gilled young of a salamander (plural: Larvae).

Lateral: The side of an animal.

Liebesspiel: A German term which means "love play;" used to describe the aquatic courtship of salamanders, such as the Ambystomatidae.

Melanism: A color condition of an animal where black pigment covers most of the body.

Mental gland: A light colored swelling below the chin on males of several species of plethodontid salamanders (usually more apparent during the breeding season).

Metamorphosis: A morphological change from a larva to an adult with the loss of larval characteristics and the acquisition of adult characteristics.

Mid-dorsal: The area in the center of the back.

Morph: The structure, shape, form or color of an animal species which may be used by a biologist for its identification.

Mullerian duct: Embryonic oviducts. Also the vestigial oviducts present along the kidneys of some male true frogs (Family Ranidae) such as the northern leopard frog.

Naso-labial groove: A groove extending downward from the nostril and across the lip in the lungless salamanders.

Neotenic: Sexually mature and able to reproduce, but retaining most of the larval form and habits.

Nocturnal: Active at night.

Ocelli: Markings on an animal that resemble eyes; round markings of concentric rings.

Oral disk: Fleshy parts of a tadpole's mouth, including anterior and posterior labia and papillae.

Osteoderm: A bony plate or scale in the dermal layer of skin in some reptiles.

Oviparous: In reference to animals that lay eggs.

Ovoviviparous: In reference to animals that produce eggs that are retained in the oviduct of the female throughout the development of the young. The young are born completely developed.

Paedogenetic: The condition of some salamanders to retain some larval characteristics and gain the ability to reproduce.

Papillae: Small fleshy projections along the labial edges of a tadpole's mouth.

Parotoid glands: The large, wartlike glands located behind each eye on toads.

Plastron: A turtle's lower shell.

Plates: The large scales that cover the upper and lower shells of turtles. These scales are lacking in softshells (*Trionyx*). Also, the anal scale of snakes, which may be single or divided.

Pond-type: Salamander larvae with characteristics of species that breed in ponds: large or wide head; large, external gills; high caudal fin.

Process: An extension of a common structure or organ. In the alligator snapping turtle, the wormlike extension of the tongue which resembles a red worm.

Resorb: In tadpoles: the loss and assimilation of the tail during metamorphosis from the tadpole form to a toadlet or froglet.

Rostral scale: The scale at the tip of the snout on lizards or snakes.

Serrate: Having projections in the shape of the teeth of a saw. Jaws of some tadpoles may be serrated.

Smooth scales: Body scales along the sides and back of some snakes which are devoid of ridges ("keels") and are smooth to the touch.

Snouth–vent length (S–V): The measurement of an animal from the tip of the nose to the cloaca. Usual method of measuring toads and frogs.

Spermatophore: A gelatinous cone with a cap consisting of sperm. Secreted by male salamanders and picked up by a female with her cloacal lips.

Spiracle: A tubelike opening on the left side of most tadpoles which allows water to pass out of the gill chambers during aquatic respiration.

Stream-type: Salamander larvae with characteristics of species that breed in cool, rocky streams: small or narrow head; small, external gills; low caudal fin.

Subcaudal: A series of scales along the ventral surface of the tail of snakes and lizards.

Subspecies: A geographic race of a species having two or more closely related forms with slightly different characteristics, but usually occurring in adjoining areas.

Symbiosis: The living together of two unrelated organisms where one or both gain some benefit (i.e., the green alga found in Ambystomatidae eggs).

Sympatric: When two or more species occupy the same geographic area.

Tadpole: The aquatic larva of toads and frogs. Gills are present but hidden behind a flap of skin. The stage of life between the egg and the tailless, young adult.

Triploid: Each cell of an animal having 1 1/2 times the normal number of chromosomes.

Troglobitic: An animal restricted to living in caves.

Tympanum: The round, flat external eardrum of most toads and frogs.

Type locality: Collection site of the original specimen used for the first published description of a species.

Vent: See cloaca.

Ventral: The lower surface or belly of an animal.

Vermiculation: Arrangement of dark pigment in a wormlike pattern.

BIBLIOGRAPHY

PART I. GENERAL WORKS

This list consists of publications which deal in a general manner with the amphibians and reptiles in this book, and is provided for those who wish to learn more about these animals.

Agassiz, L.
  1857.   Contributions to the natural history of the United States of America. Little, Brown and Co., Boston, Vol. 1-2, 452 pp.

Allen, E. R. and W. T. Neill.
  1950.   The alligator snapping turtle, *Macrochelys temminckii*, in Florida. Ross Allen's Reptile Inst. Spec. Publ. 4:15p.

Altig, R.
  1967.   Food of *Siren intermedia nettingi* in a spring-fed swamp in southern Illinois. Am. Midl. Nat., 77(1):239-241.
  1970.   A key to the tadpoles of the continental United States and Canada. Herpetologica, 26(2):180-207.

Altig, R. and R. Lohoefener.
  1983.   *Rana areolata*. Cat. American Amph. Rept., 324.1-324.4.

Anderson, J.D.
  1965.   *Ambystoma annulatum*. Cat. American Amph. Rept., 19.1-19.2.
  1967a. *Ambystoma maculatum*. Cat. American Amph. Rept., 51.1-51.4.
  1967b. *Ambystoma opacum*. Cat. American Amph. Rept., 46.1-46.2.
  1967c. *Ambystoma texanum*. Cat. American Amph. Rept., 37.1-37.2.

Anderson, P. K.
  1954.   Studies in the ecology of the narrow-mouthed toad (*Microhyla carolinensis carolinensis*). Tulane Stud. Zool., 2(2):13-38.

Ayres, D. E.
  1973.   Field behavior of the six-lined racerunner in Peoria County. Proc. Peoria Acad. Sci., 6:23-30.

Barbour, R. W.
  1971.   Amphibians and reptiles of Kentucky. Univ. Ky. Press. Lexington, x + 334 pp.

Barbour, R. W. and W. L. Gault.
  1952.   Notes on the spadefoot toad (*Scaphiopus h. holbrookii*). Copeia, (3):192.

Behler, J. L. and F. W. King.
  1979.   The Audubon Society field guide to North American reptiles and amphibians. Alfred A. Knopf. N.Y., 719 pp.

Bishop, S. C.
  1941.   The salamanders of New York. New York St. Mus. Bull., (324):1-365.

1944. A new neotenic plethodont salamander, with notes on related species. Copeia, (1):1-5.

1943. Handbook of salamanders. The salamanders of the United States, of Canada, and of lower California. Comstock Pub. Co., Inc., Ithaca., xiv + 555 pp.

Blair, W. F.
1936. A note on the ecology of *Microhyla olivacea*. Copeia, (2):115.

1976. Some aspects of the biology of the ornate box turtle, *Terrapene ornata*. Southwest. Nat., 21(1):89-104.

Blanchard, F. N.
1923. A new North American snake of the genus *Natrix*. Mich. Univ. Occas. Papers Mus. Zool., 140. 7 pp.

1935. The sex ratio in the salamander *Hemidactylium scutatum* (Schlegel). Copeia, (2):103.

Blaney, R. M.
1979. *Lampropeltis calligaster*. Cat. American Amph. Rept., 229.1-229.2.

Blem, C. R.
1981. *Heterodon platyrhinos*. Cat. American Amph. Rept., 282.1-282.2.

Bragg, A. N.
1936. The ecological distribution of some North American Anura. American Nat., 70:459-466.

1937. Observations of *Bufo cognatus* with special reference to breeding habits and eggs. American Midl. Nat., 18(2):273-284.

1940. Observations on the ecology and natural history of Anura. 1. Habits, habitat and breeding of *Bufo cognatus* Say. American Nat., 74:322-349.

1942. Life history of Hurter's spadefoot. Anat. Records, Vol. 84, p. 506 (abstract).

1944. Breeding, habits, eggs, and tadpoles of *Scaphiopus hurterii*. Copeia, (4):230-241.

1964. Further study of predation and cannibalism in spadefoot tadpoles. Herpetologica, 20(1):17-24.

Brandon, R. A.
1961. A comparison of the larvae of five northern species of *Ambystoma* (Amphibia, Caudata). Copeia, (4):377-383.

1970. *Typhlotriton* and *T. spelaeus*. Cat. American Amph. Rept., 84.1-84.2.

Brandon, R. A. and D. J. Bremer.
1966. Neotenic newts. *Notophthalmus viridescens louisianensis,* in southern Illinois. Herpetologica, 22(3):213-217.

Brandon, R. A. and J. H. Black.
1970. The taxonomic status of *Typhlotriton braggi*. (Caudata, Plethodontidae). Copeia, (2):388-391.

Breitenbach, G. L.
1982. The frequency of communal nesting and solitary brooding in the salamander, *Hemidactylium scutatum*. J. Herpetol., 16(4):341-346.

Brooks, G. R.
1975. *Scincella lateralis*. Cat. American Amph. Rept., 169.1-169.4.

Brown, L. E.
1973.   Speciation in the *Rana pipiens* complex. American Zool., 13(1):73-79.
1978.   Subterranean feeding by the chorus frog, *Pseudacris streckeri*. Herpetologica, 34(2):212-216.

Brown, L. E. and J.R. Brown.
1972a.   Mating calls and distributional records of treefrogs of the *Hyla versicolor* complex in Illinois. J. Herpetology, 6(3-4):233-234.
1972b.   Call types of the *Rana pipiens* complex in Illinois. Science, 176(4037):928-929.

Brown, L. E., J. O. Jackson and J. R. Brown.
1972.   Burrowing behavior of the chorus frog, *Pseudacris streckeri*. Herpetologica, 28:325-328.

Brown, L. E., H. M. Smith and R. S. Funk.
1976.   I.C.Z.N. to consider a proposal to conserve the name *Rana sphenocephala* Cope. Herp. Review, 7(1):5.

Burkett, R. D.
1966.   Natural history of cottonmouth moccasin, *Agkistrodon piscivorus* (Reptilia). Univ. of Kansas, Mus. of Nat. Hist., 17(9):435-491.
1969.   An ecological study of the cricket frog, *Acris crepitans*, in northeastern Kansas. Doctoral Thesis, Univ. Kansas, 111 pp.

Burt, C. E. and M. D. Burt.
1929.   A collection of amphibians and reptiles from the Mississippi valley, with field observations. Am. Mus. Novitates, (381):1-14.

Burton, T. M.
1976.   An analysis of the feeding ecology of the salamanders (Amphibia, Urodela) of the Hubbard Brook Experimental Forest, New Hampshire. J. Herpetol., 10(3):187-204.

Cagle, F. R.
1942.   Herpetological fauna of Jackson and Union counties, Illinois. American Midl. Nat., 28(1):164-200.
1950.   The life history of the slider turtle *Pseudemys scripta troostii* (Holbrook). Ecol. Monog. 20:31-54.

Christiansen, J. L.
1973.   The distribution and variation of the western earth snake, *Virginia valeriae elegans* (Kennicott), in Iowa. Proc. Iowa Acad. Sci., 80.

Christiansen, J. L. and R. R. Burken.
1979.   Growth and maturity of the snapping turtle (*Chelydra serpentina*) in Iowa. Herpetologica, 35(3):261-266.

Christman, S. P.
1982.   *Storeria dekayi*. Cat. American Amph. Rept., 306.1-306.3.

Clark, D. R., Jr.
1970.   Ecological study of the worm snake *Carphophis vermis* (Kennicott). Univ. Kansas Publ. Mus. Nat. Hist., 19(2):85-194.

Clark, D.R. and R. J. Hall.
1970.   Function of the blue tail coloration of the five-lined skink (*Eumeces fasciatus*). Herpetologica, 26(2):271-274.

Clarke, R. D.
1974. Food habits of toads, genus *Bufo* (Amphibia: Bufonidae). American Midl. Nat., 91(1):140-147.

Cochran, D. M.
1961. Living amphibians of the world. Doubleday Co., Garden City, N. Y., 199 pp.

Collins, J. T.
1982. Amphibians and reptiles in Kansas. Univ. Kansas Mus. Nat. Hist. Pub. Ed. Ser., 8:1-356

Collins, J. T., R. Conant, J. E. Huheey, J. L. Knight, E. M. Rundquist and H. M. Smith.
1982. Standard common and current scientific names for North American amphibians and reptiles. Sec. Ed. SSAR Herp. Circ., 12:1-28.

Collins, J. T. and J. L. Knight.
1980. *Crotalus horridus*. Cat. American Amph. Rept., 253.1-253.2.

Conant, R. *et al.*
1956. Common names for North American amphibians and reptiles. Copeia, (3):172-185.

Conant, R.
1958. A field guide to reptiles and amphibians. Houghton Mifflin Co., Boston, xv+ 366 pp.
1960. The queen snake, *Natrix septemvittata*, in the interior highlands of Arkansas and Missouri, with comments upon similar disjunct distributions. Proc. Acad. Nat. Sci. Philadelphia, 112:25-40.
1975. A field guide to reptiles and amphibians of eastern and central North America. Houghton Mifflin Co., Boston, xviii+ 429 pp.

Costello, David F.
1969. The prairie world. Thomas Y. Crowell Co, N. Y., 242 pp.

Cuellar, H. S.
1971. Levels of genetic compatibility of *Rana areolata* with southwestern members of the *Rana pipiens* complex (Anura: Ranidae). Evolution, 25:399-409.

Dickerson, M. C.
1907. The frog book. Doubleday, Page and Co., N. Y., xvii + 253 pp.

Ditmars, R. L.
1931. Snakes of the world. MacMillan Co., N. Y., 207 pp.
1946. A field book of North American snakes. Doubleday, Doran and Co., Inc., Garden City, 305 pp.

Dobie, J. L.
1971. Reproduction and growth of the alligator snapping turtle, *Macroclemys temminckii* (Troost). Copeia, (4):645-658.

Dodd, C. K., Jr.
1980. Notes on the feeding behavior of the Oklahoma salamander, *Eurycea tynerensis* (Plethodontidae). Southwest. Nat., 25(1):111-113.

Dowling, H. G.
1956. Geographic relations of Ozarkian amphibians and reptiles. Southwest. Nat., 1(4):174-189.

Duellman, W. E.
1979. The number of amphibians and reptiles. Herp. Review, 10(3):83-84.

Dundee, H. A.
1965a. *Eurycea multiplicata*. Cat. American Amph. Rept., 21.1-21.2.
1965b. *Eurycea tynerensis*. Cat. American Amph. Rept. 22.1-22.2.
1971. *Cryptobranchus* and *C. alleganiensis*. Cat. American Amph. Rept., 101.1-101.4.

Dunn, E. R.
1940. The races of *Ambystoma tigrinum*. Copeia, 1940:154-162.

Dyrkacz, S.
1975. Life history (litter size): *Thamnophis s. sirtalis*. Herp. Review, 6(1):20.

Easterla, D. A.
1968. Melanistic spotted salamanders in northeast Arkansas. Herpetologica, 24(4):330-331.

Elder, W. H.
1945. The spadefoot toad in Illinois. Copeia, 2:122.

Ernst, C. H.
1971. *Chrysemys picta*. Cat. American Amph. Rept., 106.1-106.4.

Ernst, C. H. and R. W. Barbour.
1972. Turtles of the United States. Univ. Kentucky Press, Lexington. x + 347 pp.

Fahey, K. M.
1980. A taxonomic study of the cooter turtles, *Pseudemys floridana* (Leconte) and *Pseudemys concinna* (Leconte), in the lower Red River, Atchafalaya River and Mississippi River Basins. Tulane studies in Zoology and Botany, 22:49-66.

Firschein, I. L.
1951. The range of *Cryptobranchus bishopi* and remarks on the distribution of the genus *Cryptobranchus*. American Midl. Nat., 45(2):455-459.

Fitch, H. S.
1954. Life history and ecology of the five-lined skink, *Eurmeces fasciatus*. Univ. Kansas Publ. Mus. Nat. Hist., 8(1):1-156.
1955. Habits and adaptations of the Great Plains skink *(Eumeces obsoletus)*. Ecol. Monog., 25(3):59-83.
1956a. A field study of the Kansas ant-eating frog, *Gastrophryne olivacea*. Univ. Kansas Publ. Mus. Nat. Hist., 8(4):275-306.
1956b. An ecological study of the collared lizard (*Crotaphytus collaris*). Univ. Kansas Publ. Mus. Nat. Hist., 8(3):213-274.
1958. Natural history of the six-lined racerunner (*Cnemidophorus sexlineatus*). Univ. Kansas Publ. Mus. Nat. Hist., 11(2):11-62.
1960. Autecology of the copperhead. Univ. Kansas Publ. Mus. Nat. Hist., 13(4):85-288.

1963a. Natural history of the racer, *Coluber constrictor*. Univ. Kansas Publ. Mus. Nat. Hist., 15(8):351-468.

1963b. Natural history of the black rat snake (*Elaphe o. obsoleta*) in Kansas. Copeia, (4):649-658.

1965. An ecological study of the garter snake, *Thamnophis sirtalis*. Univ. Kansas Publ. Mus. Nat. Hist., 15(10):493-564.

1970. Reproductive cycles in lizards and snakes. Univ. Kansas Mus. Nat. Hist. Misc. Publ., 52:1-247.

1975. A demographic study of the ringneck snake (*Diadophis punctatus*) in Kansas. Univ. Kansas Publ. Mus. Nat. Hist., 62:1-53.

1979. A field study of the prairie kingsnake (*Lampropeltis calligaster*). Trans. Kansas Acad. Sci., 81(4):353-363.

1980. *Thamnophis sirtalis*. Cat. American Amph. Rept., 270.1-270.4.

Fitch, H. S. and R. R. Fleet.
1970. Natural history of the milk snake (*Lampropeltis triangulum*) in northeastern Kansas. Herpetologica, 26(4):387-396.

Frost, D. R.
1983. *Sonora semiannulata*. Cat. American Amph. Rept., 333.1-333.4.

Frost, D. R. and T. R. VanDevender.
1979. The relationship of the ground snakes *Sonora semiannulata* and *S. episcopa* (Serpentes: Colubridae). Occas. Pap. Mus. Zool. Louisiana St. Univ., (52):1-9.

Garton, J. S.
1972. Courtship of the small-mouthed salamander, *Ambystoma texanum*, in southern Illinois. Herpetologica, 28:41-45.

Garton, J. S., E. W. Harris and R. H. Brandon.
1970. Descriptive and ecological notes on *Natrix cyclopion* in Illinois. Herpetologica, 26(4):454-461.

Garton, J. S. and R. A. Brandon.
1975. Reproductive ecology of the green treefrog, *Hyla cinerea*, in southern Illinois (Anura: Hylidae). Herpetologica, 31(2):150-161.

Gates, A. J., Jr.
1973. Algal entry into the eggs of *Ambystoma maculatum*. J. of Herpetol. 7(2):137-138.

Gehlbach, F. R.
1967. *Ambystoma tigrinum*. Cat. American Amph. Rept., 52.1-52.4.

Gehlbach, F. R., R. Gordon and J. B. Jordan.
1973. Aestivation of the salamander *Siren intermedia*. American Midl. Nat., 82:455-463.

Gehlbach, F. R. and B. Walker.
1970. Acoustic behavior of the aquatic salamander, *Siren intermedia*. Bio Science, 20:1107-1108.

Gilbert, P. W.
1942. Observations on the eggs of *Ambystoma maculatum* with special reference to the green algae found within the egg envelopes. Ecology, 23(2):215-227.

Gillingham, J. C.
  1974.   Reproductive behavior of the western fox snake, *Elaphe v. vulpina* (Baird and Girard). Herpetologica, 30(3):309-313.

Goin, C. J.
  1942.   Description of a new race of *Siren intermedia* LeConte. Ann. Carnegie Mus., 29:211-217.

Gosner, K. L.
  1960.   A simplified table for staging anuran embryos and larvae with notes on identification. Herpetologica, 16(3):183-190.

Gray, R. H.
  1971.   Fall activity and overwintering of the cricket frog (*Acris crepitans*) in central Illinois. Copeia, (4):748-750.

Green, D. M.
  1981.   Adhesion and the toe pads of treefrogs. Copeia, (4):790-796.

Grobman, A. B.
  1984.   Scutellation variation in *Opheodrys aestivus*. Bull. Florida St. Mus., Biol. Sci., 29(4):153-170.

Groves, J. D.
  1982.   Egg-eating behavior of brooding five-lined skinks, *Eumeces fasciatus*. Copeia, (4):969-971.

Hall, R. J.
  1969.   Ecological observations on Graham's water snake (*Regina grahami* Baird and Girard). American Midl. Nat., 81(1):156-163.
  1972.   Food habits of the Great Plains skink (*Eumeces obsoletus*). American Midl. Nat., 87(2):258-263.
  1976.   *Eumeces obsoletus*. Cat. American Amph. Rept., 186.1-186.3.

Hansen, K. I.
  1958.   Breeding pattern of the eastern spadefoot toad. Herpetologica, 14:57-67.

Hardy, D. F.
  1962.   Ecology and behavior of the six-lined racerunner, *Cnemidophorus sexlineatus*. Univ. Kansas Sci. Bull., 43(1):3-73.

Harris, R. N. and E. E. Gill.
  1980.   Communal nesting, brooding behavior and embryonic survival of the four-toed salamander *Hemidactylium scutatum*. Herpetologica, 36(2):141-144.

Haskell, N., Jr.
  1979.   Geographic distribution: *Sceloporus undulatus hyacinthinus*. Herp Review, 10(4):118.

Hebrard, J. J. and H. R. Mushinsky.
  1978.   Habitat use by five sympatric water snakes in a Louisiana swamp. Herpetologica, 34(3):306-311.

Hecht, M. K.
  1958.   A synopsis of the mudpuppies of eastern North America. Proc. Staten Island Inst. Arts Letters, 21(1):1-38.

342

Henderson, R. W.
1970. Feeding behavior, digestion, and water requirements of *Diadophis punctatus arnyi* Kennicott. Herpetologica, 26(4):520-526.

Highton, R.
1959. The inheritance of the color phase of *Plethodon cinereus*. Copeia, (1):33-37.
1962a. Revision of North American salamanders of the genus *Plethodon*. Univ. of Florida, Gainesville. Bull. Florida St. Mus., 6(3):235-367.
1962b. Geographic variation in the life history of the slimy salamander. Copeia, (4):597-613.

Highton, R. and P. Webster.
1976. Geographic protein variation and divergence in populations of the salamander *Plethodon cinereus*. Evolution, 30(1):33-45.

Holbrook, J. E.
1842. North American herpetology. 2nd Ed. 5 Vol. J. Dobson, Philadelphia. [Reprinted Ed. 1976, SSAR].

Holman, J. A.
1971a. *Ophisaurus attenuatus*. Cat. American Amph. Rept. 111.1-111.3.
1971b. *Ophisaurus ventralis*. Cat. American Amph. Rept., 115.1-115.2.

Holman, J. A., H. O. Jackson and W. H. Hill.
1964. *Pseudacris streckeri illinoensis* Smith from extreme southern Illinois. Herpetologica, 20(3):205.

Houseal, T. W., J. W. Bickham and M. D. Springer.
1982. Geographic variation in the yellow mud turtle, *Kinosternon flavescens*. Copeia, (3):567-580.

Hoyt, D. L.
1960. Mating behavior and eggs of the plains spadefoot. Herpetologica, 16(3):199-201.

Hutchison, V. H.
1956. Notes on the plethodontid salamanders, *Eurycea lucifuga* (Rafinesque) and *Eurycea longicauda longicauda* (Green). Occas. Papers Nat. Speleol. Soc., 3:1-24.
1958. The distribution and ecology of the cave salamander, *Eurycea lucifuga*. Ecol. Monogr., 28(1):1-20.
1966. *Eurycea lucifuga*. Cat. American Amph. Rept., 24.1-24.2.

Hutchison, V. H. and L. G. Hill.
1976. Thermal selection in the hellbender, *Cryptobranchus alleganiensis*, and the mudpuppy, *Necturus maculosus*. Herpetologica, 32(3):327-331.

Ireland, P. H.
1970. Systematics, reproduction, and demography of the salamander *Eurycea multiplicata*. Ph.D. thesis, Univ. of Arkansas, Fayetteville. 127 pp.
1974. Reproduction and larval development of the dark-sided salamander, *Eurycea longicauda melanopleura* (Green). Herpetologica, 30(3):338-343.

343

1976.   Reproduction and larval development of the gray-bellied salamander *Eurycea multiplicata griseogaster*. Herpetologica, 32(3):233-238.

1979.   *Eurycea longicauda*. Cat. American Amph. Rept., 221.1-221.4.

Iverson, J. B.
1977.   *Kinosternon subrubrum*. Cat. American Amph. Rept., 193.1-193-4.

1979a.   A taxonomic reappraisal of the yellow mud turtle, *Kinosternon flavescens* (Testudines: Kinosternidae). Copeia, (2):212-225.

1979b.   Reproduction and growth of the mud turtle, *Kinosternon subrubrum* (Reptilia, Testudines: Kinosternidae), in Arkansas. J. Herpetol., 13(1):105-111.

Jameson, E. W., Jr.
1947.   The food of the western cricket frog. Copeia, (3):212.

Jenssen, T. A. and W. D. Klimstra.
1966.   Food habits of the green frog, *Rana clamitans*, in southern Illinois. American Midl. Nat., 76(1):169-182.

Johnson, B. K. and J. L. Christiansen.
1976.   The food and food habits of Blanchard's cricket frog, *Acris crepitans blanchardi* (Amphibia, Anura: Hylidae), in Iowa. J. Herpetol., 10(1):63-74.

Johnson, C.
1966.   Species recognition in the *Hyla versicolor* complex. Texas J. Sci., 18:361-364.

Jordan, R., Jr.
1970.   Death-feigning in a captive red-bellied snake, *Storeria occipitomaculata* (Storer). Herpetologica, 26(4):466-468.

Keen, W. H.
1975.   Breeding and larval development of three species of *Ambystoma* in central Kentucky (Amphibia: Urodela). Herpetologica, 31(1):18-21.

Keenlyne, K.D.
1972.   Sexual differences in the feeding habits of *Crotalus horridus horridus*. J. Herpetol., 6(3-4):234-237.

1978.   Reproductive cycles in two species of rattlesnakes. American Midl. Nat., 100(2):368-375.

Keenlyne, K. D. and J. R. Beer.
1973.   Food habits of *Sistrurus catenatus catenatus*. J. Herpetol., 7(4):382-384.

Kezer, J.
1952.   Thyroxin-induced metamorphosis of the neotenic salamanders *Eurycea tynerensis* and *Eurycea neotenes*. Copeia, 1952: 234-237.

Klauber, L. M.
1972.   Rattlesnakes. Their habits, life histories, and influence on mankind. Second ed. Univ. California Press, Berkeley and Los Angeles. Two volumes.

Kofron, C. P.
1979.   Reproduction of aquatic snakes in south-central Louisiana. Herpetologica, 35(1):44-50.

1978. Foods and habitats of aquatic snakes (Reptilia, Serpentes) in a Louisiana swamp. J. Herpetol., 12(4):543-554.

Kofron, C. P. and J. R. Dixon.
1980. Observations on aquatic colubrid snakes in Texas. The Southwest. Nat., 25(1):107-109.

Kruse, K. C. and D. G. Dunlap.
1976. Serum albumins and hybridization in two species of the *Rana pipiens* complex in the north central United States. Copeia, (2):394-396.

Lagler, K. F.
1943. Food habits and economic relations of the turtles of Michigan with special reference to fish management. American Midl. Nat., 29:257-312.

Lagler, K. F. and J. C. Salyer, II.
1947. Food and habits of the common water snake, *Natrix s. sipedon*, in Michigan. Pap. Michigan Acad. Sci. Arts and Lett., 31:169-180.

Lang, J. W.
1969. Hibernation and movements of *Storeria occipitomaculata* in northern Minnesota. J. Herpetol., 3(3-4):196-197.

Legler, J. M.
1960. Natural history of the ornate box turtle, *Terrapene ornata ornata* Agassiz. Univ. Kansas Publ. Mus. Nat. Hist., 11(10):527-669.

Leviton, A. E.
1971. Reptiles and amphibians of North America. Doubleday and Company, New York, 251 pp.

Littlejohn, M. J. and R. S. Oldham.
1968. *Rana pipiens* complex: mating call structure and taxonomy. Science, 162:1003-1005.

Lynch, J. D.
1965. Rediscovery of the four-toed salamander, *Hemidactylium scutatum*, in Illinois: a relict population. Herpetologica, 21(2):151-153.
1978. The distribution of leopard frogs (*Rana blairi* and *Rana pipiens*) (Amphibia, Anura: Ranidae) in Nebraska. J. Herpetol., 12(2):157-162.

Mahmoud, I. Y.
1968. Feeding behavior in kinosternid turtles. Herpetologica, 24(4):300-305.

Marr, J. C.
1944. Notes on amphibians and reptiles from the central United States. American Midl. Nat., 32(2):478-490.

Martin, W. F. and R. B. Huey.
1971. The function of the epiglottis in sound production (hissing) of *Pituophis melanoleucus*. Copeia, (4):752-754.

Martof, B. S.
  1970. *Rana sylvatica.* Cat. American Amph. Rept., 86.1-86.4.
  1973. *Siren intermedia.* Cat. American Amph. Rept., 127.1-127.3.

McCoy, C. J.
  1973. *Emodoidea blandingii.* Cat. American Amph. Rept., 136.1-136.4.

McDaniel, V. R. and J. P. Karges.
  1983. *Farancia abacura.* Cat. American Amph. Rept., 314.1-314.2.

Meade, G. P.
  1937. Breeding habits of *Farancia abacura* in captivity. Copeia, (1):12.
  1940. Observations on Louisiana captive snakes. Copeia (3):165-168.

Mecham, J. S.
  1954. Geographic variation in the green frog, *Rana clamitans* Latreille. Texas J. Sci., 6:1-24.
  1967. *Notophthalmus viridescens.* Cat. American Amph. Rept., 53.1-53.4.

Mecham, J. S., M. J. Littlejohn, R. S. Oldham, L. . Brown and J. R. Brown.
  1973. A new species of leopard frog (*Rana pipiens* complex) from the Plains of the central United States. Occas. Papers Mus. Texas Tech. Univ., 18:1-11.

Merkle, D. A. and S. I. Guttman.
  1977. Geographic variation in the cave salamander *Eurycea lucifuga.* Herpetologica, 33(3):313-321.

Merkle, D. A., S. T. Guttman and M. A. Nickerson.
  1977. Genetic uniformity throughout the range of the hellbender, *Cryptobranchus alleganiensis.* Copeia, (3):549-553.

Metcalf, E. and A. L. Metcalf.
  1979. Mortality in hibernating ornate box turtles, *Terrapene ornata.* Herpetologica, 35(1):93-96.

Minton, S. A.
  1972. Amphibians and reptiles of Indiana. Indiana Acad. Sci. Monog., (3):v + 346 pp.
  1983. *Sistrurus catenatus.* Cat. American Amph. Rept., 332.1-332.2.

Moehn, L. D.
  1980. Microhabitat preference in the broadheaded skink. Bull. Chicago Herp. Soc., 15(2):49-53.

Moll, E. O.
  1962. Recent herpetological records for Illinois. Herpetologica, 18(3):207-209.
  1973. Latitudinal and intersubspecific variation in reproduction of the painted turtle *Chrysemys picta.* Herpetologica, 29(4):307-318.

Moll, D.
  1979. Subterranean feeding by the Illinois mud turtle, *Kinosternon flavescens spooneri.* J. Herpetol., 13(3):371-373.

Morris, M. A.
  1974. Observations on a large litter of the snake *Storeria dekayi.* Trans., Illinois St. Acad. Sci., 67(3):359-360.

Morris, M. A. and M. B. Morris.
    1984.   Geographic distribution: *Lampropeltis calligaster calligaster*. Herp. Review, 15(3):76.

Morris, P. A.
    1944.   They hop and crawl. The Jaques Cattell Press, York, Penn., i-xiv + 253 pp.

Mount, R. H.
    1975.   The reptiles and amphibians of Alabama. Auburn Univ., Auburn, Ala., viii + 347 pp.

Mulcare, D. J.
    1965.   The problem of toxicity in *Rana palustris*. Proc. Indiana Acad. Sci., 75:319-324.

Munyer, E. A.
    1967.   Behavior of an eastern hognose snake, *Heterodon platyrhinos*, in water. Copeia, (3):668-670.

Neill, W. T.
    1963.   *Hemidactylium scutatum*. Cat. American Amph. Rept., 2.1-2.2.

Nelson, C. E.
    1972a.   *Gastrophryne carolinensis*. Cat. American Amph. Rept., 120.1-120.4.
    1972b.   Systematic studies of the North American microhylid genus *Gastrophryne*. J. Herpetol., 6(2):111-137.
    1972c.   *Gastrophryne olivacea*. Cat. American Amph. Rept., 122.1-122.4.

Nelson, D. H. and J. W. Gibbons.
    1972.   Ecology, abundance and seasonal activity of the scarlet snake, *Cemophora coccinea*. Copeia, (3):582-584.

Nickerson, M. A. and C. E. Mays.
    1973.   The hellbenders. Milwaukee Pub. Mus., Pub. in Biol. and Geol., No. 1, viii + 106 pp.

Noble, G. K.
    1931.   The biology of the Amphibia. McGraw-Hill, New York, xiii + 577 pp.

Oliver, J. A.
    1955.   The natural history of North American amphibians and reptiles. D. Van Nostrand Co., Inc., Princeton. ix + 359 pp.

Orton, G.
    1942.   Notes on the larvae of certain species of *Ambystoma*. Copeia, (3):170-172.

Pace, A. E.
    1974.   Systematic and biological studies of the leopard frog (*Rana pipiens* complex) of the United States. Mus. Zool. Univ. Michigan Misc. Publ., 148 pp.

Palmer, W. M.
    1978.   *Sistrurus miliarius*. Cat. American Amp. Rept., 220.1-220.2.

Parmalee, P. W.
    1954.   Amphibians of Illinois. Story of Illinois No. 10, Illinois St. Mus. 1-38 pp.

Parrish, H. M.
    1963.   Analysis of 460 fatalities from venomous animals in the United States. American Jour. Med. Sci., 245(2):35-47.

Perkins, R. M. and M. J. R. Lentz
    1934.   Contribution to the herpetology of Arkansas. Copeia, (3):139-140.

Peters, J. A.
    1946.   Records of certain North American salamanders. Copeia, (2):106.

Petranka, J. W.
    1982a.   Courtship behavior of the small-mouthed salamander (*Ambystoma texanum*) in Central Kentucky. Herpetologica, 38(2):333-336.
    1982b.   Geographic variation in the mode of reproduction and larval characteristics of the small-mouthed salamander (*Ambystoma texanum*) in the east-central United States. Herpetologica, 38(4):475-485.

Pierce, B. A. and J. R. Shaywitz.
    1982.   Within and among population variation in spot number of *Ambystoma maculatum*. J. Herpetol., 16(4):402-405.

Pisani, G. R., J. T. Collins and S. R. Edwards.
    1973.   A re-evaluation of the subspecies of *Crotalus horridus*. Trans. Kansas Acad. Sci., 75(3):255-263.

Platt, D. R.
    1969.   Natural history of the hognose snakes *Heterodon platyrhinos* and *Heterodon nasicus*. Univ. Kansas Publ. Mus. Nat. Hist., 18(4):253-420.

Plummer, M. V.
    1977.   Observations on breeding migrations of *Ambystoma texanum*. Herp. Review, 8(3):79-80.
    1981.   Habitat utilization, diet and movements of a temperate arboreal snake (*Opheodrys aestivus*). J. Herpetol., 15(4):425-432.

Plummer, M. V. and D. B. Farrar.
    1981.   Sexual dietary differences in a population of *Trionyx muticus*. J. Herpetol., 15(2):175-179.

Pope, C. H.
    1944.   Amphibians and reptiles of the Chicago area. Chicago Nat. Hist. Mus. Press, Chicago, 275 pp.

Pritchard, P. C. H.
    1979.   Encyclopedia of turtles. T.F.H. Publications, Neptune, N. J., 895 pp.

Ralin, D. B.
    1968.   Ecological and reproductive differentiation in the cryptic species of the *Hyla versicolor* complex (Hylidae). Southwest. Nat., 13:283-299.

Raney, E. C. and R. M. Roecker.
    1947.   Food and growth of two species of water snakes from western
            New York. Copeia, (3):171-174.

Raveling, D. G.
    1965.   Variation in a sample of *Bufo americanus* from southwestern
            Illinois. Herpetologica, 21(3):219-225.

Reagan, D. P.
    1974.   Habitat selection in the three-toed box turtle, *Terrapene carolina
            triunguis*. Copeia, (2):512-527.

Regan, G. T.
    1972.   Natural and manmade conditions determining the range of *Acris
            crepitans* in the Missouri River basin. Unpublished doctoral thesis,
            Univ. Kansas, 130 pp.

Reinert, H. K. and W. R. Kodrich.
    1982.   Movement and habitat utilization by the massasauga, *Sistrurus
            catenatus*. J. Herpetol., 16(2):162-171.

Reynolds, S. L. and M. E. Seidel.
    1982.   *Sternotherus odoratus*. Cat. American Amph. Rept., 287.1-287.4.

Richmond, N. D.
    1947.   Life history of *Scaphiopus holbrookii holbrookii* (Harlan). Part
            1. Larval development and behavior. Ecology, 28(1):53-67.

Riemer, W. J.
    1957.   The snake *Farancia abacura*: an attended nest. Herpetologica,
            13(1):31-32.

Risley, P. L.
    1933.   Contributions on the development of the reproductive system in
            the musk turtle, *Sternotherus odoratus* (Latreille). Mikrosk. Anat.
            (Berlin) 18(4):459-541.

Robison, H. W. and N. H. Douglas.
    1978.   First record of *Eumeces obsoletus* in Arkansas. Southwest. Natl.,
            23(3):538-539.

Rose, R.
    1978.   Observations on natural history of the ornate box turtle (*Terra-
            pene o. ornata*). Abstract. Trans. Kansas Acad. Sci., 8(2):171-172.

Rossman, D. A.
    1970.   *Thamnophis proximus*. Cat. American Amph. Rept., 98.1-98.3.

Rossman, D. A. and W. G. Eberle.
    1977.   Partition of the genus *Natrix*, with preliminary observations on
            evolutionary trends in natricine snakes. Herpetologica, 33(1):34-43.

Salthe, S. N.
    1973.   *Amphiuma tridactylum*. Cat. American Amph. Rept.,
            149.1-149.3.

Sanders, H. O.
    1970.   Pesticide toxicities to tadpoles of the western chorus frog *Pseud-
            acris triseriata* and Fowler's toad *Bufo woodhousii fowleri*. Copeia,
            (2):246-251.

Schaaf, R. T.
1971.   *Rana palustris*. Cat. American Amph. Rept., 117.1-117.3.

Schaaf, R. T. and P. W. Smith.
1970.   Geographic variation in the pickerel frog. Herpetologica, 26(2):240-254.

Schmidt, K. P.
1953.   A checklist of North American amphibians and reptiles. 6th ed. A.S.I.H., viii + 280 pp.

Scott, F. and R. M. Johnson.
1972.   Geographic distribution: *Ambystoma texanum*. Herp Review, 4:95.

Scott, T. G. and R. B. Shendahl.
1937.   The black-banded skink in Iowa. Copeia, (3):192.

Seale, D. B.
1982.   Physical factors influencing oviposition by the wood frog, *Rana sylvatica*, in Pennsylvania. Copeia, (3):627-635.

Seidel, M. E.
1978.   *Kinosternon flavescens*. Cat. American Amph. Rept., 216.1-216.4.

Sexton, O. J.
1979.   Remarks on defensive behavior of hognose snake, *Heterodon*. Herp. Review, 10(3):86-87.

Sexton, O. J. and K. R. Marion.
1974.   Duration of incubation of *Sceloporus undulatus* eggs at constant temperature. Physio. Zoology, 47(2):91-98.

Shoop, C. R.
1964.   *Ambystoma talpoideum*. Cat. American Amph. Rept., 8.1-8.2.

Skorepa, A. C. and J. E. Ozment.
1968.   Habitat, habits, and variation of *Kinosternon subrubrum* in southern Illinois. Tras. Illinois St. Acad. Sci., 61:247-251.

Smith, H. M.
1946.   Handbook of lizards: lizards of the United States and Canada. Comstock Publ. Company, Ithaca, New York, xxi + 557 pp.
1950.   Handbook of amphibians and reptiles of Kansas. Misc. Publ., Univ. Kansas Mus. Nat. Hist., 2:1-336.

Smith, P. W. and D. M. Smith.
1952.   The relationships of the chorus frogs, *Pseudacris nigrita feriarum* and *Pseudacris n. triseriata*. American Midl. Nat., 48(1):165-180.

Smith, P. W.
1961.   The amphibians and reptiles of Illinois. Bull. Illinois Nat. Hist. Survey, 28(1):1-298.
1966a.   *Hyla avivoca*. Cat. American Amph. Rept., 28.1-28.2.
1966b.   *Pseudacris streckeri*. Cat. American Amph. Rept., 27.1-27.2.

Snyder, D. H.
1972.   Amphibians and reptiles of Land Between the Lakes. TVA, 90 pp.

Spotila, J. R. and R. J. Beumer.
  1970. The breeding habits of the ringed salamander, *Ambystoma annulatum* (Cope), in northwestern Arkansas. American Midl. Nat., 84(1);77-89.

Stewart, M. M.
  1983. *Rana clamitans*. Cat. American Amph. Rept., 337.1-337.4.

Tanner, W. W.
  1950. Notes on the habits of *Microhyla carolinensis olivacea* (Hallowell). Herpetologica, 6(2):47-48.

Thurow, G. R.
  1956. Comparison of two species of salamanders, *P. cinereus* and *P. dorsalis*. Herpetologica, 12:177-182.
  1957. Relationships of the red-backed and zigzag plethodons in the west. Herpetologica, 13:91-99.
  1966. *Plethodon dorsalis*. Cat. American Amph. Rept., 29.1-29.3.
  1968. On the small black *Plethodon* problem. W. Illinois Univ. Series in the Bio. Sci. Macomb, Il., No. 6.

Tihen, J. A.
  1958. Comments on the osteology and phylogeny of ambystomatid salamanders. Bull. Florida St. Mus., 3:1-50.

Trapp, M. M.
  1956. Range and natural history of the ringed salamander, *Ambystoma annulatum* Cope (Ambysotmidae). Southwest. Nat., 1:78-82.

Trauth, S. E.
  1980. Geographic variation and systematics of the lizard *Cnemidophorus sexlineatus* (Linnaeus). Ph.D. dissertation, Auburn University.

Trembley, F. J.
  1948. The effects of predation on the fish population of Pocono Mountains lakes. Proc. Pennsylvania Acad. Sci., 22:44-49.

Turnipseed, G.
  1976. Geographic distribution: *Hyla avivoca avivoca* (Western Bird-voiced Treefrog). Herp. Review, 7:178-179.

Valentine, B. D.
  1964. A preliminary key to the families of salamanders and sirenids with gills or gill slits. Copeia, (3):582-583.

Vial, J. L., T. J. Berger and W. T. McWilliams, Jr.
  1977. Quantitative demography of copperheads, *Agkistrodon contortrix* (Serpentes, Viperidae). Res. Pop. Ecol., 18(2):223-234.

Viparina, S. and J. J. Just.
  1975. The life period, growth and differentiation of *Rana catesbeiana* larvae occurring in nature. Copeia, (1):103-109.

Vogt, R. C.
  1981. Natural history of amphibians and reptiles in Wisconsin. Milwaukee Pub. Mus., Milwaukee, 205 pp.

Volpe, E. P.
    1955.   Intensity of reproductive isolation between sympatric and allopatric populations of *Bufo americanus* and *Bufo fowleri*. American Nat.,
            89:303-317.

Ward, J. P.
    1978.   *Terrapene ornata*. Cat. American Amph. Rept., 217.1-217.4.
    1984.   Relationships of chrysemyd turtles of North America (Testudines: Emydidae). Spec. Pub. Mus. Texas Tech. Univ., 21:1-50.

Wasserman, A. O.
    1968.   *Scaphiopus holbrookii*. Cat. American Amph. Rept., 70.1-70.4.

Webb, R. G.
    1962.   North American Recent soft-shelled turtles (Family trionychidae). Univ. Kansas Publ. Mus. Nat. Hist. 13(10):429-611.
    1970.   Reptiles of Oklahoma. Stovall Mus. Publ., (2):xi + 370 pp.
    1973a.   *Trionyx muticus*. Cat. American Amph. Rept., 139.1-139.2.
    1973b.   *Trionyx spiniferus*. Cat. American Amph. Rept., 140.1-140.4.

Wells, K. D.
    1977.   Territoriality and male mating success in the green frog (*Rana clamitans*). Ecology, 58(4):750-762.

Wendelken, P. W.
    1978.   On prey-specific hunting behavior in the western ribbon snake, *Thamnophis proximus* (Reptilia, Serpentes: Colubridae). J. Herpetol., 12(4):577-578.

Wharton, C. H.
    1960.   Birth and behavior of a brood of cottonmouths, *Agkistrodon piscivorus piscivorus*, with notes on tail-luring. Herpetologica, 16:125-129.

Williams, K. L.
    1978.   Systematics and natural history of American milk snakes, *Lampropeltis triangulum*. Milwaukee Pub. Mus., Pub. in Biol. and Geol. No. 2., 258 pp.

Williams, T. A. and J. L. Christiansen.
    1981.   The niches of two sympatric softshell turtles, *Trionyx muticus* and *Trionyx spiniferus* in Iowa. J. Herpetol., 15(3):303-308.

Wilson, L. D.
    1973.   *Masticophis flagellum*. Cat. American Amph. Rept., 145.1-145.4.
    1978.   *Coluber constrictor*. Cat. American Amph. Rept., 218.1-218.4.

Wright, A. H.
    1929.   Synopsis and descriptions of North American tadpoles. Proc. U. S. National Mus., 74 Art., 11:1-70.

Wright, A. H. and A. A. Wright.
    1949.   Handbook of frogs and toads of the U. S. and Canada. Ithaca, Comstock Pub. Assoc., Cornell Univ. Press, vi + 286 pp.
    1957.   Handbook of snakes of the United States and Canada. Comstock Pub. Company, Ithaca, two volumes.

Wyman, R. L.
    1971.   The courtship behavior of the small-mouthed salamander, *Amby-stoma texanum*. Herpetologica, 27(4):491-498.

Zug, G. R. and A. Schwartz.
    1971.   *Deirochelys, D. reticularia*. Cat. American Amph. Rept., 107.1-107.3.

BIBLIOGRAPHY

PART II. MISSOURI REFERENCES

This list consists of publications about the amphibians and reptiles of Missouri, and is provided for those who wish to learn more about the herpetofauna of Missouri.

Aldridge, R. D. and D. E. Metter.
    1973.   The reproductive cycle of the western worm snake, *Carphophis vermis*, in Missouri. Copeia, (3):472-477.

Alt, A.
    1910.   On the histology of the eye of *Typhlotriton spelaeus*, from Marble Cave, Mo. Trans. Acad. Sci. St. Louis, 19:83-96.

Anderson, P.
    1941.   The cottonmouth in northern Missouri. Copeia, (3):178.
    1942.   Amphibians and reptiles of Jackson County, Missouri. Bull. Chicago Acad. Sci., 6(11):203-220.
    1945.   New herpetological records for Missouri. Bull. Chicago Acad. Sci., 7:271-275.
    1950a.   A range extension for the ringed salamander, *Ambystoma annulatum* Cope. Herpetologica, 6:55.
    1950b.   A record for the northern prairie skink, *Eumeces septentrionalis septentrionalis* (Baird) in Missouri. Herpetologica, 6(2):53.
    1957.   A second list of new herpetological records for Missouri. Chicago Acad. Sci. Nat. Hist. Misc., 161:5 pp.
    1965.   The reptiles of Missouri. Univ. Missouri Press, Columbia. xxiii+ 330 pp.

Besharse, J. C. and R. A. Brandon.
    1974a.   Postembryonic eye degeneration in the troglobitic salamander *Typhlotriton spelaeus*. J. Morphol., 144(4):381-405.
    1974b.   Size and growth of the eyes of the troglobitic salamander *Typhlotriton spelaeus*. Int. J. Speleol., 6:255-264.

Blanchard, F.N.
    1925.   A collection of amphibians and reptiles from southeastern Missouri and southern Illinois. Michigan Acad. Sci. Arts and Let. Pap., 4:533-541.

Boyer, D. A. and A. A. Heinze.
    1934.   An annotated list of the amphibians and reptiles of Jefferson County, Missouri. Trans. Acad. Sci. St. Louis, 28(4):185-201.

Brandon, R. A.
    1966.   A re-evaluation of the status of the salamander, *Typhlotriton nereus* Bishop. Copeia, (3):555-561.
    1971.   Correlation of seasonal abundance with feeding and reproductive activity in the grotto salamander (*Typhlotriton spelaeus*). American Midl. Nat., 86(1):93-100.

Buchanan, A. C.
    1980.   Mussels (naiades) of the Meramec River basin, Missouri. Mo. Dept. of Cons., Aqu. Ser. 17, 69 pp.

Cary, D. L., R. L. Clawson, and D. Grimes.
    1981.   An observation of snake predation on a bat. Trans. Kansas Acad. Sci., 84(4):223-224.

Clawson, M. E. and T. S. Baskett.
    1982.   Herpetofauna of the Ashland Wildlife Area, Boone County. Trans. Missouri Acad. Sci., 16:5-16.

Conway, C. H. and D. E. Metter.
    1967.   Glands associated with breeding in *Microhyla carolinensis*. Copeia, (4):672-673.

Drda, W. J.
    1968.   A study of snakes wintering in a small cave. J. Herpetol., 1(4):64-70.
    1979.   Geographic distribution, *Agkistrodon piscivorus leucostoma* (Missouri). Herp. Review, 10(4):118.

Dundee, H. A. and D. S. Dundee.
    1965.   Observations on the systematics and ecology of *Cryptobranchus* from the Ozark Plateaus of Missouri and Arkansas. Copeia, (3):369-370.

Dyrkacz, S. E.
    1973.   Geographic distribution: *Gastrophryne carolinensis* (Missouri). HISS News-J., 1:152.

Easterla, D. A.
    1970.   Albinistic small-mouthed salamander from southeastern Missouri. Trans. Missouri Acad. Sci., 4:93-94.
    1971.   A breeding concentration of four-toed salamanders, *Hemidactylium scutatum*, in southeastern Missouri. J. Herpetology, 5(3-4):194-195.
    1972.   Herpetological records for northwest Missouri. Trans. Missouri Acad. Sci., 6:158-160.

Easterla, D. A., and H. Gregory.
    1967.   First record of the mole salamander for Missouri. Herpetologica, 23(3):239-240.

Evans, P. D.
    1940.   Notes on Missouri snakes. Copeia (1):53-54.

Evans, P. D., and H. K. Gloyd.
    1948.   The subspecies of the massasauga, *Sistrurus catenatus* in Missouri. Bull. Chicago Acad. Sci., 8(9):225-232.

Ewert, M. A.
1979.   Geographic distribution: *Chrysemys picta belli x marginata*. Herp.
         Review, 10(3):101-102.

Femmer, S., and D. Metter.
1979.   Geographic distribution: *Gastrophryne carolinensis, Bufo cognatus*
         and *Scaphiopus bombifrons*. Herp. Review, 10(1):23.

Funk, R. S.
1974.   Addendum to a checklist of Missouri amphibians and reptiles. St.
         Louis Herp. Soc. Newsl., 1(8):2-5.
1975.   The leopard frogs of Missouri. St. Louis Herp. Soc. Newsl., 2(3):2-6.
1979.   Geographic distribution: *Ambystoma annulatum* (Missouri). Herp
         Review, 10(3):101.

Henning, W. L.
1938.   Amphibians and reptiles of a 2,220-acre tract in central Missouri.
         Copeia, (2):91-92.

Hoy, P. R.
1865.   Journal of an exploration of western Missouri in 1854, under the
         auspices of the Smithsonian Institution. Ann. Rept. Smithsonian
         Inst., 1864:431-438.

Hurter, J.
1893.   Catalogue of reptiles and batrachians found in the vicinity of St.
         Louis, Missouri. Trans. St. Louis Acad. Sci., 6(11):251-261.
1897.   A contribution to the herpetology of Missouri. Trans. St. Louis
         Acad. Sci., 7(19):499:503.
1903.   A second contribution to the herpetology of Missouri. Trans. St.
         Louis Acad. Sci., 13(3):77-86.
1911.   Herpetology of Missouri. Trans. St. Louis Acad. Sci., 20(5):59-274.

Jerrett, D. P., and C. E. Mays.
1973.   Comparative hematology of the hellbender, *Cryptobranchus*
         alleganiensis, in Missouri. Copeia, (2):331-337.

Johnson, T. R.
1974a.   A checklist of Missouri toads and frogs. St. Louis Herp. Soc.
         Newsl., 1(2):6-7.
1974b.   A preliminary checklist of the salamanders of Missouri. St. Louis
         Herp. Soc. Newsl., 1(3):8-9.
1975a.   Record size mudpuppy for Missouri. St. Louis Herp. Soc. Newsl.,
         2(2):3-4.
1975b.   Fall choruses of *Hyla crucifer* in Missouri. St. Louis Herp. Soc.
         Newsl., 2(12):5-6.
1977.   The amphibians of Missouri. Univ. Kansas Mus. Nat. Hist. Pub.
         Ed. Ser., 6:1-134.
1978.   Missouri's mountain boomer. Missouri Conservationist, 39(6):6-7.
1979a.   Missouri turtles . . . an exercise in contrast. Missouri Conserva-
         tionist, 40(2):6-7.
1979b.   Geographic distribution: *Cemophora coccinea* (Missouri). Herp.
         Review., 10(2):60.
1979c.   Missouri's venomous snakes. Missouri Conservationist, 40(6):4-7.
1979d.   Notes on an egg clutch and new county record for the broadhead
         skink (*Eumeces laticeps*). St. Louis Herp. Soc. Newsletter, 7(1):12.

1979e. Several rare species of Missouri reptiles rediscovered. St. Louis Herp. Soc. Newsletter. 6(3&4):10-11.

1980. Snakes of Missouri. Missouri Conservationist, 41(4):11-22.

1981. Missouri's Turtles. Missouri Conservationist, 42(6):11-22.

1982. Missouri's Toads and Frogs. Missouri Conservationist, 43(6):11-22.

1983. Courtship under water. (salamanders). Missouri Conservationist, 44(2):22-24.

Johnson, T. R. and R. N. Bader.
1974. Annotated checklist of Missouri amphibians and reptiles. St. Louis Herp. Soc. special issue 1:1-16 pp.

Johnson, T. R., R. N. Bader and D. J. Coxwell.
1975. Amphibians and reptiles in captivity. St. Louis Herp. Soc., special issue 2:1-38.

Jones, J. M.
1967. A western extension of the known range of Kirtland's watersnake. Herpetologica, 23(1):66-67.

Kangas, D. A., B. Miller and D. Noll.
1980. A report on the 1980 studies of the Illinois mud turtle in Missouri. Unpublished report to the Missouri Dept. of Cons.

Kangas, D. A. and K. R. Palmer.
1982. Field studies of the distribution and ecology of the Illinois Mud Turtle in northeast Missouri. Unpublished report to the Missouri Dept. of Cons., 1-62 pp.

Kiester, A. R., C. W. Schwartz and E. R. Schwartz.
1982. Promotion of gene flow by transient individuals in an otherwise sedentary population of box turtles (*Terrapene carolina triunguis*). Evolution, 36(3):617-619.

Kofron, C. D. and A. A. Schreiber.
1982. Ecology of aquatic turtles in a northeastern Missouri marsh, with special reference to *Kinosternon flavescens* and *Emydoidea blandingii*. Unpublished report to the Missouri Dept. of Cons.

Korschgen, L. J. and D. L. Moyle.
1955. Food habits of the bullfrog in central Missouri farm ponds. American Midl. Nat. 54(2):332-341.

Korschgen, L. J. and T. S. Baskett.
1963. Foods of impoundment- and stream-dwelling bullfrogs in Missouri. Herpetologica, 19(2):89-99.

Krohmer, R. W. and R. D. Aldridge.
1985a. Male reproductive cycle of the lined snake, *Tropidoclonion lineatum*. Herpetologica, in press.

1985b. Female reproductive cycle of the lined snake, *Tropidoclonion lineatum*. Herpetologica, in press.

Laposha, N. A. and R. Powell.
1982. Record size *Virginia valeriae*. Herp. Review, 13(3):97.

Lodato, M. J.
1983. Geographic distribution: *Ophisaurus attenuatus attenuatus*. (Missouri). Herp Review, 14(4):123.

Marion, K. R.
  1970. The reproductive cycle of the fence lizard, *Sceloporus undulatus*, in eastern Missouri. Unpublished Ph.D. dissertation, Washington Univ., St. Louis. vi + 191 pp.

Metter, D. E., W. R. Morris and D. A. Kangas.
  1970. Great plains anurans in central Missouri. Copeia, (4):780-781.

Mittleman, M. B.
  1950. Cavern-dwelling salamanders of the Ozark Plateau. Bull. Nat. Speleolog. Soc., 12(1):1-14.

Myers, C. W.
  1958. Amphibians in Missouri caves. Herpetologica, 14:35-36.
  1959. Amphibians and reptiles of Montauk State Park and vicinity, Dent County, Missouri. Trans. Kansas Acad. Sci., Vol. 62(1):88-90.

Nickerson, M. A.
  1967. The scarlet snake, *Cemophora coccinea*, in Missouri. Herpetologica, 23(1):74.
  1972. Geographic distribution: *Eurycea longicauda melanopleura*. (Missouri). Herp. Review, 4(5):170.

Nickerson, M. A. and R. Krager.
  1972. Additional noteworthy records of Missouri amphibians and reptiles with a possible addition to the herpetofauna. Trans. Kansas Acad. Sci., 75(3):276-277.
  1971. Noteworthy records of Missouri reptiles. Trans. Kansas and Acad. Sci., 74(1):99-101.
  1975. The Lake Erie water snake "phenotype" in central Missouri. Herp. Review, 6(3):75.

Nickerson, M. A. and C. E. Mays.
  1973. A study of the Ozark hellbender *Cryptobranchus alleganiensis bishopi*. Ecology, 54(5):1164-1165.

Orton, G. L.
  1951. Notes on some tadpoles from southwestern Missouri. Copeia (1):71-72.

Owens, V.
  1949. New snake records and notes, Morgan County, Missouri. Herpetologica, 5(2):49-50.

Paukstis, G. L.
  1977. Geographic distribution: *Sistrurus miliarus streckeri*. (Missouri). Herp. Review, 8(1):14.

Peters, J. A.
  1946. Reptiles and amphibians of Sam A. Baker State Park, Wayne County, Missouri. Copeia, (1):44.

Pingleton, M., J. Roth and A. Rogers.
  1975. Bullfrog found in Cliff Cave. St. Louis Herp. Soc. Newsl., 2(10 & 11):14.

Powell, R., K. P. Bromeier, N. A. Laposha, J. S. Parmerlee and B. Miller.
  1982. Maximum sizes of amphibians and reptiles from Missouri. Trans. Missouri Acad. Sci., 16:99-106.

Resetarits, W. J., Jr.
    1984.   Ecology and reproductive biology of the pickerel frog, *Rana palustris* LeConte, in an Ozark Cave. unpub. M.S. thesis. Saint Louis Univ., St. Louis, Mo.

Schroeder, E. E.
    1975.   The reproductive cycle in the male bullfrog, *Rana catesbeiana* in Missouri. Trans. Kansas Acad. Sci., 77(1):31-35.

Schroeder, E. E. and T. S. Baskett.
    1965.   Frogs and toads of Missouri. Missouri Conservationist, 11 pp.

Schuette, B.
    1978.   Two black rat snakes from one egg. Herp. Review, 9(3):92.
    1979.   Extension of Missouri's Ozark faunal region. Trans. Missouri Acad. Sci., 13:37-40.
    1980a.   Two broad-headed skink nests. J. St. Louis Herp. Soc., 7(3 & 4):13-14.
    1980b.   Geographic distribution: *Ambystoma annulatum, A. maculatum, A. opacum, Hemidactylium scutatum, Scincella lateralis,* and *Virginia valeriae elegans* (Missouri). Herp. Review, 11(4):114-115.

Schwartz, C. W. and E. R. Schwartz.
    1974.   The three-toed box turtle in Central Missouri: its population, home range and movements. Missouri Dept. Cons., Ter. Ser. No. 5:28.
    1984.   The three-toed box turtle in Central Missouri, Part II: A nineteen-year study of home range, movements and population. Missouri Dept. Cons., Ter. Ser. No. 12:28.

Seigel, R. A.
    1981.   The status of the massasauga (*Sistrurus catenatus*) at the Squaw Creek National Wildlife Refuge, 1979-1981. Unpublished report to the Missouri Dept. of Cons.
    1983.   Final report on the ecology and management of the massasauga, *Sistrurus catenatus*, at the Squaw Creek National Wildlife Refuge, Holt County, Missouri. Unpublished report to the Missouri Dept. Cons. pp. 1-14.

Sexton, O. J., N. Shannon and S. Shannon.
    1976.   Late season hatching success of *Elaphe o. obsoleta.* Herp Review, 7(4):171.

Sexton, O. J. and S. R. Hunt.
    1980.   Temperature relationships and movements of snakes (*Elaphe obsoleta, Coluber constrictor*) in a cave hibernaculum. Herpetologica, 36(1):20-26

Smith, D. D.
    1974.   Geographic distribution: *Kinosternon flavescens flavescens* (Missouri). Herp. Review, 5(3):69.

Smith, P. W.
    1948.   Food habits of cave dwelling amphibians. Herpetologica, 4:205-208.
    1955.   *Pseudacris streckeri illinoensis* in Missouri. Trans. Kansas Acad. Sci., 58(3):411.
    1956.   A second record of *Hemidactylium scutatum* in Missouri. Trans. Kansas Acad. Sci., 59:463-464.

Stejneger, L.
1893. Preliminary description of a new genus and species of blind cave salamander from North America. Proc. U.S. National Mus. (for 1892), 15:115-117.

Topping, M. S. and C. A. Ingerol.
1981. Fecundity in the hellbender, *Cryptobranchus alleganiensis.* Copeia, (4):873-876.

Taber, C. A., R. F. Wilkinson Jr. and M. S. Topping.
1975. Age and growth of hellbenders in the Niangua River, Missouri. Copeia, (4):633-639.

Thom, R. H. and J. H. Wilson.
1980. The natural divisions of Missouri. Trans. Missouri Acad. of Sci. 14:9-23.

Watkins, L. C.
1969. A third record of the four-toed salamander, *Hemidactylium scutatum,* in Missouri. Trans. Kansas Acad. Sci., 72:264-265.

Watkins, L. C. and L. L. Hinesley.
1970. Notes on the distribution and abundance of the Sonoran Skink, *Eumeces obsoletus,* in Western Missouri. Trans. Kansas Acad. Sci., 73(1):118-119.

Wiley, J. R.
1968. Guide to the amphibians of Missouri. Mo. Speleology, Jefferson City, Mo., 1(4):132-172.

Willis, Y. L., D. L. Moyle and T. S. Baskett.
1956. Emergence, breeding, hibernation, movement and transformation of the bullfrog, *Rana catesbeiana* in Missouri. Copeia, (1):30-41.

Index

363

What kind of frog is that? The Missouri Department of Conservation makes available additional aids for identifying the frogs and toads of Missouri by sight and sound.

The "Talking Toad and Frog Poster and Cassette," depicting 20 species of Missouri toads and frogs* can be ordered from the address below. The colorful wall poster is accompanied by a cassette recording identifying the call of each species pictured.

To order, send $4.00** (Missouri residents add 25 cents sales tax) to:

"Talking Toad and Frog Poster"
Missouri Department of Conservation
P.O. Box 180
Jefferson City, MO 65102–0180

*poster and recording do not include the northern leopard frog, a species that occurs rarely in northern Missouri

**price subject to change without notice